Vernon Lee

Belcaro

Being Essays on Sundry Aesthetical Questions

Vernon Lee

Belcaro
Being Essays on Sundry Aesthetical Questions

ISBN/EAN: 9783744746496

Printed in Europe, USA, Canada, Australia, Japan

Cover: Foto ©Thomas Meinert / pixelio.de

More available books at **www.hansebooks.com**

TO

A. MARY F. ROBINSON.

CONTENTS.

I HAVE to thank the Editors of the *Cornhill* and of *Fraser's Magazines*, and of the *Contemporary Review*, for kind permission to republish such of these studies as have previously appeared in print.

THE BOOK AND ITS TITLE.

A LITTLE while ago I told you that I wished this collection of studies to be more especially yours: so now I send it you, a bundle of proofs and of MS., to know whether you will have it. I wish I could give you what I have written in the same complete way that a painter would give you one of his sketches; that a singer, singing for you alone, might give you his voice and his art; for a dedication is but a drop of ink on a large white sheet, and conveys but a sorry notion of property. Now, this book is intended to be really yours; yours in the sense that, were it impossible for more than one copy of it to exist, that one copy I should certainly give to you. Because these studies represent the ideas I have so far been able to work out for myself about art, considered not historically, but in its double relation to the artist and the world for whom he works; ideas which it is my highest ambition should influence those young enough and powerful enough to act upon them; and, this being the case, my first thought is to place them before you: it is, you see, a matter of conversion,

A

and the nearest, most difficult, most desired convert, is
yourself.

To you, therefore, before any one else, must I explain
what manner of book this is, what are its origin and its
aims. And first, the meaning of its title. Logically,
this title means nothing; it is a mere negation, a mere
arbitrary combination of letters chosen from sheer despair to find any name which should tell, what this title
certainly does not, what is the contents of the volume.
Yet, a meaning the name has: a meaning of association.
For, even as a snatch of melody will sometimes, for no
apparent reason, haunt us while we are about any particular work, follow us while we are travelling through
a definite tract of country (as, two years since, Wagner's
Spinning Chorus travelled with me from Mantua to
Verona, and from Verona to Venice) in such a way that
the piece of work, the tract of country, bring with their
recollection the haunting tune to our mind; so, also,
during the time of making up this volume, I have been
haunted by the remembrance of that winter afternoon,
when last we were together, on the battlements of
Belcaro. Perhaps (if we must seek a reason), because,
while driving to the strange, isolated villa castle, up and
down, and round and round the hills of ploughed-up
russet earth, and pale pink leafless brushwood, and
bright green pine-woods, where every sharp road-turning
surprises one with a sudden glimpse of Siena, astride,
with towers and walls and cupolas, on her high, solitary
ridge; while dashing up the narrow hedged lanes
whose sere oak and ilex branches brushed across our
faces; or, while looking down from the half-fortified old
place on to the endless, vague, undulating Sienese fields

and oak-woods ; perhaps, because at that moment I may, unconscious to myself, have had a vague first desire to put together more of the helter-skelter contents of the notes over which we had been looking, and give it you in some intelligible shape.   Perhaps this may have served to set up the association ; or perhaps it was something wholly different, unguessed, trumpery, in- scrütable.   Be this as it may, the fact remains that dur- ing the dull months of planning and putting together this book, I have been haunted, as by a melody, by the remembrance, the vision, the consciousness of that after- noon, warm and hazy, of early December, on the battle- ments of Belcaro castle, when we looked down over the top of the dense mural crown of sprouting pale green acorned ilex on to the hills and ravines, with the sere oak-woods reddened with the faint flush of sun-light, and the vague, white thinned olives and isolated golden-leaved oaks, and distant solitary belfries and castles ; away towards Siena, grey on the horizon, beneath the grey, pinked, wet cloud masses, lurid and mysterious like Beccafumi's frescos, as if the clouds, if one looked at them long, might gather into clustered angels with palm-shaped wings and flushed faces and reddened pale locks.   Thus have I been haunted by this remembrance, this inner sight, this single moment continuing, in a way, to exist alongside of so many and various other moments ; so that, when it has come to giving a name to this book, I find that there is already indissolubly associated with it, the name of Belcaro.

So far of the title : now of the book itself, of what it is, and why it is such.   When, two summers since, I wrote the last pages of my first book, it was, in a way, as if I had been working out the plans of another dead individual. The myself who had, almost as a child, been insanely bewitched by the composers and singers, the mask actors and pedants, and fine ladies and fops, the whole ghostly turn-out of the Italian 18th century; who had, for years, in the bustle of self-culture, I might almost say, of childish education, never let slip an opportunity of adding a new miscrospic dab of colour to the beloved, quaint, and ridiculous and pathetic century-portrait which I carried in my mind; this myself, thus smitten with the Italian 18th century, had already ceased to exist. Another myself had come instead, to whom this long accumulated 18th century lore had been bequeathed, but who would never have taken the pains, or had the patience, to collect it; who carried out with a sort of filial piety the long cherished plan of making into a book all that inherited material, seeing the while in this 18th century lore what the original collector had never guessed: illustrations, partial explanations, of questions of artistic genesis and evolution, of artistic right and wrong, which were for ever being discussed within me. This new myself, this heir to the task of putting into shape the historical materials collected by an extinct individuality, is the myself by whom has been written this present book: this present book represents the thoughts, the problems, the doubts, the solutions, which were haunting me while writing that first book from which this new one so completely differs. To plan, to work for such a book as that first one, seems to me now about the most incomprehensible of all things; to care for one particular historical moment, to study the details of one particular civilisation, to worry about finding out the exact when and how of any definite event; above all, to feel (as I felt) any desire to teach any specified thing to anybody; all this has become unintelligible to my sympathies of to-day. And it is natural: natural in mental growth that we are, to some extent, professorial and professorially self-important and engrossed, before becoming restlessly and sceptically studious : we may teach some things before we even know the desire of learning others. Thus I, from my small magisterial chair or stool of 18th century-expounder, have descended and humbly gone to school as a student of æsthetics.

To school, where, and with whom ? A little to books, and this (excepting a few psychological works not bearing directly upon my subject) with but small profit ; mainly to art itself, to pictures and statues and music and poetry, to my own feelings and my own thoughts ; studying, in seemingly desultory fashion, in discussions with my friends and with myself. This volume BELCARO is the first fruit of these attempts at knowing: it is not the Sir-Oracle manual of a professor, with all in its right place, understood or misunderstood, truth and error all neatly systematised for the teaching of others; but rather the scholar's copy book, the fragmentary and somewhat helter-skelter notes of what, in his listenings and questionings, he has been able to understand, and which he hands over to his fellow-pupils, who may have understood as much of the lessons as himself, but have in all probability understood different portions or in different ways. Such a collection of notes this volume most unmetaphorically is : it is literally a selection of such pages out of my commonplace books as seemed

(though written at various moments) to converge upon
given points of æsthetical discussion ; to coalesce, con-
glomerate naturally, and to admit of some sort of setting,
or resetting. I say setting or resetting, because these
thoughts, these questionings, these discussions, though
in their written shape merely copied out from a confusion
of quite heterogeneous notes, have nearly all had, while
they were living, while thought or asked or discussed,
a real setting of some sort. For the ideas have come
mainly in the presence of works of art, or in discussions
with friends : they have come, sometimes unperceived at
the moment, together with the sight of a picture, the
hearing of a bar or two of music, the reading of an
accidentally met, familiar quotation ; a reason, a long
sought explanation has been suddenly struck out by a
sentence, a word from a friend. Oh yes, a setting they
have had, these ideas, such as they are: a real, living,
shimmering setting of tones and looks, and jests and
passion, and anecdote and illustration, and irrelevant
streakings and veinings of description and story ; a
setting too of place and time and personality. For they
have come out of real desultory talks : re-echoed by the
bare walls of glaring galleries and sounding statue cells ;
or whispered on the steps before the withdrawn curtain
of some altar-piece, while the faint mass bell tinkled
from distant chapels, or great waves of litany responses
rushed roaring down the nave, and broke in short repeated echoes against the pillars of the aisle ; or, never
clearly begun or ended, between one piece of music and
another, with the hands still on the keys, and the eyes
still on the score ; talks desultory, digressive, broken off
by the withdrawing of the curtain from a fresh picture,.

by the prelude of another piece, by a cart blocking up
the street or a cat in behind a window grating; by something often utterly trumpery, senseless and for the
moment all important. And they have come also,
these scattered ideas, in long discussions, rambling but
eager (their seriousness shivered ever and anon by a
sudden grotesque image or cutting answer, or inane
pun, or diverted off, no one knew how, into anecdotes or
folk tales), in the fire-lit winter afternoons, with the
crackle of wood and the crackling of sparks; or, in the .
August-heated, shuttered room, with the midday drowsy
silence brought home more completely by the never
flagging saw of the cicalas on the vine-bearing poplars,
by the uniform clatter of the wooden frame crushing the
brittle silvery hemp straw in the dark courtyard outside.
This manner of setting they have had; and a far finer
than any that could artificially be given to them. In
order to endure, they had, these ideas, to be removed
out of all this living frame-work; to be written down,
that is to say, to be made quite lifeless and inorganic,
and dry and stiff, like some stuffed animal or bird.
And when it came to sorting them, to preparing
them to show to other folk; the vague melancholy sense
of how different they now looked, my poor art thoughts
all dreary in their abstractness, from what they had
been when they had first come into my head; this sense
of difference made me wish and try to replace them in a
setting, an artificial one, which should in a manner be
equivalent to that original real setting of place and
moment, and individuality and digression : equivalent
as an acre of garden, with artificial rocks, streams,
groves, grottoes, places for losing your way, flower-beds

etc., is equivalent for all the country you can travel over
in five or six years.   I have done as best I could, merely
to satisfy my own strong feeling that art questions
should always be discussed in the presence of some definite
work of art, if art and its productions are not to become
mere abstractions, logical counters wherewith to reckon ;
also, that discussions should be, what real discussions
are, a gradual unravelling of tangled questions, either
alone or with others' assistance, not a mere exposition
of a cut and dry system.   I have always, in putting together these notes, had a vision of pictures or statues or
places, had a sound of music in my mind, or a page of
a book in my memory ; I have always thought, in
arranging these discussions, of the real individuals with
whom I should most willingly have them : I have always felt that some one else was by my side to whom I
was showing, explaining, answering ; hence, the use of the
second person plural, of which I have vainly tried to be
rid : it is not the oracular *we* of the printed book, it is
the *we* of myself and those with whom, for whom, I am
speaking; it is the constantly felt dualism of myself and
my companion.

Thus much of the form into which, as the only one
which, however imperfectly, suited my liking, I have
worked these notes, taken from out of the confusion of
my commonplace books.   Now, as to the notes, or rather
as to the ideas which they embody.   These ideas, I re-
peat, are not a system; they are mere fragmentary think-
ings out of æsthetic questions.   Yet, they have, taken
altogether, a certain uniformity of tendency, a certain
logical shape : they look like a system.   But if a logical
shape they have, it is not because they have been

deliberately fitted into each other, but because they have been homogeneously evolved ; if a system they appear, it is because the same individual mind, in its attempt to solve a series of closely allied problems, must solve them in a self-consistent way.   Hence, while dreading beyond all things to cramp my still growing, and therefore altering, ideas in the limits of a system, I find that I have, nevertheless, evolved for myself a series of answers to separate questions, which constitute a sort of art-philosophy.   An art-philosophy entirely unabstract, unsystematic, essentially personal, because evolved unconsciously, under the pressure of personal circumstances, and to serve the requirements of personal tendencies.   I have, of course, read a good deal about art, perhaps more than other people ; and I have consciously and unconsciously assimilated a good deal of the books that I read ; but I have never deliberately accepted (except in the domain of art-history and evolution, of which I have not, treated in this book which deals only of art in its connection with the individual artist and his public) a whole theory, and set myself either to developing or correcting it : the ideas of others enter largely into the answers to my self-questionings, but they do so because they had become part and parcel of my own thought ; and the questions and their answers have always been asked by myself and answered by myself.   For, with respect to æsthetic training, I have been circumstanced differently from most writers on the subject, nay, from most readers of our generation.   I was taught as little about art, I heard as little talk about pictures, statues, or music, as any legendary calvinist child of the 17th century ; I jostled art of one kind or

another as much as any child well can : I was familiar
with art, cared about it (to the extent of requiring it)
before well knowing that art existed : reversing the
training of these days of culture and eclecticism and
philosophy, according to which one usually knows all
about art, all about its history, ethics, philosophy, schools,
epochs, moral value, poetic meaning, and so forth, before
one knows art itself, long before one cares a jot for it.
To me, art was neither a technical study, nor a philosophic puzzle, nor a rhetorical theme, nor a fashionable
craze : it was something natural, familiar ; indifferent at
first, then enjoyed ; only later read and thought about.
It was only when I began to read what other people had
thought and felt on the subject, that I began to discover
(with surprise and awe) that there was something rare,
wonderful, exotic, sublime, mysterious, ineffable about
art.   I read a great many books about all the arts, and
about each art in particular, from Plato to Lessing, from
Reynolds to Taine, from Hegel to Ruskin ; I read,
re-read, annotated, extracted, compared, refuted ; I filled
copy books with transcendental, romantic, and positiv-
istic æsthetics ; I began to feel, to understand art and
all its wonderful mysteries ; I began to be able to express in words all the vague sublimities which I felt.
Any one reading my notes, hearing my conversation,
would have sworn that I was destined to become an art
philosopher.   But it was not to be.   Much as I read,
copied, annotated, analysed, imitated, I could not really
take in any of the things which I read ; or if I took
them in, they would remain pure literary flourishes.   As
soon as I got back into the presence of art itself, all my
carefully acquired artistic philosophy, mystic, romantic,

or transcendental, was forgotten : I looked at pictures and statues, and saw in them mere lines and colours, pleasant or unpleasant ; I listened to music, and when, afterwards, I asked myself what strange moods it had awakened in my soul, what wondrous visions it had conjured up in my mind, I discovered that, during that period of listening, my mind had been a complete blank, and that all I could possibly recollect were notes. My old original prosaic, matter-of-fact feeling about art, as something simple, straightforward, enjoyable, always persisted beneath all the metaphysics and all the lyrism with which I tried to crush it. I continued, indeed, to study art, to think about what it really was ; but gradually I perceived that this thinking of mine, instead of developing my faculties for seeing in art all the wonderful things seen in it by others, tended more and more to confirm my original childish impression that art was a simple thing to be simply enjoyed. My thinking was mainly negative : instead of discovering new things in art, I discovered every day the absence in it of some of the strange properties with which I had learned to invest it; I perceived more and more distinctly that half of the ideas of æstheticians had merely served to hide the real nature of the art about which they wrote ; I understood that while analysing psychological meanings in pictures, they were shutting their eyes to the form and the colour ; that while they were dreaming about woods and lakes, and love and death, they were not listening to the music. I gradually took in the fact that most writers on art were simply substituting psychological or mystic or poetic enjoyment, due to their own literary activities, for the simple artistic enjoyment which was

alone and solely afforded by art itself. I saw that the
more value any work of art possessed in itself, and the
greater the amount of pleasure which it could afford, the
more extraneous and impertinent was the sort of interest with which æstheticians tried to invest it. I
became aware that writers, being unable to awaken with
their machinery of thoughts and feelings and words the
activities awakened by the intrinsic qualities, visible or
audible, of statues or pictures or music, had unconsciously substituted an appeal to other mental activities
with which the works of art had at best but little
connection. This gradual discovery amused me, but
it also made me indignant. Had mankind appeared to
me to be merely placidly enjoying as artistic effects
those which were not artistic effects at all, it would have
been a mere matter for amusement; but it seemed to me
that as a consequence of this mankind was entirely
missing much of the enjoyment which art could give,
and, moreover, which could be given only by art. Besides, art was for ever attempting really to produce those
imaginary, imagined effects : sculpture was trying to
give psychological amusement, music was trying to play
tragedies and paint landscapes, and write religious medi-
tations ; and in so doing art was incapacitating itself for
its real work, even as mankind was incapacitating itself
for appreciating the real powers of art. Hence, in so far
as I thought at all about art in its absolute relations to
artist and public (as distinguished from art as a psychological, historical, merely scientific study) my thoughts
all tended towards getting rid of those foreign, extra-
artistic, irrelevant interests which æstheticians have
since the beginning of time interposed between art and

those who are intended to enjoy it ;. my work has, unconsciously enough, been to logically justify that perfectly simple, direct connection between art and ourselves, which was the one I had felt, as a child, before
learning all the wonderful fantastications of art philo-
sophers. My own art philosophy is therefore simply to
try and enjoy in art what art really contains, to obtain
from art all that it can give, by refraining from asking
it to give what it cannot. To this end have tended all
those most harum-scarum notes, written during the last
six years, which I have here collected and tried to group
according to the particular art, or the particular portion
of an art, to which they referred. Some are about
painting, some about music, some about poetry, some
about art in general, some inextricably combined
and mixed up with other subjects. They have been
written at different times, hence with varying amount
of experience and information; occasionally they may
even be contradictory in a trifle. Thus, when I
wrote the notes on musical expression incorporated in
the essay called after Hoffmann's Kapell-Meister
Kreisler, I was not yet acquainted with the discoveries
of Mr. Herbert Spencer on the subject; discoveries
which have infinitely cleared my ideas, and which serve
to correct, in the adjoining essay called *Cherubino*, much
that was vague, and perhaps equivocal, in my earlier
notes. Had I been constructing a system, I should
have recast all the old (or suppressed all the new); but I
am merely collecting notes, so I have let them stand as
they were written. My object is not to teach others,
but to show them how far I have taught myself, and
how far they may teach themselves. I must always return

to my comparison of the copy books of the boy attending a course of lectures: this is not all that I conceive can be said on the subject; it is merely as much as I have been able to understand thereof; and the more I have listened and questioned, the more what I have understood has become connected within itself and seemed to indicate connections with unstudied problems belonging to different orders of thought. Thus, after having thought and written only about art; about what each art can and cannot do, about the relations of the various arts amongst each other and to their artists, I have gradually found myself thinking and writing about what art as a whole can do and should do; about the relations between all art and life taken as a whole: after the purely æsthetical questions has come the question, no æsthetical question this time—what value, in this world of good and evil, of doubt and certainty, of action and inaction, in this world struggling for physical and social and moral good, what value have æsthetical questions at all? And with these notes, written latest of all, and threatening to divert me more than they should from my present field of study to the wider, nobler, far more intricate and dangerous field of ethics, I have thought it best to close my book; since these latest notes supply the explanation—felt all along, but only vaguely formulated till now—of my whole æsthetic, because of my whole philosophic, tendencies: the greatest amount of good work to be obtained from everything, and this possible only by all being seen in its right light, and consequently used in its right place.

This is what my new book is, and this is how such it has come to be. And just because it is what it is, be-

cause it is not a mere piece of work, not a mere something made by me and thrust away, in its systematic cut
and dryness, from my living personality ; but a certain
proportion of my growing, altering, enlarging, disjointed,
helter-skelter thoughts, of the thoughts which come to
me whether I will or not; because it is not a real book
but a collection of notes, do I wish it to be read by you.
So now I tie together and make a packet of all the
pages of proofs and sheets of MS., and send it all to
you. The summer has come round : the tall grass,
brocaded like some rough, rich mediæval stuff, with
yellow buttercups and blue sage flowers, is already beginning to be scythed and raked away ; the last clusters
of hawthorn, which, a few days since, still stood out
white and crisp against the blue of the sky, fall to pieces
as soon as one tries to gather them ; the Tuscan country
has already got its summer sheen of pale green poppied
wheat, and pale green budding vine, and dim
blue distance, and pervading faint yellow haze ; the
hills of Siena are green with sprouting arbutus and
ilex and fern and hellebore bells ; the oakwoods that
we saw russet under the reddening light, are in tender,
yellowish new leaf; the olives are in blossom from
which we broke the fruit-laden twigs ; it seems so long,
so very long, since that soft grey winter day when last
we were together, looking down from the battlements of
the old Sienese villa ; and yet the memory of that
winter day seems as real as the present reality of this
summer one ; and haunts me still, as I write these
words, even as it has haunted me throughout the putting
together of this book, which I have called, from that
haunting remembrance, and, perhaps, a little also that

the association might make it more pleasant in your
eyes, by the name of that strange, isolated, ilex-circled
castle villa of Belcaro.   And now, unroll the tight-rolled
manuscript and smooth out the rumpled proof sheets;
read, and tell me whether or not what you have read is
ever to be read by any one else.

FLORENCE, *May*, 1881.

THE CHILD IN THE VATICAN.

THERE were a lot of children in the Vatican this morning : small barbarians scarce out of the nursery, who should have been at home, at their lessons, or reading fairy books, or carpentering, or doll-educating, or boat-sailing, or amusing themselves in the hundred nondescript ways which we seem to forget (remembering only ready-made toys and ready-made stories) when we grow up. Some were left to their own devices, and scampered, chattering and laughing, through the gallery ; jumping up three steps at a time, clambering up to windows, running round isolated statues, feretting into all the little nook and corner rooms, peeping into the lidless sarcophagi and the great porphyry baths, with the rough-hewn rings and lions' heads. The others were being led by their elders : talking in whispers, or silent: demure, weary, vacant, staring about with dreary, vague little faces ; these, who were not permitted to rush about like the others, seemed chilled, numbed by a sort of wonder unaccompanied by curiosity, oppressed by a sense of indefineable desolation. And, indeed, it is a desolate place, this Vatican, with its long, bleak, glaring corridors; its half-lit, chill, resounding halls; its damp little Belvedere Court, where green lichen fills up the fissured pavement ; a dreary labyrinth of brick and mortar, a sort of over-ground catacomb of stones, constructed in our art-studying, rather than art-loving times where once—when Michael Angelo was stretched painting on the creaking scaffolding slung from the roof of the Sixtine—the poppies waved scarlet among the trailing vines of the pope's orchard, and the white butterflies, like wind-blown blossoms, swarmed in the tall grass beneath the bending apple trees, and the fire-flies danced in luminous spirals among the wild rose-hedges. A dismal scientific piece of ostentation, like all galleries ; a place where art is arranged and ticketed and made dingy and lifeless even as are the plants in a botanic collection. Eminently a place of exile, or worse, of captivity, for all this people of marble : these athletes and nymphs and satyrs, and warriors and poets and gods, who once stood, each in happy independence, against a screen of laurel or ilex branches, or on the sun-heated gable of a temple, where the grass waved in the fissures and the swallows nested, or in a cresset-lit, incense-dim chapel, or high against the blue sky above the bustle of the market place ; poor stone captives cloistered in monastic halls and cells, or arranged, like the skeletons of Capuchins, in endless rows of niche, shelf, and bracket. Galleries are necessary things, to save pictures and statues (or the little remaining of them) from candle smoke, sacristans' ladders, damp, worms, and street boys, but they are evil necessities ; and the sense of a sort of negative vandalism always clings to them, specially to the galleries of statues, so uninhabited, so utterly sepulchral. Going to a gallery of sculpture, we must be prepared to isolate what we wish to enjoy, to make for it a fitting habitation in our fancy : it is like going to read a page of Homer, or the Georgics, or Shelley, in some great musty, dusty library, redolent of crumbling parchment and forgotten rubbish. Such is this Vatican, even for us accustomed to it and knowing what we do and do not want: for us grown-up creatures, familiar with such matters, and with powers of impression quite deadened by culture. What, therefore, must not this Vatican be for a child : a quite small, ignorant barbarian such as has never before set its feet in a gallery, to whom art and antiquity have been mere names, to whom all this world of tintless stone can give but a confused, huge, overpowering impression of dreariness and vacuity. An impression composed of negative things : of silence and absence of colour, of lifelessness, of not knowing what it all is or all means ; a sense of void and of unattractive mystery which chills, numbs the little soul into a sort of emotionless, inactive discomfort. What we were, how we felt, how we understood and vaguely guessed things, as children, we can none of us know. The recollection of ourselves when we were so different from ourselves, this tradition handed down from a dim, far-off creature of whom we know, without feeling it, that he, was our *ego*, this mysterious tradition remains to us only in fragments, has been printed into our memory only by desultory patches : at one point we can read, at another the ink has not taken ; we know as distinctly as the sensation and impressions of this very morning this or that sensation or impression of so many, many years ago ; and we ask ourselves at the same time—"how did such another thing affect our mind?"—with the utter hopelessness of answer with which we should try to look into the soul of a dog or a cat. Thus it is with our small barbarian child in the Vatican : how did it feel? Alas, we should, in order to know, first have to find that little

obscure, puzzled soul again ; and where is it gone?
this thing which may once have been ourselves, whither
has it disappeared, when has it been extinguished ? So
we can only speculate and reconstruct on a general
basis. Certain it is that to this child, to any child, this
Vatican must have been the most desolate, the most
unintelligible of places. For, strange as it may seem,
this clear and simple art of sculpture, born when the
world was young and had not yet learned to
think and talk in symbolical riddles, this apparently so outspoken art is, to the childish soul of our
days, the most silent art of any. To the child, the
modern child, it is speechless ; it knows not a word of
the language understood by the child's fancy. For this
fancy language of our modern child is the language of
colour, of movement, of sound, of suggestion, of all the
broken words of modern thought and feeling : and the
statue has none of these. The child does not recognise
in it anything familiar: these naked, or half-naked, limbs
are things which the child has never seen, at least, never
observed ; they do not, in their unfamiliarity, their
vagueness, constitute an individual character ; the dress,
the furrowed face, the coloured hair, the beard, these are
the things which the child knows, and by which it recognises ; but in these vague, white things, with their
rounded white cheek, and clotted white hair, with their
fold of white drapery about them, the child recognises
nothing : men ? women ? it does not ask : for it, they
are mere things, figures cut out of stone. And thus, in
their vagueness, their unfamiliarity, they seem also to be
all alike, even as, on first acquaintance, we sometimes
ask ourselves whether those sisters or brothers we know

are four or only three ; for in the unknown there is no
diversity. Mysterious things, therefore, these statues for
the child ; but theirs is a mystery of mere vacuity, one
which does not haunt, does not seek a solution. For
they are dull things, in their dirty whiteness : they are
doing nothing, these creatures, merely standing or sitting
or leaning, they are looking at nothing with their
pupilless white eyes, they have no story to tell, no name
to be asked. The child does not say to them, as to the
people in pictures, the splendid people in strange
colours, and holding strange things, "Who are you? why
are you doing that?" It does not even ask or answer
itself whether these white things, who seem to be all the
same, are dead or alive : they are not ghosts, they are
things which, for aught the child knows or cares, have
never been born and never will die. A negation, op-
pressive and depressing, that is all ; and in the infinite
multitude of statues in such a place as this Vatican,
their sense must become actively painful to the child.
Hence, the children we meet either rush headlong
through corridor and hall, looking neither to the right
nor to the left, or let themselves be passively led
through, listless, depressed, glancing vaguely about,
looking wistfully at the little glimpses of sunlit garden
outside, at the clipped box hedges and trim orange trees
in the court of the Pine Cone. For there, outside, is life,
movement, green ; little hedged beds to run round ;
fountains to be made to spirt aside by sticking fingers
into their pipes ; walls on which to walk balanced, and
benches to jump over : there is field and food for the
child's fancy, and here, within, among all these cut
stones, there is none.

Hence it is that the child, who will one day become
ourselves, rarely cares to return to these sculpture
galleries ; or, if it care to return to any, it is to mixed
galleries like those of Florence, where, instead of the
statues, it looks at the pictures.   And out of pictures,
out of the coarse blurs of colour in picture-books, out
of the black, huddled, infinitively suggestive engravings
in bible and book of travel ; out of fine glossy
modern pictures which represent a definite place, or
tell a definite story; out of all this, confused with
haunting impressions, of things seen or heard of
(the strange, deeply significant sights and words of our
childhood), do we get our original, never really alterable
ideas and feelings about art ; for much as we may clip,
trim, and bedizen our minds with borrowed things, we
can never change, never even recast its solid material :
a compact, and seemingly homogeneous soul mass, made
up of tightly-pressed, crushed odds and ends of impression ; broken, confused, pounded bits of the sights and
sounds and emotions of our childhood.   To the statues
we return only quite late, when this long-formed, long-
moulded soul of ours has been well steeped in every sort
of eclectic and artificial culture ; has been saturated with
modern art and modern criticism, with mysticism and
realism and sentiment and cynicism, with Dante and
Zola, and Mozart and Wagner and Offenbach, saturated
with every kind of critically distilled æsthetic essence,
till there is not a flavour and not a scent, good or bad,
sweet or foul, which may not be perceived in this strange
soul of ours.   Then we return to the statues ; and, having imbibed (like all things) a certain amount of Hellenic,
Pagan, antique feeling, we try also to assimilate the

spirit of the statues of Phidias or Praxiteles ; we expound the civilisation, the mode of thought ; we trace
the differences of school, we approve and condemn, we
speak marvellously well, with subtlety or passion ; we
imagine all manner of occult, ineffable virtues and vices
in this antique art, we dabble deliciously in alternate
purity and impurity (this being the perfection of artistic
pleasure), as we even occasionally, for a few moments, feel
actual, simple, unreasoning, wholesome pleasure in the
sight of the old broken marbles. All this we do, and
most often are therewith satisfied. Yet if, weighing our
artistic likings and dislikings, comparing together our
feelings towards so many and so various manifestations,
trying to determine what is fresh and wholesome food to
our depraved æsthetic (and æsthetico-moral) palate,
and what is mere highly flavoured, spicy or nauseous
drug-stuff, if, in such a moment of doubt, we ask ourselves, overheard by no one, whether in reality this
antique art is, in the life of our feelings, at all important,
comforting, influential? we shall, for the most part,
whisper back to ourselves that it is not so in the very
least. But could it ever have been ? Could this, or any
art have been for us more than merely one of a hundred
feebly enjoyed, more or less exotic mental luxuries ;
than an historic fossil, by study of which, as with the
bone of a pterodactyl or an ichthyosaurus, we can
amuse ourselves reconstructing the appearance and
habits of a long dead, once living civilisation? Or
might these statues have been much more to us? Might
they, perhaps, have shaped and trained our souls with
their unspoken lessons?

Well, once upon a time (let us invent a fairy tale), a

child was brought to the Vatican : just such an one, only perhaps a trifle more wayward, than those we met this morning, demurely led about, or scampering through the galleries : its name signifies nothing, suffice it that it was a child.   Now, it so happened, that upon that day the statues (who, as our forefathers of the middle ages knew) are merely stone imprisoned demons, dethroned gods of antiquity, were bent upon getting some small amount of amusement in their dreary lives : all the more dreary since the great joyful hope of restoration in the hearts of men which they had conceived when Winckelmann and Goethe came to them and adored, had been slowly disappointed by seeing that what men cared for was not them, but merely their own impertinent theories and grandiloquent speeches.   The Statue-demons were sick of the bitter amusement of watching the follies of their pretended or deluded worshippers.   So they sorely wanted excitement, diversion of some sort ; and in their idleness, they capriciously determined to amuse themselves, no longer with grown men, but with children. So, as a toy for the moment, they singled out this particular child we are speaking of, who was wandering wearily through the gallery, overpowered like its companions by the sense of negativeness, of greyness, of silence, of want of character and movement and story, and as it passed them, the statue-demons looked at each other with their pupilless eyes, as much as to say: "This is the one we shall take," and determined to cast a spell upon it which would make it theirs.   How they did is more than any of us can tell : there was a little gurgling fountain in the garden outside, where a broken-snouted dragon spirted a trickle of water through the maiden-

hair choking up the basin, and of this water the child did
drink a little in the palm of its hand, the rest running
up its sleeve; there was also an old noseless Vertumnus
in a corner, on whose pedestal a great tuft of wild grass
had shot up, and round whose arms and neck an ivy
plant had cast its green trailing leaves; and one of these
bitter glossy leaves that child did certainly munch; but
whether the charm was in the water or the leaf, or in
neither, and only a mysterious spell, a sort of invisible
winged seed of passion which they cast direct into that
little soul, no one may ever decide. Be it as it may,
the child remained for a while conscious of nothing at
all, never dreaming that it had in any way come in contact with that demon world imprisoned in the stone. It
lived its child life of romping and day dreams and
lessons and punishments, and, with its companions,
fretted to get away from this dreary, horrible Rome of
the popes : this warm, wet place with its sordid houses,
its ruins embedded in filth and nettles; its tawdry, stuffy
churches, filled with snuffling of monks and jig-quaver-
ing of strange, cracked, sickening-sweet voices; its whole
atmosphere of decay and sloth, as of a great marsh-
pond, sprinkled with bright green weed and starred
with flaunting nauseous yellow lilies. The child
wondered at all these things : dug bits of porphyry and
serpentine out of gutters, collected pieces of potshard
from the Palatine ; read and re-read the stories of ship-
wrecks and red Indians and volcanoes: played in dressing-
gowns and shawls, at processions of cardinals and pre-
lates, and, with yelling companions in pinafores and
napkins, at church music, with tremendous time-beating
with rolls of paper ; laughed and pouted and quarrelled

as children do ; quite unconscious of being the chosen
one, the changeling, the victim of the statues. But little
by little, into its everyday life, stole strange symptoms ;
sometimes there would come like a sudden stop, as of a
boat caught in the rushes, a consciousness of immobility
in the midst of swirling, flowing movement, a giddy
brain-swimming feeling ; and then things went on
again just as before. But the symptoms returned, and
others with them. What was the matter? A vagueness, a want ; a seeking, a clinging, but seeking for,
clinging to the unknown. In the evenings of early
spring, when the children had returned from their
scrambling walks, and were waiting for supper, chattering,
looking at books, or strumming tunes ; this child would
watch the bank of melting colours, crimson, and smoke-
purple and gold, left by the sun behind the black dome
of St. Peter's ; and as the white vapours rose from the
town below and gathered on the roofs like a veil, it
would feel a vague, acheless pain within it ; and at any
stray, trifling word or bar of dance music, its eyes and
its whole little soul would fill with a mist of tears. The
spell cast by the statues was not idle, the mysterious
philter which they had poured into it was working
throughout that childish soul : the child was in love ; in
love with what it had hated ; in love intensely, passionately, with Rome. And as a part of Rome it loved,
blindly, for no other reason, that desolate Vatican ; to the
statues it returned, and in a way, grew up in their presence. And one day the child looked at itself, and perceived that it was a child no longer ; knew all of a sudden, that in those drowsy years of childish passion and
day dreams, it had been learning something which others

did not know. For it heard one day a few pages of a symphony of Mozart's; the first it had ever heard save much more modern music; and those bars of symphony were intelligible words, conveyed to the child a secret. And the secret was: "we are the brethern, the sounding ones of the statues: and all we who are brethren, whether in stone, or sound, or colour, or written word, shall to thee speak in such a way that thou recognise us, and distinguish us from others; and thou shalt love and believe only in us and those of our kin." Then the child went forth from the Vatican, and went in among the pictures, and among the poems and the music, and did indeed find that all those who were of the same kin as the statues spoke to it intelligible words, and returned its love by making it happy. This came of the statues having had the whim of giving to that child the love potion which had made it love Rome.

All this is a fairy tale, a very meagre one indeed, quite inferior to any told us by nurse or peasant woman; but a fairy tale nevertheless; for, of course, we all know that statues cannot give love philters, nor children fall in love with towns, nor symphonies talk about having brothers in marble or colour. All this is rubbish of the same sort as the dancing water, the singing apple, the dragon Fafner's blood which made Sigurd understand the language of the birds, the enchanted lake into which Charlemagne sat gazing out his life, because of the ring cast into it; mere rubbish, and, consequently, not to be examined into or reasoned about. But as the wise men of to-day tell us that in all our nursery tales (Heaven forbid that anything so appalling be true) there is a hidden, sensible meaning; perhaps, also, there

may be one in this absurd little story of the child in the
Vatican, and that we may see. And so, now, we must
be serious and examine methodically into the matter.

To grow up in the presence of the statues ; to become
acquainted with antique art long before any other ; to
perceive the beauty and enjoyableness of a statue
before seeking for the beauty and enjoyableness of a
picture or a piece of music ; this is the reverse of the
artistic training which every individual man or woman
obtains consciously or unconsciously in our own day ;
for we begin with the art born nearest our time, then
proceed to those further ; we go from music to painting,
and from painting to sculpture. But humanity at
large received the opposite training in the last four-and-
twenty centuries, since humanity knew beauty in the
statue before knowing beauty in the picture, and beauty
in the picture before beauty in music. The first
standard of artistic right and wrong (since architecture,
being a thing partly for use, and only partly for beauty,
has a mixed morality of its own) was the standard
of sculpture. Let us see what that was, and how we
must alter and enlarge it (as humankind has done),
in order to obtain the standard of right and wrong
in painting and that in music. The statues, in our
fairy tale, told the child that they had brethren in sound,
brethren which, knowing them, he should also know
from the resemblance. But first, what like are these
first born of art, these statues ? What is this character
in them which, found in the younger things, in painting
and music, shall show that even these are of the same
stock as the statues ? What like are these statues ?
What a question ! it is perfectly insulting to any one

of us most æsthetic creatures. What like are these
statues? Does any of us require to ask or to be taught
that? And to begin with, the very question is a gross
error, an unendurable blunder: statues, antique statues . .
. . . . You think that so simple, do you? You think,
perhaps, like the people of the sixteenth century, that
there is only one kind of antique statue ; know, most
impudent of ignoramuses, that there are innumerable
sorts of statues and antique statues, there are good
statues and bad statues, and early statues and late
statues, there are Dedalian statues and Æginete
statues, and immediately pre-Phidian and Phidian, and
immediately post-Phidian and Praxitelian statues, and
statues of the school of Pergamus, and statues of the
school of Rhodes, and Græco-Roman statues, and
statues of the Græco-Egyptian revival under Hadrian,
and statues. . . . . Enough, enough! We have been
talking of the teachings of the statues themselves, of
the lesson which they, with their unchangeable attitude
and gesture, their lines and curves and lights and
shadows of body, their folds and plaits of drapery, have
silently, slowly taught to a child ; and the statues themselves, who have never read Winckelmann, nor Quatre-
mère, nor Ottfried Müller, do not know all these
wondrous classifications of schools of which (with their
infinite advantage of teaching us to admire only one
or two schools, and abominate all the others as barbarous, decaying, Græculan, etc., without even looking
at them) we are so justly proud. Oh, yes, the statues
which taught the child were a very mixed company,
such as the carefully-trained of our day, who can endure
only Phidias, and next to Phidias, only Clodion or

Carpeaux, would scarcely like to know at all. Not
Phidian, all of them, nor even, alas, Praxitelian ; they
were not the Elgin marbles nor the Venus of Milo, sole
objects of the feeble love of us good, learned folk ; they
were those extremely harum-scarum statues of the
Vatican : a few of them copies of lost, irreproachable
originals, like the Doryphoros, the Minerva, the Amazon,
the Satyr ; a certain number of impostors of now exploded reputation, the Apollo, the Laocoön, the
Antinous, and a whole host of quite despicable others,
of every degree of lateness of epoch and baseness of
work. And what is still worse, the child was taught,
not merely by this multifarious company, but by heaven
knows what dreadful statues besides ; things to shudder
at, things, hewn stones (for the right-minded cannot call
them statues) out in gardens, noseless, armless things
under artificial ruined temples, in niches of clipped box,
or half-swathed up with ivy and creeping roses. All
these said to that child that, although some of them
were quite artistic patricians and princes, and others the
merest ragtag and bobtail, nay, unspeakable ruffians and
outcasts, they yet belonged to the same stock, they all
being antique ; and that all of them, according to their
degree and power, some in unspoken words perfect as any
of Plato's, and others in horrible, jumbled slang, mala-
prop gibberish, would teach him the same lesson, if he
would listen to them all : the lesson of their own nature
and kinship. And from all of them, insensibly, slowly,
without archæologic or æsthetic formulæ, in the simple
manner in which children learn all that is most important to know, this child learned. So that, without
desire for archæologic and æsthetic answers, we now ask,

referring to this lesson learnt by the child—"What like *are* the statues?" What like? Why, of course—well, they are like—like—like—what in the world should statues *be* like?—things cannot be defined in that cut and dry fashion—why, statues are like—. In short, such questions can neither be asked nor answered by intelligent folk. They can be put only by people who believe in love philters and symphonies which talk, and children who fall in love with towns; idiotic questions like "Why should there be sin?"—and "Why love our neighbours when they are nasty?"—which only children ask—questions to answer which as they deserve, you had better get hold of your eternal fairy-story child, and ask him what the statues said they were like. Nay, do not lose all patience. And see, since you think that the question, "What like are the statutes?" is fit to be answered only by the child of the fairy tale, we will pretend, for a moment, that the fairy tale is true, and play, for your benefit, the part of that child. And the things which that child would have learned, scarce consciously, in the course of its own growth, and during years of familiarity with all this host of statues, we will try and explain in an hour or so, by examining together a single work of ancient sculpture. This work is the Niobe group; and we have chosen it, after a little thought, for the purpose, because, from the complication of the story and of the group itself, it will enable us to illustrate a greater number of points than could well be done in the examination of isolated antique figures, or groups of merely two or three, such as there are plenty of here in Rome. But the Niobe is not in Rome, you will say; why not take some statue or group of statues

here in the Vatican? Because the Niobe can teach us
most in least time; and because also, you need not think
of the group as it stands in the gallery in Florence.
Indeed, you must not think of that group at all, spread
out as it is, in idiotic confusion, round the walls of Peter
Leopold's oblong hall. What you must think of, look
at, is this—See: here we have all the figures composing
the group, very fairly copied in terra-cotta, the largest
not much longer than your arm ; and these figures we
have placed, according to their relative size, in this
rough wooden model of the triangular gable of a Greek
temple ; following approximately the design of the
restored temple front which Cockerell made years ago
for the Florentine gallery.

Come and stand at a little distance from the table on
which the wooden gable and statues are set. So, now we
can get an idea (which in the gallery we cannot) of the
general effect of the group. It seems so simple, but it
is not : it is in sculpture something like what a fugue is
in music: it is a homogeneous form due to the extremely
skilful co-ordination of various forms ; it is a harmonious
whole, because the parts are combined just at the point
where their diversities coalesce. For, as the various
voices of the fugue, some subtly insinuating themselves
half whispered, while the others are thundering their
loudest or already dying away into silence, meet and
weave together various fragments of the same melody,
so also do the figures of the group, some standing,
some reclining, some kneeling, some rising, some draped,
some nude, meet our sight in various ways so as to constitute in their variety, one great pattern ; balance each
other on opposite sides of the gable, slope and taper

down towards the extremities, grow and rise higher towards the middle where the vertix of the triangular
temple front, the triumphant centre of the rhythm and
harmony of lines, is formed by the majestic, magnificent
mother between her two eldest, most beautiful daughters.
And now, think no more of this terra-cotta than, having
learned the shape of a hymn by Bach or a psalm by
Marcello on the piano, you would think of the poor
miserable piano-notes which you hear with your ears, instead of the mass of voices which you hear with your
fancy. Think of this Niobe group, twice humansized,
standing on the weather-mellowed, delicately painted
marble temple front ; the amber-tinted figures against
the dark hollow formed by the projecting roof; the sunshine drawing on the black back-ground, as with a
luminous pencil, the great solemn masses of light and
shadow, the powerfully rhythmed attitudes, the beautiful
combinations of lines and light and shade produced by
the gesture, which now raises, now drops the drapery,
opposing to the large folds, heavy and severe, the minute,
most supple, and most subtle plaits ; and to the strong
broken shadows of the drapery, the shining smoothness
of the nude. Think of that, and remember then the
single figures in their best examples, the mother and
eldest daughter of Florence, the headless younger
daughter of the Vatican, the exquisite dying boy of
Munich ; and think, by recollecting these dispersed
noblest copies, what must the lost original have been. And
thus, looking at the little rough terra-cotta model, and
magnifying it in fancy into the great superb group such
as it must have stood on the temple, there comes home
to us, filling, expanding our mind, an almost ineffable

c

sense of perfection of line and curve, and light and shade, perfection as of the sweeping wave of some great mountain, distant and deep blue against the pale sky ; perfection as of the pearled edge of the tiny pink cyclamen petal ; as of the single small voice, swelling and diminishing in crisp exquisiteness every little turn and shake, and again as of the many chords of multitudinous voices rolling out in great joyous sound billows ; perfection of whole in harmony and graduation of perfect parts : perfection of visible form.

But by the side of this overwhelming positive sense of beauty there creeps into our consciousness an irritating little sense of negation.   For the more intense becomes our perception of the form, the vaguer becomes our recollection of the subject ; the strong imaginative realization of the story of Niobe, conjured up by the mere mention of her name, dwindles to nothing in the presence of the group representing the chief incident of history ; the shrieks and desperate scuffling of feet, which we had heard in our fancy, gradually die into silence ; our senses cease to shrink with horror, our sympathies cease to vibrate with pity, as we look upon this visible embodiment of the terrible tragedy.   We are no longer feeling emotion; we are merely perceiving beauty.   How has this come to pass ?   Shall we look into ourselves and analyze in the darkness of our consciousness ?   Nay, rather first look for an explanation in the materially visible, the clear, easily examined work of art.   Come and look at the group once more : this time not to understand its beauty, but to understand why there is in it nothing beyond this beauty.

Certainly, the group answers very well to the general

idea [x] of the massacre of the Niobides: the figures
have the attitudes of men and women overtaken by a
sudden danger against which they seek, but vainly, to
shield themselves : the mother clasps the cowering,
clinging, youngest girl, and tries to cover her with her
mantle, her arms, her whole body, to let the child melt
into herself and be lost; the youngest son sinks, panting
and helpless, on to one knee ; the eldest daughter bends
forward to throw her veil over a dead brother ; the
younger daughter mechanically raises her draped arm
to ward off the shafts from her face ; another son hastens
away, looking bewildered around him, trying to see from
which side come the arrows, which come from all sides.
All this is perfectly correct in expression ; we are bound
to admit that these are the probable movements and
gestures of people situated like Niobe and her children.
We cannot find fault with anything, yet we feel a vague
sense of unreality.   Unreality to ourselves ?   Nay,
rather, unreality to the artist : we perceive, little by little,
that every one of these evident indications of a catastrophe
is connected with a grand gesture, a noble fold, a harmonious combination of masses: the mother raising
the arm covered with her cloak and clasping the child
with the other, produces thereby a magnificent contrast
between the round, bunched fold of the mantle, and
the straight, narrow folds of her skirt, nay, between the
simple and ample drapery covering her own bosom, and
the minute clinging crinkles on the back of the little
one ; the wounded youth sinks down in such a way as to
display the grand muscles of his throat and shoulders ;
the girl covering her naked dead brother, forms with
him, a powerfully-balanced mass of brightly-lit nude

and broken, shadow-furrowed drapery; and all the remaining children stoop and cower and stretch forth
their arms in such a way as to produce the inclination of
the two sides of the triangle crowning the temple.
Moreover, the pathetic, upward movement of the
mother's head, by slightly drawing down the jaw, and
in upturning the eyes, contracting the brows into a
triangular furrow, accentuates the grandeur of the grand
features, and prevents the light from above falling upon
a mere flat expanse of cheek and forehead; the eldest
daughter stooping tenderly over the dead boy produces,
in so doing, an incomparable curve of neck and
shoulders; and thus, with all the other figures, the
gesture is invariably productive of a definite beauty of
form.   And, on the other hand, there is not present a
single one of the gestures or attitudes which would
certainly produce definite ugliness of form, and would
yet be as appropriate and inevitable to the situation as
these.   There is not, in this group, any movement, any
effect, of which we could decidedly say that it would not
arise in a scene like this ; but, in a scene like this, there
would certainly be a great many movements and effects
which cannot be found in the group.   Hence, the
dramatic expression of the work is essentially negative :
in the mind of the artist the realisation of the scene,
the bringing home of the story, has been a purely
secondary thing, and therefore the realisation of the
scene, the bringing home of the story, is secondary
also to us, the spectators.   The impression produced
in us is exactly corresponding to the interest dominant
in the artist: he has cared for the subject only inasmuch
as it afforded suggestions for beautiful forms ; and we

therefore have perceived the beautiful forms, and forgotten the subject. The object of the artist has been,
whether or not he formulated it clearly to himself, not to
bring home the situation to the fancy; not to awaken
an emotion; but to present to the eye and the mind a
mere beautiful form. And that such has been his
object, is the first and main lesson which we have
learned from the Niobe group, as it was the first and
main lesson learned by the child of our fairy tale from
the innumerable statues which, during those long years
in the Vatican, were its silent teachers.

To present to the eye and the mind a mere beautiful
form, this seems a terribly low and limited definition of
the aim of a great artist, of a whole great national art.
Surely not this. The aim of the artist, of the innumerable artists constituting antique art, must have been
nobler: the form for them must have been the mere
physical embodiment of the ideas and the presentation
of the beautiful idea must have been their real object.
You think so? well; the child of our fairy tale pretends
that the statues told him the contrary; told him that
form was the real artistic aim, and that the idea was
arranged, clipped, sometimes even mangled, to make it
fit the form. We can judge for ourselves. You say
idea, and oppose it to form; hence, the *idea* is, we must
presume, what the *form* is not, and since the form is the
sensible, the visible, the concrete, the outwardly existing,
the idea must be the invisible, the abstract, the merely
intellectually existing. In this sense, what is the *idea*,
the abstract intellectual conception of the Niobe group?
Merely the fact of the slaughtering of the Niobides by
Apollo and Artemis in the presence of their mother,

keep this fact (if you can) in your mind without mentally investing with any shape the Niobides, the gods,
or the mother; conceiving the mere bare fact, without
conceiving what it would look like; do this and when
you have succeeded, as far as any creature not born
blind can succeed, you will have the *idea* of the Niobe
group.   Such an idea does not require for its conception
that you be a great sculptor; indeed you understand
that for the idea to be nothing beyond an idea, it requires a man born blind, that is to say, totally deficient;
that activity of plastic conception which is possessed in
the highest degree by the artist.   Now what is the product of that very plastic activity of mind which the
artist possesses in the highest degree, and which you
required to deaden in yourself in order to conceive the
idea in its perfect abstract purity, what is that product
of plastic activity? what is it which is for ever hovering
before your mental vision, getting between you and the
mere idea, interfering with the abstract conception,
turning that abstract idea into something (even in your
mind) concrete, perceptible by the senses?   That something was the *form*.   When you involuntarily said to
yourself—"the mother looked in such a way, the sons in
such another, this that you were conceiving was no
longer the mere *idea*, it was the *form*: not the action,
but the visible appearance presented by the action.   To
conceive the mere *idea*, all plastic fancy must be in
abeyance; to conceive the *form*, all plastic fancy must
be active; and as the artist is the man in whom plastic
fancy is more than usually active, that which the artist
conceives is not the idea, but the form: not the abstract
intellectual side of the action, but the concrete, the

visible. The idea, the fact of the action, and all its non-visible, psychological details, come to the artist from without; the knowledge that Niobe saw her children slaughtered by the gods, and the psychological inferences therefrom that Niobe, being a mother, and mothers, feeling anguish at the sufferings of their children, must have undergone great anguish at thus seeing her children slaughtered—this fact by its psychologic developments, comes from without to the artist, it may come from the same individual man of whom the artist is a portion, but even in this case it comes equally from without the artist; if Mr. Rossetti invent a story about a Blessed Damozel, and then paint a picture representing her looking down from heaven, the story, the idea of the Blessed Damozel is given by Mr. Rossetti, the poet, that is the man who conceives facts and their psychologic developments, to Mr. Rossetti, the painter, that is the man who conceives the visible appearance of actions; the two artists happen to be united in one person, but they are two distinct artists nevertheless, and the painter is *not* the artist who conceives the idea of the action, but the one who conceives the *form* of the action. Thus, the artist is the man who conceives the form. Now, since his activity is entirely limited to the form, since, as an artist, he can produce only the form, how is this artist to do what behoves every man and every artist: his best? How is he to give the world the greatest possible benefit of his special endowment? Evidently, since his endowment is for the creation of form, the result of the greatest activity of his endowment will be seen in the form; if he do his best, he will do his best with the only thing which, inasmuch as he is an artist, he can control, namely, the form. But how do his best with the form? Clearly, by making the form as good as possible. Good in what way? Shall we say as expressive as possible? Nay, but the expressiveness is a mere correspondence between the idea and the form, it is not an inherent quality of the form itself; given only the form, without the idea, we cannot judge of its expressiveness: to judge whether or not the Niobe group is expressive, we must first be told that which it might or might not express; the idea, the fact and its psychologic developments, which do not lie within the domain of the man of mere form. Thus the goodness of the form must not be a fittingness to something outside and separate from the form, it must be intrinsic in the form itself. And what is this excellence which can be intrinsic to the form, which can be fully appreciated in the contemplation of that mere form, which requires no comparison with anything outside the form? Not expressiveness, we have seen; not likeness, for that, like expressiveness, is an extrinsic quality of which we can judge only by bringing into comparison something besides this form; still less fittingness to some material or moral use. We must look for the intrinsic possibilities of form, that is for the effect which the form can, without intermediary or collateral help, produce upon the spectator; shall we say clearness? Clearness is an intrinsic quality of form, but it is not an ultimate quality. That a form is clear means that we can see it well; but the question remains, why should we care to see it well? what is the intrinsic quality of form in obtaining which the artist is doing the utmost which, in his capacity of mere artist, he can do? What is that which can make it desirable for us to see clearly a form isolated from any extraneous interest of expressiveness, resemblance or utility? That highest intrinsic quality of form is beauty; and the highest merit of the artist, of the mere form creator, is to make form which is beautiful.

Can the Niobe teach us more? Has your Vatican child learned any more from the statues? you ask, contemptuous at this definition, narrow, as must be all definitions of duty. Perhaps the Niobe may teach us next how this highest artistic quality of beauty, this sole aim of the artist, is to be attained? Be not so contemptuous. The Niobe can teach us something about the mode of attaining to this end; it cannot, indeed, teach us what to do, for the knowledge of that, the knowledge of how to combine lines and curves and lights and shades, is the secret belonging to the artist, to be taught and learned only by himself; but it can teach us what not to do, teach us the conditions without which those combinations of lines and curves and lights and shades, cannot be created. Let us return to the Niobe once more : let us see the group clearly in its general composition, and then, with the group before us, let us ask ourselves what plastic form is conceived in our imagination when there comes home to it the mere abstract idea of the sudden massacre of the Niobides, by Apollo and Artemis. Nothing, perhaps, very clear at first, but clearer if we try to draw what we see or to describe it in words. In the first place, we see, more or less vaguely, according to our imaginative endowment, a scene of very great confusion and horror : figures wildly shuffling to and fro, clutching at each other, writhing, grimacing with convulsed agony, skriek-

ing, yelling, howling; we see horrible wounds, rent, raw
flesh, arrows sticking in torn muscles, dragging forth
hideous entrails, spirting and gushing and trickling of
blood; we see the mother, agonised into almost beast-
like rage and terror, the fourteen boys and girls, the god
and the goddess adjusting their shafts and drawing their
bows; we see all, murderous divinities, writhing victims,
impotent, anguished mother.   If we see it, how much
more fully and more clearly, in every detail, is it not
seen in the mind of the sculptor, of the man whose
special gift is the conception of visible appearances?
Oh, yes, he sees it: here the mother, here the elder
daughters, there the other children, further off, Apollo
and Artemis, sees how each stands, moves, looks, sees
the convulsed features, the rumpled garments, the fear,
the pain, the anger, the hopelessness, the pitilessness.
He takes three planks, nails together their extremities:
this is the gable of the temple, the triangular cavity
or box into which he must fit his group; then, with
thumb and fingers, roughly moulds a certain number of
clay puppets, places them in the triangular box, removes
them, alters them, replaces them, takes them out once
more, throws some away, elaborates others; works for
hours, days, weeks, till we return to his workshop,
and find a number of models, tiny moulded dolls in the
plank triangle; large statuettes, half-finished, roughly-
worked heads—drawings, perhaps, of parts of the group.
And we examine it all.   It is the rudiment of the
Niobe group.   But see: of all those things which we
saw in our fancy, which the artist, being an artist, must
have seen with infinitely more completeness and clearness, only a portion has here been reproduced.   Of all

the movements and gestures there remain but a very
few : the convulsions, the writhings, and grimacings are
gone ; there is no trampling, no clutching, no howling,
no grimacing, there are no quivering limbs, or disembowelled bodies. Why so ? Ask the artist. Because,
he will answer, all those movements and gestures were
radically ugly ; because all that howling and grimacing
in agony entirely ruined the beauty of the features ;
because the situation could not be adequately represented, except to the utter detriment of the form.
Hence, if all the movements and gestures which had
presented themselves to his inner vision, at the first
mention of the story of Niobe, the artist has rejected
those which were at all detrimental to the beauty of the
form, and accepted those others which were conducive
thereto. He has cast aside a whole portion of the
real appearance of the event, because it interfered with
his, perhaps unspoken and unformulated, but instinctively imperious artistic aim : to create beautiful
form.

But this is not all. He has left out something else
which was a most essential, nay, an all important part of
his first mental vision of the scene. He has actually left
out—guess what—some son or daughter of Niobe ?—has
run counter to the tradition of the seven girls and seven
boys ?—oh, in comparison, that would be nothing. He
has actually and absolutely left out the god and goddess—
left out the murderers from the representation of the
murder. Why in the world has he done this ? Granting
that he need not transfer to his group all the terrible
details he has seen in his mind, why should he leave out
Apollo and Artemis ? They need not be convulsed, or

writhing, or grimacing ; on the contrary, they ought to be quite calm and passionless in their cruel beauty. There is nothing unbeautiful in Apollo and Artemis surely. No : not in Apollo and Artemis, taken in themselves; but in Apollo and Artemis considered as part of this group. Listen : we will explain. Since Apollo and Artemis are, between them, slaughtering all the Niobides, closing them in with their arrows, it is obvious that Apollo and Artemis must be placed in such a manner as to command the whole family of Niobides ; there must be no Niobides behind them, for that would mean that there are Niobides who are out of danger and can escape. So the god and goddess must be placed in one of three ways : either back to back in the very centre of the group, each shooting down one half of the family ; or else entirely separated, each at one extremity of the group, so as to face each other and enclose all the Niobides between them ; or else above the Niobides, floating in mid air and raining down arrows like hail. Now, which of these three arrangements shall the sculptor select ? He rejects at once the plan of placing the god and goddess back to back in the centre of the group, and we agree with him ; for the two figures, thus applied to each other, each more or less in profile, would form the most ludicrous double-headed Janus. Place, then, Apollo at one end and Artemis at the other. There is nothing ugly in that, is there ? There would not be were the sculptor modelling the oblong bas-relief of a sarcophagus ; but there would be something very ugly now that, as it happens, he is modelling a group for the triangular gable of a temple. For, as the sides of the triangle slope sharply down, the figures beneath them necessarily become smaller and less erect in proportion to their distance from the vertex ; so the god and goddess, if placed at the extremity of the group, must be flattened down in the acute angles of the base, must crouch and squat with their bows barely on a level with the knees of their victims. So this arrangement will not do ; there remains the third plan of placing Apollo and Artemis above the Niobides. This is an admirable idea : the vertex of the triangle is filled by the floating figures of the gods, who appear calm, beautiful, mysterious, showering down death from inaccessible heaven. Will this do ? Alas, much less than either of the others. The arrangement would be beautiful if the triangle of the gable, instead of being filled with a group of statues, were walled up, plastered, and could be painted on in fresco. The colour, light and shade, and perspective of painting, by creating a seeming depth of back-ground, by hiding one figure partially behind another, so as to make them appear not in actual contact, by piling up ætherial clouds or waving light draperies, would permit the artist to show the Niobides on solid ground below, and the gods in the air, high, distant above. But the sculptor, without any such means, could only suspend Apollo and Artemis (at tremendous expense of iron clamps) in such a way that they should seem to be standing on the shoulders of the Niobides ; or interpose between them a thick bolster of marble clouds, a massive flutter of streaming marble draperies. Now do you think that the marble clouds and the marble fluttering drapery would be conducive to the beauty of the group, to the perfection of visible forms ? Certainly not. And, therefore, Apollo and Artemis, gods though they are and chief actors in the story, have simply been left out in this its artistic representation.

For beauty of form has a double origin: it is not only an intellectual conception, but also a physical embodiment; and the intellectual conception is altered by the nature of the material in which it is embodied. The abstract form which will be infinitely delicate and life-like in the brown clay, which receives every minute dimple and crease from the finger of the artist, which presents a soft, uniform tint to the spectator; this same abstract form will be coarse and lifeless in the purple speckled porphyry, against whose hard grain the chisel is blunted, and the mottled colour and salt-like sparkle of which hide from the eye the real relations of line and curve, of concave and projection. The Mercury who, in the green bronze, floats upwards like a bubble, would jump like a clodhopper in the dingy white plaster. And these, remark, are differences only in one category of material and handling; change the sort of material and manner of handling and the differences become still greater. Statues, whether in clay, bronze, porphyry, or plaster, are always similar in the fact of being wholly free—round as Vasari calls them—of being interfered with by no complications of shadows like the figures of a high, middle or bas-relief; hence, as soon as the figures cease to be round, as soon as they are attached to a background, the whole composition is altered by the consideration how the different degrees of projection, and the consequent play of light and shadow, will affect the apparent shape of the figures. And yet we are still within the domain of sculpture. How great a difference of form will not result when, instead of the tintless, tangible projections of stone, we get to the mere semblance of infinite depth and distance cunningly obtained by light and shade, colour and perspective, on a flat surface; where the light, instead of existing variable and confusing outside the work, is within that very work, inside the picture, combining, graduating every detail, making form melt gently into form, or stand out in triumphant relief? Thus the things which can be done in bronze must not be attempted in porphyry, the group of statues must be conceived differently from the bas-relief; the picture is different from the statue; for the beauty of form depends not only on the conception but upon the embodiment: if the material is violent, the conception is warped; and the same beauty can be obtained in all the arts only by remembering that those arts are different that, with the material and modes of handling, must change the conception.

Thus we have seen that the sculptor of the Niobe deliberately refused to embody his complete mental vision of the scene of massacre; that he selected among the attitues and gestures and expressions suggested to him by this scene, rejected those which were inherently ugly, and accepted those which were intrinsically beautiful; and that he left out of his representation of the incidents its principal actors, because he could not have introduced them without either violating the nature of the whole composition to which he was bound, or violating the nature of the material in which he was working, and by so doing sacrificing the perfection of visible form which, being the only intrinsic quality to which his art could independently attain, was the one object of his desires and efforts. Such is the logical conclusion which we have consciously and perhaps wearisomely obtained from our analysis of the mode of conception and treatment of the Niobe group ; and such the lesson which, unconsciously, vaguely, the child of our fairy tale must have learned from its marble teachers in the Vatican : That the only intrinsic perfection of art is the perfection of form, and that such perfection is obtainable only by boldly altering, or even casting aside, the subject with which this form is only imaginatively, most often arbitrarily, connected ; and by humbly considering and obeying the inherent necessities of the material in which this form is made visible or audible. That by such artistic laws they themselves had come into existence, and that all other things which had come into existence by the same laws, were their brethren, was the secret which those statue-demons imparted to that child ; the secret which enabled it to understand those symphony notes of Mozart's, when they said : " we also, the sounding ones, are the brethren of the statues ; and all we who are brethren, whether in stone, or sound or colour, shall to thee speak in such a way that thou recognize us, and distinguish us from all others ; and thou shalt love and believe only in us and those of our kin ; in return we will give thee happiness." And this, as we have told you, came to pass solely because the statues took the whim of bewitching that child into falling in love with Rome.

ORPHEUS AND EURYDICE.

THE LESSON OF A BAS-RELIEF.

No Greek myth has a greater charm for our mind than
that of Orpheus and Eurydice. In the first place, we
are told by mythologists that it is a myth of the dawn,
one of those melancholy, subdued interpretations of
the eternal, hopeless separation of the beautiful light
of dawn and the beautiful light of day, which forms the
constantly recurring tragedy of nature, as the tremendous struggle between light and darkness forms her
never-ending epic, her Iliad and Nibelungenlied. There
is more of the purely artistic element in these myths of
the dawn than in the sun myths. Those earliest poets,
primitive peoples, were interested spectators of the great
battle between day and night. The sun-hero was truly
their Achilles, their Siegfried. In fighting, he fought
for them. When he chained up the powers of darkness
the whole earth was hopeful and triumphant; when he
sank down dead, a thousand dark, vague, hideous
monsters were let loose on the world, filling men's
hearts with sickening terror; the solar warfare was
waged for and against men. The case is quite different
with respect to the dawn tragedy. If men were moved
by that, it was from pure, disinterested sympathy. The
dawn and the day were equally good and equally
beautiful; the day loved the dawn, since it pursued her
so closely, and the dawn must have loved the day in

return, since she fled so slowly and reluctantly. Why, then, were they forbidden ever to meet? What mysterious fate condemned the one to die at the touch of the other—the beloved to elude the lover, the lover to kill the beloved? This sad, sympathising question, which the primitive peoples repeated vaguely and perhaps scarce consciously, day after day, century after century, at length received an answer. One answer, then another, then yet another, as fancy took more definite shapes. Yes, the dawn and the morning are a pair of lovers over whom hangs an irresistible, inscrutable fate—Cephalus and Procris, Alcestis and Admetus, Orpheus and Eurydice.

And this myth of Orpheus and Eurydice is, to our mind, the most charming of the tales born of that beautiful, disinterested sympathy for the dawn and the morning, the one in which the subdued, mysterious pathos of its origin is most perfectly preserved; in which no fault of infidelity or jealousy, no final remission of doom, breaks the melancholy unity of the story. In it we have the real equivalent of that gentle, melancholy fading away of light into light, of tint into tint. Orpheus loses Eurydice as the day loses the dawn, because he loves her; she has issued from Hades as the dawn has issued from darkness; she melts away beneath her lover's look even as the dawn vanishes beneath the look of the day.

The origin of the myth of Orpheus and Eurydice is beautiful ; the myth itself, as evolved by spontaneous poetry, is still more so, and more beautiful still are the forms which have successively been lent it by the poet, the sculptor, and the musician. Its own charm adds to that of its embodiments, and the charm of its embodiments adds in return to its own; a complete circle of beautiful impressions, whose mysterious, linked power it is impossible to withstand. The first link in the chain are those lines of Virgil's, for which we would willingly give ten Æneids, those grandly simple lines, half-hidden in the sweet luxuriance of the fourth book of the *Georgics*, as the exquisitely chiselled fragment of some sylvan altar might lie half-hidden among the long grasses and flowers, beneath the flowering bays and dark ilexes, broken shadows of boughs and yellow gleams of sunlight flickering fantastically across the clear and supple forms of the sculptured marble "And " already upwards returning, he had escaped all mishaps, " and the given-back Eurydice was coming into the upper " air, walking behind him, for Proserpina had made this " condition. When, of a sudden, a madness seized on the " unwily lover—pardonable, surely, if ghosts but knew " how to pardon. He stood, and back on his Eurydice, " already in our sunlight, he looked, forgetful, alas ! and " broken of will. Then was all the work undone, broken " was the compact with the unkind lord, and vainly had " he thrice heard the waters of hell sounding. Then " she—'What madness has ruined me, wretched one, " and thee, also, Orpheus? For I am called by the cruel " Fates to return, and sleep closes my swimming eyes. " So, farewell. I am borne away muffled in thick night, " stretching forth to thee (alas, thine no longer !) my " helpless hands.' She spoke, and from his sight sud- " denly, even as thin smoke mingles with air, disappeared; " nor him, vainly clasping the shadows, and many things " wishing to say, did she see again." These lines suggest

a bas-relief to us, because a real bas-relief is really
connected with them in our mind, and this connection
led to a curious little incident in our æsthetic life,
which is worth narrating. The bas-relief in question
is a sufficiently obscure piece of Greek workmanship,
one of those mediocre, much-degraded works of art
with which Roman galleries abound, and among which,
though left unnoticed by the crowd that gathers round
the Apollo, or the Augustus, or the Discobolus, we
may sometimes devine a repetition of some great lost
work of antiquity, some feeble reflection of lost perfection. It is let into the wall of a hall of the Villa
Albani, where people throng past it in search of the
rigid, pseudo-Attic Antinous. And it is as simple as
the verses of Virgil: merely three figures slightly
raised out of the flat, blank back-ground, Eurydice
between Orpheus and Hermes. The three figures stand
distinctly apart and in a row. Orpheus touches
Eurydice's veil, and her hand rests on his shoulder,
while the other hand, drooping supine, is grasped by
Hermes. There is no grouping, no ·embracing, no
violence of gesture—nay, scarcely any gesture at all;
yet for us there is in it a whole drama, the whole pathos
of Virgil's lines. Eurydice has returned, she is standing
beneath our sun—*jam luce sub ipsa*—but for the last
time. Orpheus lets his lyre sink, his head drooping
towards her—*multa volens dicere*—and holds her veil,
speechless. Eurydice, her head slightly bent, raises her
eyes full upon him. In that look is her last long
farewell :—

Jamque vale, feror ingenti circumdata nocte,
Invalidas tibi tendens, heu ! non tua, palmas.

Behind Eurydice stands Hermes, the sad, though youthful messenger of the dead. He gently takes her hand ;
it is time ; he would fain stay and let the parting be
delayed for ever, but he cannot. Come, we must go.
Eurydice feels it ; she is looking for the last time at
Orpheus, her head and step are prepared to turn away—
jamque vale. Truly this sad, sympathising messenger
of Hades is a beautiful thought, softening the horror of
the return to death.

And we look up again at the bas-relief, the whole
story of Orpheus laying firmer hold of our imagination ;
but as our eyes wander wistfully over the marble, they
fall, for the first time, upon a scrap of paper pasted at
the bottom of it, a wretched, unsightly, scarce legible
rag, such as insult some of the antiques in this gallery,
and on it is written :—"Antiope coi figli Anfione e
Zeto." A sudden, perplexed wonder fills our mind—
wonder succeeded by amusement. The bunglers, why,
they must have glued the wrong label on the bas-relief.
Of course ! and we turn out the number of the piece in
the catalogue, the solemn, portly catalogue—full of
references to Fea, and Visconti, and Winckelmann.
Number—yes, here it is, here it is. What, again ?

"Antiope urging her sons, Amphion and Zethus, to
avenge her by the murder of Dirce."

We put down the catalogue in considerable disgust.
What, they don't see that that is Orpheus and Eurydice!
They dare, those soulless pedants, to call *that* Antiope
with Amphion and Zethus ! Ah !—and with smothered
indignation we leave the gallery. Passing through the
little ilex copse near the villa, the colossal bust of
Winckelmann meets our eyes, the heavy, clear-featured,

strong-browed head of him who first revealed the world
of ancient art. And such profanation goes on, as it
were, under his eyes, in that very Villa Albani which
he so loved, where he first grew intimate with the
antique! What would he have said to such heartless
obtuseness?

We have his great work, the work which no amount
of additional learning can ever supersede, because no
amount of additional learning will ever enable us to feel
antique beauty more keenly and profoundly than he
made us feel it—we have his great work on our shelf,
and as soon as we are back at home, our mind still
working on Orpheus and Eurydice, we take it down
and search for a reference to our bas-relief. We search
all through the index in vain; then turn over the pages
where it may possibly be mentioned, again in vain; no
Orpheus and Eurydice. Ah! "A bas-relief at the
Villa Albani"—let us see what that may be. "A bas-
relief," &c., &c.—horror beyond words! The bas-
relief—our bas-relief—deliberately set down as Antiope
with Amphion and Zethus—set down as Antiope with
Amphion and Zethus, by Winckelmann himself!

Yes, and he gravely states his reasons for so doing.
The situation is evidently one of great hesitation; there
is reluctance on the one hand, persuasion on the other.
Moreover, the female figure is that of a mourner, of a
supplicant, draped and half-veiled as it is; the figure
with the lyre, in the Thracian or Thessalian costume,
must necessarily be Amphion, while the other in the
loose tunic of a shepherd, must as evidently be his
brother, Zethus; and if we put together these facts,
we cannot but conclude that the subject of the bas-

relief is, as previously stated, Antiope persuading Amphion and Zethus to avenge her on Dirce.

The argument is a good one, there can be no denying it, although it is very strange that Winckelmann should not have perceived that the bas-relief represented Orpheus and Eurydice. But, after all, we ask ourselves, as the confusion in our minds gradually clears up : how do we know that this *is* Orpheus and Eurydice, and not Antiope and her sons ? How ! and the answer rises up indignantly, Because we see to the contrary ; because we know that it must be Orpheus and Eurydice · because we feel morally persuaded that it is. But a doubt creeps up. We are morally convinced, but whence this conviction ? Did we come to the bas-relief not knowing what it was, and did we then cry out, overcome by its internal evidence, that it must represent Orpheus and Eurydice ? Did we ourselves examine and weigh the evidence as Winckelmann did ? And we confess to ourselves that we did none of these things. But how, then, explain this intense conviction, and the emotion awakened in us by the bas-relief ? Yet that emotion was genuine ; and now we have, little by little, to own that we had read in a book, by M. Charles Blanc, that such and such a bas-relief at the Villa Albani represented Orpheus and Eurydice, and that we had accepted the assertion blindly, unscrutinisingly, and coming to the bas-relief with that idea, did not dream of examining into its truth. And did we not then let our mind wander off from the bas-relief to the story of Orpheus, and make a sort of variation on Virgil's poem, and mistake all this for the impression received from the bas-relief itself ? May this not be the

explanation of our intense conviction? It seems as if
it were so. We have not only lost our sentimental
pleasure in the bas-relief, but we have been caught by
ourselves (most humiliating of all such positions) weaving
fantastic stories out of nothing at all, decrying great
critics for want of discernment, when we ourselves had
shown none whatever.

It may have been childish, but it was natural to feel
considerable bitterness at this discovery; you may smile,
but we had lost something precious, the idea that art
was beginning to say more to us than to others, the budding satisfaction of being no longer a stranger to the
antique, and this loss was truly bitter; nay, in the first
bitterness of the discovery, we had almost taken an aversion to the bas-relief, as people will take an aversion to
the things about which they know themselves to have
been foolish. However, as this feeling subsided, we
began to reflect that the really worthy and dignified
course would be to attain to real certainty on the subject,
and finding that our recollection of the bas-relief was not
so perfectly distinct as to authorise a final decision, we
determined coolly to examine the work once more, and
to draw our conclusions on the spot.

The following Tuesday, therefore, we started betimes
for the Villa Albani, intending to have a good hour to
ourselves before the arrival of the usual gaping visitors.
The gallery was quite empty; we drew one of the heavy
chairs robed in printed leather before the bas-relief, and
settled ourselves deliberately to examine it. We were
now strangely unbiassed on the subject, for the reaction
against our first positive mood, and the frequent turning
over one view, then the other, had left in us only a very

strong critical curiosity, the desire to unravel the tangled reason of our previous unexplained conviction. Of course we found that our memory had failed in one or two particulars, that the image preserved in our mind was not absolutely faithful, but we could discover nothing capable of materially influencing our views. We looked at the bas-relief again and again ; strictly speaking, there is in it nothing beyond a woman standing between two men, of whom the one touches her veil, and the other, to whom she turns her back, grasps her right hand, while her left hand rests lightly on the shoulder of the first male figure ; so far there is reason for saying that the bas-relief represents either Orpheus and Eurydice, or Antiope and her sons ; indeed, all that could fairly be said is that it represents a woman between two men, with one of whom she appears to be in more or less tender converse, whereas she is paying no attention to the other, who is taking her passively drooping hand. There is, however, the additional circumstance that one of the men holds a lyre and is dressed in loose trousers and mitre-like head-dress, while the other man wears only a short tunic, leaving the arms and legs bare, and his head is uncovered and shows closely-cut curly locks ; the woman being entirely draped, and her head partially covered with a veil. Now, we know that this costume of trousers and mitre-shaped head-gear was that of certain semi-barbarous peoples connected with the Greeks, amongst others the Thracians and Phrygians, while the simple tunic and the close-cut locks were distinctive of Hellenic youths, especially those admitted to gymnastic training. Moreover, we happen to know that Orpheus was a Thracian, and that Hermes

on the other hand, although in one capacity conductor
of the souls to Hades, was also the patron divinity of
the Greek ephebi of the youths engaged in gymnastic
exercises. Now, if we put together these several facts, we
perceive great likelihood of these two figures—the one
in the dress of a barbarian, which Orpheus is known to
have been, and holding a lyre, which Orpheus is known
to have played, and the other in the dress of a Greek
ephebus, which Hermes is known to have worn—of these
two figures really being intended for Orpheus and
Hermes. At the same time, we must recollect that
Amphion also is known to have worn this barbaric costume and to have played the lyre, while his brother,
Zethus, is equally known to have worn the habit of the
ephebus; so that Winckelmann has quite as good
grounds for his assertion as we have for ours. If only
the sculptor had taken the trouble to give the figure in
the tunic a pair of winged sandals or a caduceus, or a
winged cap; then there could remain no doubt of his
being Hermes, for it is a positive fact that no one except Hermes ever had these attributes; the doubt is
owing to the choice of insufficiently definite and distinctive peculiarities. But it now strikes us: all this is
founded upon the supposition that we know that the
barbarians wore trousers and mitres, that Orpheus was a
sort of barbarian, that Greek ephebi wore tunics and
short-cut hair, that Hermes was a sort of ephebus, that,
moreover, he was a conductor of souls; now, supposing
we knew none or only some of these facts, which we certainly should not, if classical dictionaries had not taught
them us, how could we argue that this is Orpheus and
that Hermes? Is the meaning of a work of Art to de-

pend on Lempriere and Dr. William Smith? At that
rate the sculptor might as well have let alone all such
distinctions, and merely written under one figure
Orpheus or *Amphion*, whichever it might be, under the
the other *Hermes* or *Zethus ;* this would not have pre-
supposed more knowledge on our part, since it seems
even easier to learn the Greek alphabet than the precise
attributes of various antique gods and demi-gods, and
then, too, no mistake would have been possible, we
should have had no choice, the figure *must* be either
Orpheus or Amphion, Hermes or Zethus, since the artist
himself said so. But this would be an admission of the
incapacity of the art or the artist, like the old device of
writing—" This is a lion," " This is a horse ; " well, but,
after all, how are we able to recognise a painted lion or
a horse ? Is it not, thanks to previous knowledge, to our
acquaintance with a live horse or live lion ? if we had
never seen either, could we say, " This is a lion," " That
is a horse ? " evidently not. But then, most people can
recognise a horse or a lion, while they cannot be expected to recognise a person they have never seen,
especially a purely imaginary one ; the case is evidently
one of degree ; if we had never seen a cow, and did not
know that cows are milked, we should no more understand the meaning of a representation of cow-milking
than we should understand the meaning of a picture of
Achilles in Scyros if we knew nothing about Achilles.
The comprehension of the subject of a work of art would
therefore seem to require certain previous information ;
the work of art would seem to be unable to tell its story
itself, unless we have the key to that story. Now, this
is not the case with literature ; given the comprehen-

sion of the separate words, no further information is required to understand the meaning, the subject of prose
or verse ; Virgil's lines pre-suppose no knowledge of the
story of Orpheus, they themselves give the knowledge of
it   The difference, then, between the poem and the
bas-relief is that the story is absolutely contained in the
former, and not absolutely contained in the latter ; the
story of Orpheus is part of the organic whole, of the existence of the poem ; the two are inseparable, since the
one is formed out of the other ; whereas, the story of
Orpheus is separate from the organic existence of the
bas-relief, it is arbitrarily connected with it, and they
need not co-exist.   What then is the bas-relief?   A
meaningless thing, to which we have wilfully attached a
meaning which is not part or parcel of it—a blank sheet
of paper on which we write what comes into our head,
and which itself can tell us nothing.

As we look up perplexedly at the bas-relief, which,
after having been as confused, has now become well
nigh as blank as our mind, we are startled by hearing
our name from a well-known voice behind us.   A young
painter stands by our side, a creature knowing or thinking very little beyond his pencils and brushes, serenely
unconscious of literature and science in his complete
devotion to art.   A few trivial sentences are exchanged,
during which we catch our friend's eye glancing at the
bas-relief.   "I never noticed that before," he remarks,
"Do you know, I like it better than anything else in this
room.   Strange that I should not have noticed it
before."

"It is a very interesting work," we answer ; adding,
with purposely feigned decision, " Of course you see that

it represents Orpheus and Eurydice, not Antiope and her sons."

The painter, whose instinctive impression on the point we have thus tried to elicit, seems wholly unmoved by this remark; the fact literally passes across his mind without in the least touching it.

"Does it? Ah, what a splendid mass of drapery! That grand, round fold and those small, fine vertical ones. I should like to make a sketch of that."

A sort of veil seems suddenly to fall off our mental eyes; these simple, earnest words, this intense admiration seem to have shed new light into our mind.

This fellow, who knows or cares apparently nothing whatever about either Orpheus or Antiope, has not found the bas-relief a blank; it has spoken for him, the clear, unmistakeable language of lines and curves, of light and shade, a language needing no interpreters, no dictionaries; and it has told him the fact, the fact depending on no previous knowledge, irrefutable and eternal, that it is beautiful. And as our eyes follow his, and we listen to his simple, unaffected, unpoetical exclamations of admiration at this combination of lines, or that bend of a limb, we recognise that if poetry has its unchangeable effects, its power which, in order to be felt, requires only the comprehension of words; art also has its unchangeable effects, its power, its supreme virtue, which all can feel who have eyes and minds that can see. The bas-relief does not necessarily tell us the story of Orpheus and Eurydice, as Virgil's lines do, that is not inherent in its nature as in theirs; but it tells us the fact of its beauty, and that fact is vital, eternal, and indissolubly connected with it.

To appreciate a work of art means, therefore, to appreciate that work of art itself, as distinguished from appreciating something outside it, something accidentally or arbitrarily connected with it ; to appreciate Virgil's lines means to appreciate his telling of the story of Orpheus, his choice of words and his metre; to appreciate the bas-relief means to appreciate the combination of forms and lights and shades ; and a person who cared for Virgil's lines because they suggested the bas-relief or for the bas-relief because it suggested Virgil's lines, would equally be appreciating neither, since his pleasure depended on something separate from the work of art itself.

Yet this is what constantly happens, and happens on account of two very simple and legitimate movements of the mind : that of comparison and that of association. Let us examine what we have called, for want of a more definite word, the movement of comparison. You are enjoying a work of art, plastic and musical ; what you enjoy is the work of art itself, the combination of lines, lights and shades and colours in the one case, the combination of modulations and harmonies in the other ; now, as this enjoyment means merely the pleasing activity of your visual and æsthetic, or acoustic and æsthetic organism, you instinctively wish to increase the activity in order to increase the pleasure; the increase of activity is obtained by approximating as much as possible to the creative activity of the original artist, by going over every step that he has gone over, by creating the work of art over again in the intensity of appreciation. If it be a plastic work, you produce your pencil and brushes and copy it; if it be a musical composition, you try and reproduce it by means of your voice or your instrument ; and you thus obtain the highest degree of æsthetical activity and pleasure compatible with mere appreciation. But supposing you can neither draw, nor sing, nor play ; supposing you have only another set of faculties, those dealing with thoughts and images, those of the artist in words, of the writer. How will you obtain that high degree of æsthetical activity, how will you go over the steps of the original creator ? You will find that words cannot copy the work of art, plastic or musical ; that lines and lights and shades, or modulations and harmonies, must be seen or heard to be appreciated ; that, in short, you have no means of absolutely reproducing what you have seen or heard ;—instinctively, unintentionally, unconsciously, you will seek for an equivalent for it ; you will try and produce with the means at your disposal something analogous to the work of art, you will obtain your æsthetic activity from another set of faculties ; not being able to draw or to sing, you will think and feel, and, in default of producing a copy, you will produce an equivalent. But the same result is not obtainable by different means ; a painter, copying a statue, will produce not a statue but a picture ; a sculptor copying a picture will produce a model, not a sketch ; yet the difference between the *modus operandi* of painting and sculpture is as nothing compared with that between the *modus operandi* of art which appeals to the eye or the ear, and art which appeals direct to the mind ; of art which deals with visible or audible shapes, and of art which deals with purely abstract thoughts and images. How much greater, then, must not also be the difference in the result ! Instead of a statue you have, not a picture, but a poem, a work of art of totally different nature from the one which you originally tried to reproduce. Instead of visual or audible forms, you have feelings and fancies; and if you compare your equivalent with the original work of art you will probably find that it has little in common with it : you had seen a beautifully chiselled head, and you say that you had perceived a beautiful emotion ; you had heard a lovely modulation, and you have written that you witnessed a pathetic parting ; instead of your eye and your ear, your imagination and feeling have been active, and the product of their activity is a special, separate one. So, in your desire to appreciate a work of art, you have, after a fashion, created a new one, good or bad, and having created it, there are a hundred chances against one that you will henceforward perceive your creation and not the original work ; that you will no longer perceive lines or sounds, but fancies and feelings, in short, that instead cf appreciating the work of art itself, you will appreciate merely your intellectual equivalent of it, that is to say, something which most distinctly and emphatically is *not* the work of art.

The process of association is even commoner : you have taken interest in some story, or some form, your mind has worked upon it ; you are shown a work of art whose name, often nothing more, connects it with this story or poem, and your thoughts being full of the latter, you apply to the work of art the remarks you had made about the story or poem ; you see in the work of art the details of that story or poem ; you look at it as a mere illustration ; very often you do not look at it at all ; for although your bodily eyes may be fixed on the picture or statue, your intellectual eyes are busy with some recollection or impression in your mind; it is the case of the bas-relief of the Villa Albani, of the pleasure received from Virgil's lines being re-awakened by the mere circumstance of the bas-relief being called, rightly or wrongly, Orpheus and Eurydice; it is the story of a hundred interpretations of works of art, of people seeing a comic expression in a certain group at the Villa Ludovisi because they imagined it to represent Papirius and his mother, while other people found the same group highly tragic, because they fancied it represented Electra and Orestes; it is the old story of violent emotion, attributed to wholly unemotional music, because the words to which it is arbitrarily connected happen to be pathetic; the endless story of delusions of all sorts, of associations of feelings and ideas as accidental as those which make certain tunes or sights depress us because we happened to be in a melancholy mood when we first saw or heard them.

What becomes of the real, inherent effect of the work of art itself in the midst of such concatenations of fancies and associations? How can we listen to its own magic speech, its language of lines and colours and sounds, when our mind is full of confused voices telling us of different and irrelevant things? Where, at such times, is our artistic appreciation, and what is it worth? Should we then, if such a thing were possible, forbid such comparisons, such associations? Should we voluntarily deprive ourselves of all such pleasure as is not given by the work of art itself?

No, but we should restrain such impressions; we should, as far as we can, remain conscious of the fact that they are mere effects of comparison and association, that

E

they are not the work of art, but something distinct from
it, and that the work of art itself exists in the lines, tints,
lights and shades of the picture or statue, in the modulations
and harmonies of a composition, and that all the rest is
gratuitously added by ourselves. Nay, we should remember
that there could not even have been that very comparison,
that very association if there had been no previous real
artistic perception ; that unless we had first cared for
Virgil's Orpheus for its own sake, we could not afterwards have cared for the bas-relief on its account.

We confess that we have ourselves become instinctively
jealous of such foreign causes of pleasure in art, jealous
because we have been pained by their constant encroach-
ment ; the feeling may be an exaggerated one, but it is
a natural reaction. We have thus caught ourselves
almost regretting that pictures should have any subjects ;
we have sometimes felt that the adaptation of music to
the drama is a sort of profanation ; and all this because we have too often observed that the subject
seemed to engross so much attention as to make people
forget the picture, and that the drama made people mis-
interpret the music ; and that criticism itself, instead of
checking this tendency, has done much to further it.
Yes, critics, grave and emphatic thinkers, have spoken as
if the chief merit of the painter had consisted in clearly
expressing some story, which in all probability was not
worth expressing, some dull monkish legend which his
genius alone could render tolerable ; as if the chief aim
of the composer were to follow the mazes of some
wretched imbecile libretto, which has become endurable
thanks only to his notes ; as if the immortal were to be
chained to the mortal, and mediocrity, inferiority, mere

trumpery fact or trumpery utility were to bridle and be-
stride the divine hippogriff of art, and, like another
Astolfo, fly up on its back into the regions of immortality. Artists themselves have been of this way of
thinking, we cannot say of feeling, for, as long as they
were true artists, their instinctive feelings must have pro-
pelled them in a very different direction. Gluck, that
great dramatist, who was greatest when least dramatic,
thought that music was made for the sake of the drama,
that its greatest glory was to express the difference, as
he himself wrote, between a princess and a waiting-maid
between a Spartan and a Phrygian, to follow the steps
of a play as its humble retainer and commentator. Gluck
composed his music for the sake of the dramas ; but, O
irony of art ! the dramas are recollected only for the sake
of his music. Let the artist be humble, mistrustful of his
own art, let him believe it to be subservient to something outside it, devote it magnanimously to some purpose of utility, or some expression of fact, sacrifice it
throughout ; it will be all in vain ; if his work be excellent, it will subordinate all to itself, it will swallow
up every other interest, throw into the shade every other
utility.

One day the Pope's banker, Agostino Chigi, came to
Master Rafael of Urbino, and said to him—" I am building a little pleasure villa in which to entertain my
friends. Baldassare Peruzzi has made the plans,
Sebastiano del Piombo has designed the arabesques,
Nanni da Udine will paint me the garlands of fruit and
flowers ; it must be perfection. You shall paint me the
walls of the open hall looking out on the Tiber, that it
may be a fit place wherein to sup and make merry with

popes and cardinals and princes." "Very good," answered Rafael.

The object was to obtain a dining-hall, and the fresco
was to be there merely as an ornament; but Rafael
painted his Galatea, and behold, the hall could no
longer be used as a dining-room; every one crowded
into it to see the fresco; the hall has now become a
gallery, and the real property, less of its owners, who
cannot make use of it, than of the whole world, who
insist on entering it; the room now exists only for the
sake of the fresco, yet the fresco was originally intended
to exist only for it.　This is the inevitable course of art;
we call in beauty as a servant, and see, like some strange
dæmon, it becomes the master; it may answer our call,
but we have to do its bidding.

We have strayed far away from Orpheus and Eurydice, while thus following the train of ideas suggested by
the story of the bas-relief.　Yet we may return to the
subject, and use it as an illustration of our last remark.
We have said much against the common tendency
towards transporting on to a work of art an interest
not originally due to it, because, by this means, we
are apt to lose the interest which does belong to the
work of art.　But, if only each could get its due, each
exert its power unimpaired, there could be nothing more
delightful than thus to enjoy the joint effect of several
works of art; not, according to the notion of certain
æsthetic visionaries—who do not see that singers cannot
be living Greek statues nor librettists poets, nor scene-
painters Poussins—in one clumsy ambiguous monster
spectacle, but in our minds, in our fancy; if, conscious
of the difference between them, we could unite in one

collection the works of various arts: people the glades and dingles of Keats with the divinities we have seen in marble, play upon the reed of the Praxitelian Faun the woodland melodies of Mozart's Tamino. It would thus be the highest reward for self-scrutinising æsthetic humility, for honest appreciation of each art for itself, for brave sacrifice of our own artistic whimsies and vanities, to enable us to bring up simultaneously the recollection of Virgil's nobly pathetic lines, of the exquisitely simple and supple forms of the bas-relief, of the grand and tender music of Gluck, and to unite them in one noble pageant of the imagination, evoked by the spell of those two names: Orpheus and Eurydice.

FAUSTUS AND HELENA.

THERE is a story, well-known throughout the sixteenth century, which tells how Doctor Faustus of Wittemberg, having made over his soul to the fiend, employed him to raise the ghost of Helen of Sparta, in order that she might become his paramour. The story has no historic value, no scientific meaning ; it lacks the hoary dignity of the tales of heroes and demi-gods, wrought, vague, and colossal forms, out of cloud and sunbeam, of those tales narrated and heard by generations of men deep hidden in the stratified ruins of lost civilisation, carried in the races from India to Hellas, and to Scandinavia. Compared with them, this tale of Faustus and Helena is paltry and brand-new ; it is not a myth, nay, scarcely a legend ; it is a mere trifling incident added by humanistic pedantry to the ever-changing mediæval story of the man who barters his soul for knowledge, the wizard, alchemist, philosopher, printer, Albertus, Bacon, or Faustus. It is a part, an unessential, subordinate fragment, valued in its day neither more nor less than any other part of the history of Doctor Faustus, narrated cursorily by the biographer of the wizard, overlooked by some of the ballad rhymers, alternately used and rejected by the playwrights of puppet-shows ; given by Marlowe himself no greater importance than the other marvellous deeds, the juggling tricks and magic journeys of his hero.

But for us, the incident of Faustus and Helena has a meaning, a fascination wholly different from any other portion of the story; the other incidents owe everything to artistic treatment: this one owes nothing. The wizard Faustus, awaiting the hour which will give him over to Hell, is the creation of Marlowe; Gretchen is even more completely the creation of Goethe; the fiend of the Englishman is occasionally grand, the fiend of the German is throughout masterly; in all these cases we are in the presence of true artistic work, of stuff rendered valuable solely by the hand of the artist, of figures well defined and finite, and limited also in their power over the imagination. But the group of Faustus and Helena is different; it belongs neither to Marlowe nor to Goethe, it belongs to the legend. It does not give the complete and limited satisfaction of a work of art; it has the charm of the fantastic and fitful shapes formed by the flickering firelight or the wreathing mists; it haunts like some vague strain of music, drowsily heard in half-sleep. It fills the fancy, it oscillates and transforms itself; the artist may see it, attempt to seize and embody it for evermore in a definite and enduring shape, but it vanishes out of his grasp, and the forms which should have inclosed it are mere empty sepulchres, haunted and charmed merely by the evoking power of our own imagination. If we are fascinated by the Lady Helen of Marlowe, walking, like some Florentine goddess, with embroidered kirtle and madonna face, across the study of the old wizard of Wittemberg; if we are

pleased by the stately pseudo-antique Helena of
Goethe, draped in the drapery of Thorwaldsen's statues,
and speaking the language of Goethe's own Iphigenia,
as she meets the very modern Faust, gracefully
masqued in mediæval costume ; if we find in these
attempts, the one unthinking and imperfect, the other
laboured and abortive, something which delights our
fancy, it is because our thoughts wander off from them
and evoke a Faustus and Helena of our own, different
from the creations of Marlowe and of Goethe; it is
because in these definite and imperfect artistic forms,
there yet remains the suggestion of the subject with
all its power over the imagination. We forget Marlowe,
and we forget Goethe, to follow up the infinite suggestion of the legend. We cease to see the Elizabethan
and the pseudo-antique Helen ; we lift our imagination
from the book and see the mediæval street at Wittemberg, the gabled house of Faustus, all sculptured with
quaint devices and grotesque forms of apes and cherubs
and flowers ; we penetrate through the low brown
rooms, filled with musty books and mysterious ovens
and retorts, redolent with strange scents of alchemy,
to that innermost secret chamber, where the old wizard
hides, in the depths of his mediæval house, the immortal
woman, the god-born, the fatal, the beloved of Theseus
and Paris and Achilles ; we are blinded by this sunshine of Antiquity pent up in the oaken-panelled
chamber, such as Dürer might have etched ; and all
around we hear circulating the mysterious rumours of
the neighbours, of the burghers and students, whispering
shyly of Dr. Faustus and his strange guest, in the beer-
cellars and in the cloisters of the old university town.

And gazing thus into the fantastic intellectual mist which has risen up between us and the book we were reading, be it Marlowe or Goethe, we cease, after a while, to see Faustus or Helena, we perceive only a chaotic fluctuation of incongruous shapes ; scholars in furred robes and caps pulled over their ears, burghers wives with high sugar-loaf coif and slashed boddices, with hands demurely folded over their prayer-books, and knights in armour and immense plumes, and haggling Jews, and tonsured monks, descended out of panels of Wohlgemüth and the engravings of Dürer, mingling with, changing into processions of naked athletes on foaming short-maned horses, of draped Athenian maidens carrying baskets and sickles, and priests bearing oil-jars and torches, all melting into each other, indistinct, confused, like the images in a dream ; vague crowds, phantoms following in the wake of the spectre woman of Antiquity, beautiful, unimpassioned, ever young, luring to Hell the wizard of the Middle Ages.

Why does all this vanish as soon as we once more fix our eyes upon the book? Why can our fancy show us more than can the artistic genius of Marlowe and of Goethe? Why does Marlowe, believing in Helen as a satanic reality, and Goethe, striving after her as an artistic vision, equally fail to satisfy us? The question is intricate : it requires a threefold answer, dependent on the fact that this tale of Faustus and Helena is in fact a tale of the supernatural—a weird and colossal ghost-story, in which the actors are the spectre of Antiquity, ever young, beautiful, radiant, though risen from the putrescence of two thousand years ; and the

Middle Ages, alive, but toothless, palsied, and tottering. Why neither Marlowe nor Goethe have succeeded in giving a satisfactory artistic shape to this tale is explained by the necessary relations between art and the supernatural, between our creative power and our imaginative faculty ; why Marlowe has failed in one manner and Goethe in another is explained by the fact that, as we said, for the first the tale was a supernatural reality, for the second a supernatural fiction.

What are the relations between art and the supernatural? At first sight the two appear closely allied: like the supernatural, art is born of imagination ; the supernatural, like art, conjures up unreal visions. The two have been intimately connected during the great ages of the supernatural, when instead of existing merely in a few disputed traditional dogmas, and in a little discredited traditional folklore, it constituted the whole of religion and a great part of philosophy. Gods and demons, saints and spectres, have afforded at least one-half of the subjects for art. The supernatural, in the shape of religious mythology, had art bound in its service in Antiquity and the Middle Ages ; the supernatural, in the shape of spectral fancies, regained its dominion over art with the advent of romanticism. From the gods of the *Iliad* down to the Commander in *Don Giovanni,* from the sylvan divinities of Praxiteles to the fairies of Shakespeare, from the Furies of Æschylus to the Archangels of Perugino, the supernatural and the artistic have constantly appeared linked together. Yet, in reality, the hostility between the supernatural and the artistic is well-nigh as great as the hostility between the supernatural and the logical. . Critical reason is a solvent, it reduces the phantoms of the imagination to their most prosaic elements; artistic power, on the other hand, moulds and solidifies them into distinct and palpable forms: the synthetical definiteness of art is as sceptical as the analytical definiteness of logic. For the supernatural is necessarily essentially vague, and art is necessarily essentially distinct: give shape to the vague and it ceases to exist. The task set to the artist by the dreamer, the prophet, the priest, the ghost-seer of all times, is as difficult, though in the opposite sense, as that by which the little girl in the Venetian fairy tale sought to test the omnipotence of the emperor. She asked him for a very humble dish, quite simple and not costly, a pat of butter broiled on a gridiron. The emperor desired his cook to place the butter on the gridiron and light the fire; all was going well, when, behold! the butter began to melt, trickled off, and vanished. The artists were asked to paint, or model, or narrate the supernatural; they set about the work in good conscience, but see, the supernatural became the natural, the gods turned into men, the madonnas into mere mothers, the angels into armed striplings, the phantoms into mere creatures of flesh and blood.

There are in reality two sorts of supernatural, although only one really deserves the name. A great number of beliefs in all mythologies are in reality mere scientific errors—abortive attempts to explain phenomena by causes with which they have no connection—the imagination plays not more part in them than in any other sort of theorising, and the notions that unlucky accidents are due to a certain man's glance, that certain formulæ will bring rain or sunshine, that miraculous images will dispel

pestilence, and kings of England cure epilepsy, must be
classed under the head of mistaken generalizations, not
very different in point of fact from exploded scientific
theories, such as Descartes' vortices, or the innate ideas
of scholasticism.   That there was a time when animals
spoke with human voice may seem to us a piece of fairy-
lore, but it was in its day a scientific hypothesis as brilliant and satisfying as Darwin's theory of evolution.
We must, therefore, in examining the relations between
art and the supernatural, eliminate as far as possible this
species of scientific speculation, and consider only that
supernatural which really deserves the name, which is
beyond and outside the limits of the possible, the rational,
the explicable—that supernatural which is due not to
the logical faculties, arguing from wrong premises, but
to the imagination wrought upon by certain kinds of
physical surroundings.   The divinity of the earlier races
is in some measure a mistaken scientific hypothesis of the
sort we have described, an attempt to explain phenomena
otherwise inexplicable.   But it is much more : it is the
effect on the imagination of certain external impressions,
it is those impressions brought to a focus, personified, but
personified vaguely, in a fluctuating ever-changing manner ; the personification being continually altered, rein-
forced, blurred out, enlarged, restricted by new series of
impressions from without, even as the shape which we
puzzle out of congregated cloud-masses fluctuates with
their every movement—a shifting vapour now obliterates
the form, now compresses it into greater distinctness :
the wings of the fantastic monster seem now flapping
leisurely, now extending bristling like a griffon's ; at one
moment it has a beak and talons, at others a mane and

hoofs ; the breeze, the sunlight, the moonbeam, form, alter, and obliterate it. Thus is it with the supernatural : the gods, moulded out of cloud and sunlight and dark- ness, are for ever changing, fluctuating between a human or animal shape, god, or goddess, cow, ape, or horse, and the mere natural phenomenon which impresses the fancy. Pan is the weird, shaggy, cloven-footed shape which the goat-herd or the huntsman has seen gliding among the bushes in the grey twilight ; his is the piping heard in the tangle of reeds, marsh lily, and knotted nightshade by the river side : but Pan is also the wood, with all its sights and noises, the solitude, the gloom, the infinity of rustling leaves, and cracking branches; he is the greenish- yellow light stealing in amid the boughs ; he is the breeze in the foliage, the murmur of unseen waters, the mist hanging over the damp sward, the ferns and grasses which entangle the feet, and the briars which catch in the hair and garments are his grasp; and the wanderer dashes through the thickets with a sickening fear in his heart, and sinks down on the outskirts of the forest, gasping, with sweat-clotted hair, overcome by this glimpse of the great god.

In this constant renewal of the impressions on the fancy; in this unceasing shaping and reshaping of its creations, consisted the vitality of the myths of paganism, from the scorching and pestilence-bearing gods of India to the divinities shaped out of tempest and snowdrift of Scandi- navia ; they were constantly issuing out of the elements, renewed, changed, ever young, under the exorcism not only of the priest and of the poet, but of the village boor ; and on this unceasing renovation depended the sway which they maintained, without ethical importance to help them,

despite philosophy and Christianity. Christianity, born
in an age of speculation and eclecticism, removed its
divinities, its mystic figures, out of the cosmic surroundings of paganism ; it forbade the imagination to touch
or alter them, it regularised, defined, explained, placed
the Saviour, the Virgin, the saints and angels, into a kind
of supersensuous world of logic, logic adapted to Heaven,
and different therefore from the logic of earth, but logic
none the less.   Christianity endowed them with certain
definite attributes, not to be found among mortals, but
analogous in a manner to mortal attributes ; the Christian supernatural system belongs mainly to the category
of mistaken scientific systems ; its peculiarities are due,
not to overwrought fancy, but to overtaxed reason.   Thus
the genuine supernatural was well-nigh banished by
official Christianity, regulated as it was by a sort of con-
gress of men of science, who eliminated, to the best of
their powers, any vagaries of the imagination which
might show themselves in their mystico-logic system.
But the imagination did work nevertheless, and the supernatural did reappear, both within and without the Christian system of mythology.   The Heaven of theology
was too ethical, too logical, too positive, too scientific, in
accordance with the science of the Middle Ages, for the
minds of humanity at large ; the scholars and learned
clergy might study and expound it, but it was insufficient for the ignorant.   The imagination reappeared
once more.   To the monk arose out of the silence and
gloom of the damp, lichen-grown crypt, out of the fœtid
emanations of the charnal-house, strange forms of horror
which lurked in his steps and haunted his sleep after
fasting and scourging and vigils ; devils and imps

horrible and obscene, which the chisel of the stonecutter vainly attempted to reproduce, in their fluctuating abomination, on the capitals and gargoyles of cloister and cathedral. To the artisan, the weaver pent up in some dark cellar into which the daylight stole grey and faint from the narrow strip of blue sky between the over-hanging eaves, for him, the hungry and toil-worn and weary of soul, there arose out of the hum of the street above, out of the half-lit dust, the winter damp and summer suffocation of the underground workshop, visions and sounds of sweetness and glory, misty clusters of white-robed angels shedding radiance around them, swaying in mystic linked dances, mingling with the sor-did noises of toil seraphic harmonies, now near, now dying away into distance, voices singing of the sunshine and flowers of Paradise. And for others, for the lean and tattered peasant, with the dull, apathetic resignation of the starved and goaded ox or horse, sleeping on the damp clay of his hut and eating strange flourless bread, and stranger carrion flesh, there came a world of the supernatural, different from that of the monk or the artisan, at once terrifying and consoling ; the divinities cast out by Christianity, the divinities for ever newly be-gotten by nature, but begotten of a nature miserably changed, born in exile and obloquy and persecution, fostered by the wretched and the brutified ; differing from the gods of antiquity as the desolate heath, barren of all save stones and prickly furze and thistle, differs from the fertile pasture-land ; as the forests planted over the cornfield, whence issue wolves, and the Baron's harvest-trampling horses, differ from the forests which gave their oaks and pines to Tyrian ships ; divinities

warped, and crippled, grown hideous and malignant and
unhappy in the likeness of their miserable votaries.

This is the real supernatural, born of the imagination
and its surroundings, the vital, the fluctuating, the potent;
and it is this which the artist of every age, from Phidias
to Giotto, from Giotto to Blake, has been called upon to
make known to the multitude. And there had been artistic
work going on unnoticed long before the time of any
painter or sculptor or poet of whom we have any record ;
mankind longed from the first to embody, to fix its
visions of wonder, it set to work with rough unskilful
fingers moulding into shape its divinities. Rude work,
ugly, barbarous, blundering scratchings on walls,
kneaded clay vessels, notched sticks, nonsense rhymes ;
but work nevertheless which already showed that art
and the supernatural were at variance, the beaked and
clawed figures outlined on the wall were compromises
between the man and the beast, but definite compromises, so much and no more of the man, so much
and no more of the beast ; the goddess on the clay
vessels became a mere little owl ; the divinities even
in the nonsense verses were presented now as very
distinct cows, now as very distinct clouds, or very
distinct men and women ; the vague, fluctuating impressions oscillating before the imagination like the
colours of a dove's wing, or the pattern of a shot silk,
interwoven, unsteady, never completely united into one,
never completely separated into several, were rudely
seized, disentangled by art ; part was taken, part thrown
aside ; what remained was homogeneous, definite, un-
changing ; it was what it was and could never be aught
else.

Goethe has remarked, with a subjective simplicity of irreverence which is almost comical, that as God created man in his image, it was only fair that man, in his turn, should create God in *his* image. But the decay of pagan belief was not, as Hegel imagines, due to the fact that Hellenic art was anthropomorphic. The gods ceased to be gods not merely because they became too like men, but because they became too like anything definite. If the ibis on the amulet, or the owl on the terra-cotta, represents a more vital belief in the gods than does the Venus of Milo or the Giustiniani Minerva, it is not because the idea of divinity is more compatible with an ugly bird than with a beautiful woman, but because whereas the beautiful woman, exquisitely wrought by a consummate sculptor, occupied the mind of the artist and of the beholder with the idea of her beauty, to the exclusion of all else, the rudely-engraven ibis, or the badly-modelled owlet, on the other hand, served merely as a symbol, as the recaller of an idea; the mind did not pause in contemplation of the bird, but wandered off in search of the god: the goggle eyes of the owl and the beak of the ibis were soon forgotten in the contemplation of the vague, ever transmuted visions of phenomena of sky and light, of semi-human and semi-bestial shapes, of confused half-embodied forces; in short, of the supernatural. But the human shape did most mischief to the supernatural, merely because the human shape was the most absolute, the most distinct of all shapes: a god might be symbolised as a beast, but he could only be pourtrayed as a man; and if the portrait was correct, then the god was a man, and nothing more. Even the most fantastic among pagan supernatural creatures,

F

those strange monsters who longest kept their original
dual nature—the centaurs, satyrs, and tritons—became,
beneath the chisel of the artist, mere aberrations from
the normal, rare, and curious types like certain fair-booth
phenomena, but perfectly intelligible and rational ; the
very Chimæra, she who was to give her name to every
sort of unintelligible fancy, became, in the bas-reliefs
of the story of Bellérophon a mere singular mixture
between a lion, a dog, and a bird—a cross-breed which
happens not to be possible, but which an ancient might
well have conceived as adorning some distant zoological
collection.   How much more rationalised were not the
divinities in whom only a peculiar shape of the eye, a
certain structure of the leg, or a definite fashion of
wearing the hair remained of their former nature.
Learned men, indeed, tell us that we need only glance
at Hera to see that she is at bottom a cow ; at Apollo,
to recognise that he is but a stag in human shape : or at
Zeus, to recognise that he is, in point of fact, a lion.
Yet it remains true that we need only walk down the
nearest street to meet ten ordinary men and women
who look more like various animals than do any
antique divinities, and who can yet never be said to
be in reality cows, stags, or lions.   The same applies to
the violent efforts which are constantly being made to
show in the Greek and Latin poets a distinct recollection of the cosmic nature of the gods, construing the
very human movements, looks, and dress of divinities
into meteorological phenomena, as has been done even
by Mr. Ruskin, in his *Queen of the Air*, despite his
artist's sense, which should have warned him that no
artistic figure, like Homer's divinities, can possibly be

at the same time a woman and a whirlwind. The gods did originally partake of the character of cosmic phenomena, as they partook of the characters of beasts and birds, and of every other species of transformation, such as we may watch in dreams; but as soon as they were artistically embodied, this transformation ceased, the nature had to be specified in proportion as the form became distinct; and the drapery of Pallas, although it had inherited its purple tint from the storm-cloud, was none the less, when it clad the shoulders of the goddess, not a storm-cloud, but a piece of purple linen. "What do you want of me?" asks the artist. "A god," answers the believer. "What is your god to be like?" asks the artist. "My god is to be a very handsome warrior, a serene heaven, which is occasionally overcast with clouds, which clouds are sometimes very beneficial, and become (and so does the god at those moments) heavy-uddered cows; at others, they are dark, and cause annoyance, and then they capture the god, who is the light (but he is also the clouds, remember), and lock him up in a tower, and then he frees himself, and he is a neighing horse, and he is sitting on the prancing horse (which is himself, you know, and is the sky too), in the shape of two warriors, and also——" "May Cerberus devour you!" cries the artist. "How can I represent all this? Do you want a warrior, or a cow, or the heavens, or a horse, or do you want a warrior with the hoofs of a horse and the horns of a cow? Explain, for, by Juno, I can give you only one of these at a time."

Thus, in proportion as the gods were subjected to artistic manipulation, whether by sculptor or poet, they

lost their supernatural powers. A period there doubtless
was when the gods stood out quite distinct from nature,
and yet remained connected with it, as the figures of a
high relief stand out from the background; but gradually they were freed from the chaos of impressions which
had given them birth, and then, little by little, they
ceased to be gods; they were isolated from the world of
the wonderful, they were respectfully shelved off into the
region of the ideal, where they were contemplated, ad-
mired, discussed, but not worshipped, even like their
statues by Praxiteles and their pictures by Parrhasius.
The divinities who continued to be reverenced were the
rustic divinities and the foreign gods and goddesses; the
divinities which had been safe from the artistic dese-
cration of the cities, and the divinities which were
imported from hieratic, unartistic countries like Egypt
and Syria; on the one hand, the gods shaped with the
pruning-knife out of figwood, and stained with ochre or
wine-lees, grotesque mannikins, standing like scarecrows,
in orchard or corn-field, to which the peasants crowded in
devout procession, leading their cleanly-dressed little
ones, and carrying gifts of fruit and milk, while the listless Tibullus, fresh from sceptical Rome, looked on from
his doorstep, a vague, childish veneration stealing over
his mind; on the other hand, the monstrous goddesses,
hundred-breasted or ibis-headed, half hidden in the
Syrian and Egyptian temples, surrounded by mysterious
priests, swarthy or effeminate, in mitres and tawny robes,
jangling their sistra and clashing their cymbals, moving
in mystic or frenzied dances, weird, obscene, and unearthly, to the melancholy drone of Phrygian or Egyptian
music, sending a shudder through the atheist Catullus,

and filling his mind with ghastly visions of victims of
the great goddess, bleeding, fainting, lashed on to madness by the wrath of the terrible divinity. These were
the last survivors of paganism, and to their protection
clung the old gods of Greece and Rome, reduced to
human level by art, stripped naked by sculptor and poet
and muffling themselves in the homely or barbaric garments of low-born or outlandish usurpers; art had been
a worse enemy than scepticism: Apelles and Scopas had
done more mischief than Epicurus.

Christian art was, perhaps, more reverent in intention,
but not less desecrating in practice; even the Giottesques
turned Christ, the Virgin, and the Saints, into mere Florentine men and women; even Angelico himself, although
a saint, was unable to show Paradise except as a flowery
meadow, under a highly gilded sky, through which
moved ladies and youths in most artistic but most
earthly embroidered garments; and Hell except as a
very hot place where men and women were being boiled
and broiled and baked and fried and roasted by very
comic little weasel-snouted fiends, which on a carnival
car would have made Florentines roar with laughter.
The real supernatural was in the cells of fever-stricken,
starved visionaries; it was in the contagious awe of the
crowd sinking down at the sight of the stained napkin
of Bolsena; in that soiled piece of linen was Christ, and
God, and Paradise; in that and not in the panels of
Angelico and Perugino, or in the frescoes of Signorelli
and Filippino.

Why? Because the supernatural is nothing but ever-
renewed impressions, ever-shifting fancies; and that art
is the definer, the embodier, the analytic and synthetic

force of form. Every artistic embodiment of impressions
or fancies implies isolation of those impressions or fancies, selection, combination and balancing of them ; that
is to say, diminution—nay, destruction of their inherent
power. As, in order to be moulded, the clay must be
separated from the mound ; as, in order to be carved, the
wood must be cut off from the tree ; as, in order to be
re-shaped by art, the mass of atoms must be rudely
severed ; so also the mental elements of art, the mood,
the fancy must be severed from the preceding and succeeding moods or fancies ; artistic manipulation requires
that its intellectual, like its tangible materials, cease to
be vital, but the materials, mental or physical, are not
only deprived of vitality and power of self-alteration ;
they are combined in given proportions, the action of
the one on the other destroys in great part the special
power of each ; art is proportion, and proportion is restriction. Last of all, but most important, these isolated,
no longer vital materials, neutralised by each other, are
further reduced to insignificance by becoming parts of a
whole conception ; their separate meaning is effaced by
the general meaning of the work of art ; art bottles
lightning to use it as white colour, and measures out
thunder by the beat of the chapel-master's roll of notes.
But art does not merely restrict impressions and fancies
within the limits of form ; in its days of maturity and
independence it restricts yet closer within the limits of
beauty. Partially developed art, still unconscious of its
powers and aims, still in childish submission to religion,
sets to work conscientiously, with no other object than to
embody the supernatural ; if the supernatural suffers in
the act of embodiment, if the fluctuating fancies which

are Zeus or Pallas are limited and curtailed, rendered
logical and prosaic even in the wooden pre-historic idol
or the roughly kneaded clay owlet, it is by no choice of
the artist—his attempt is abortive, because it is thwarted,
by the very nature of his art. But when art is mature,
things are different; the artist, conscious of his powers,
instinctively recognising the futility of aiming at the
embodiment of the supernatural, dragged by an irresistible longing to the display of his skill, to the imitation
of the existing and to the creation of beauty, ceases to
strain after the impossible and refuses to attempt anything beyond the possible. The art, which was before a
mere insufficient means, is now an all-engrossing aim ;
unconsciously, perhaps, to himself, the artist regards the
subject merely as a pretext for the treatment; and
where the subject is opposed to such treatment as he
desires, he sacrifices it. He may be quite as conscientious
as his earliest predecessor, but his conscience has become
an artistic conscience, he sees only as much as is within
art's limits ; the gods, or the saints, which were cloudy
and supernatural to the artist of immature art, are definite and artistic to the artist of mature art; he can
think, imagine, feel only in a given manner; his religious
conceptions have taken the shape of his artistic creations;
art has destroyed the supernatural, and the artist has
swallowed up the believer. The attempts at supernatural
effects are almost always limited to a sort of symbolical
abbreviation, which satisfies the artist and his public
respecting the subject of the work, and lends it a traditional association of the supernatural ; a few spikes
round the head of a young man are all that remains of
the solar nature of Apollo ; the little budding horns and

pointed ears of the satyr must suffice to recall that he was once a mystic fusion of man and beast and forest ; a gilded disc behind the head is all that shows that Giotto's figures are immortals in glory ; and a pair of wings is all that explains that Perugino's St. Michael is not a mere dainty mortal warrior ; the highest mysteries of Christianity are despatched with a triangle and an open book, to draw which Raphael might employ his colour-grinder, while he himself drew the finely-draped baker's daughter from Trastevere.

In all these cases the artist refused to grapple with the supernatural, and dismissed it with a mere stereotyped symbol, not more artistic than the names which he might have engraved beneath each figure. Religious associations were thus awakened without the artist, whether of the time of Pericles or of the time of Leo X., giving himself further trouble ; the diffusion of religious ideas and feeling spared art from being religious. Let us, therefore, in order to judge fairly of what art can or cannot do for the supernatural, seek for one of the very rare instances in which the artist has had no symbolical abbreviations at his disposal, and has been obliged, if he would awaken any idea in the mind of the spectator, to do so by means of his artistic creations. The number of such exceptional instances is extremely limited in the great art of antiquity and the Renaissance, when artistic subjects were almost always traditionally religious or plainly realistic, and consequently intelligible at first sight. There is, however, an example, and that example is a masterpiece. It is the engraving by Agostino Veneziano, after a lost drawing by Raphael, generally called " Lo Stregozzo," and representing a witch going to the

Sabbath. Through a swampy country, amidst rank and barren vegetation, sweeps the triumphal procession— strange, beautiful, and ghastly ; a naked boy dashes headlong in front, bestriding a long-haired he-goat, and blowing a horn, little stolen children packed behind on his saddle ; on he dashes, across the tufts of marsh-lily and bulrush, across the stagnant pools of water, clearing the way and announcing his mistress the witch. She thrones, old, parched, lank, high on the top of an un-earthly car, made of the spine and ribs of some antediluvian creature, with springs and traces of ghastly jaw and collar and thigh bones, supported on either side by galloping skeletons, skeletons made up of skeletons, of all that is strangest in the bones and beaks of beasts and birds, on which ride young fauns and satyrs. To her chariot, by a yoke of human bones, are harnessed two stalwart naked youths, and two others sustain its plough-like end ; grand, magnificently moving figures, bounding forward like wild horses, the unearthly carriage swinging and creaking as they go. And, as they go, brushing through the high, dry, maremma-grass, the witch cowers on her chariot, clutching in one hand a heap of babies, in the other a vessel filled with fire, whose smoke, mingling with her long, dishevelled hair, floats behind, sweeping through the rank vegetation, curling and eddy-ing into vague, strange semblances of lions, apes, chim-æras. Forward dashes the outrunner on his goat, onward bound the naked litter-bearers ; up gallop the fauns and satyrs on the fleshless, monstrous carcases ; up and down sways the creaking, cracking chariot of bones ; one moment more, and the wild, splendid, hideous triumph will have swept out of sight, leaving behind only trampled

marsh-plants and a trail of fantastic, lurid smoke among
the ruffled, moaning reeds and grasses.

Such is Raphael's *Stregozzo*. It is a master-piece of
drawing and of pictorial fancy, it is perhaps the highest
achievement of great art in the direction of the supernatural: for Dürer is often hideous, Rembrandt always
obscure, and the moderns, like Blake and Doré, distinctly run counter to the essential nature of art in their
attempts after vagueness. When once told the subject
of the print, by Agostino Veneziano, our imagination
easily flies off on to the track of the supernatural; but,
in so doing, it leaves the work behind, and on return to
it we experience a return to the natural. If, on the
other hand, we are not told the subject of the print, we
very possibly see nothing supernatural in it: there are
splendid figures worthy of Michael Angelo, and grotesque
fancies, in the shape of the skeletons and coach of bones,
worthy of Leonardo; as a whole, the print is striking,
beautiful, and problematic, but it falls short of the effect
which would be produced by the mere words "a witch
riding through a marsh on a chariot of bones," if left to
insinuate themselves into the imagination. Of the
really supernatural, there is in it but one touch: and that
in the only part of the drawing which is left vague; it is
the confused shapes assumed by the eddying smoke
among the rushes. All the rest is outside the region of
the supernatural : it is problematic in subject, but clear,
harmonious, and beautiful in treatment; the imagination
may wander off from it, but in its presence it must remain passive. With this masterpiece we would fain
compare a picture which seems to deal with a cognate
subject; a picture as suggestive as it is absolutely

artistically worthless. We saw it once, many years ago, among a heap of rubbishy smudges at a picture-dealer's in Rome, and we have never forgotten it—a picture painted by some German smearer of the early sixteenth century; very ugly, stupid, and unattractive; ill drawn, ill composed, of a uniform hard, vulgar brown. It represented, with no attempt at perspective, a level country spread out like a map, dotted here and there with little spired and turretted towns, also a castle or two, a few trees and some rivers, disposed with a child's satisfaction with their mere indication, as much as to say—"here is a town, there is a castle." Some peasants were represented working in the fields, a little train of horsemen coming out of a castle, and near one of the chess-board castles a grass plot with half-a-dozen lit stakes, to which tiny figures were carrying faggots, while men-at-arms and burghers, no bigger than flies, looked on. In the foreground of the great flat expanse lay a boor, a fellow dressed like a field-labourer, in heavy sleep on the ground. Round him on the grass were marked curious circles, and in them was moving a strange figure, in cloak and helmet, with clawed wings and horns, leering horridly, moving round on tiptoe, his arms outstretched, as if gradually encircling the sleeper in order to pounce upon him; despite the complete absence of artistic skill, the gradual inevitable approach of the demon, the irresistible network of circles with which he was surrounding his prey, was perfectly indicated. Above, in the sky, two figures, half demon, half dragon, floated leisurely, like a moored boat, as if a guard of the devil below. What is the exact subject of this picture? No one can tell; but its meaning is intense for the imagination, it has the frightful suggestiveness of some old book on witchcraft, prosaic and curt ; of a page opened at random of Sprenger's *Malleus Malificarum.* Yes; over the plain, the towns, and castles, monotonous and dull, the fiends are hovering ; even over the stakes where their votaries are being burnt ; and see, the peasant asleep in the field, with his spade and hoe beside him, is being surrounded by magic circles, by the invisible nets of the demon, who prowls round him like a kite ready to pounce on to its quarry.

Why is there no need to write the word *witchcraft* beneath this picture ? Why can this nameless smearer succeed where Raphael has failed ? Because he is content to suggest to the imagination, and lets it create for itself its world of the supernatural ; because he is not an artist, and because Raphael is ; because he suggests everything and shows nothing, while Raphael creates, defines, perfects, gives form to that which is by its nature formless.

If we would bring home to ourselves this action of art on the supernatural, we must examine the only species of supernatural which still retains vitality, and can still be deprived of it by art. That which remains to us of the imaginative workings of the past is traditional and well-nigh effete : we have poems and pictures, Vedic hymns, Hebrew psalms, and Egyptian symbols ; we have folk-lore and dogma ; remnants of the supernatural, some labelled in our historic museums, where they are scrutinised, catalogue and eye-glass in hand ; others dusty on altars and in chapels, before which we uncover our heads and cast down our eyes : relics of dead and dying faiths, of which some are daily being transferred from the church

to the museum ; art cannot deprive any of these of that
imaginative life and power which they have long ceased
to possess. We have forms of the supernatural in which
we believe from acquiescence of habit, but they are not
vital ; we have a form of the supernatural in which, from
logic and habit, we disbelieve, but which is vital ; and
this form of the supernatural is the ghostly. We none
of us believe in ghosts as logical possibilities, but we
most of us conceive them as imaginative probabilities ; we
can still feel the ghostly, and thence it is that a ghost is
the only thing which can in any respect replace for us
the divinities of old, and enable us to understand, if only
for a minute, the imaginative power which they possessed,
and of which they were despoiled not only by logic, but
by art. By *ghost* we do not mean the vuglar apparition
which is seen or heard in told or written tales ; we mean
the ghost which slowly rises up in our mind, the haunter
not of corridors and staircases, but of our fancies. Just
as the gods of primitive religions were the undulating,
bright heat which made mid-day solitary and solemn as
midnight ; the warm damp, the sap-riser and expander
of life ; the sad dying away of the summer, and the leaden,
suicidal sterility of winter ; so the ghost, their only
modern equivalent, is the damp, the darkness, the silence,
the solitude ; a ghost is the sound of our steps through a
ruined cloister, where the ivy-berries and convolvulus
growing in the fissures sway up and down among the sculptured foliage of the windows, it is the scent of mouldering
plaster and mouldering bones from beneath the broken
pavement ; a ghost is the bright moonlight against which
the cypresses stand out like black hearse-plumes, in which
the blasted grey olives and the gnarled fig-trees stretch

their branches over the broken walls like fantastic, knotted, beckoning fingers, and the abandoned villas on the outskirts of Italian towns, with the birds flying in and out of the unglazed windows, loom forth white and ghastly; a ghost is the long-closed room of one long dead, the faint smell of withered flowers, the rustle of long-unmoved curtains, the yellow paper and faded ribbons of long-unread letters . . . each and all of these things, and a hundred others besides, according to our nature, is a ghost, a vague feeling we can scarcely describe, a something pleasing and terrible which invades our whole consciousness, and which, confusedly embodied, we half dread to see behind us, we know not in what shape, if we look round.

Call we in our artist, or let us be our own artist; embody, let us see or hear this ghost, let it become visible or audible to others besides ourselves; paint us that vagueness, mould into shape that darkness, modulate into chords that silence—tell us the character and history of those vague beings . . . . set to work boldly or cunningly. What do we obtain? A picture, a piece of music, a story; but the ghost is gone. In its stead we get oftenest the mere image of a human being; call it a ghost if you will, it is none. And the more complete the artistic work, the less remains of the ghost. Why do those stories affect us most in which the ghost is heard but not seen? Why do those places affect us most of which we merely vaguely know that they are haunted? Why most of all those which look as if they might be haunted? Why, as soon as a figure is seen, is the charm half-lost? And why, even when there is a figure, is it kept so vague and mist-like? Would you know Hamlet's

father for a ghost unless he told you he was one? and
can you remember it long while he speaks in mortal words?
and what would be Hamlet's father without the terrace
of Elsinore, the hour, and the moonlight? Do not these
embodied ghosts owe what little effect they still possess
to their surroundings, and are not the surroundings the
real ghost?

Throw sunshine on to them, and what remains?
Thus we have wandered through the realm of the supernatural in a manner neither logical nor business-like, for
logic and business-likeness are rude qualities, and scare
away the ghostly; very far away do we seem to have
rambled from Dr. Faustus and Helen of Sparta; but in
this labyrinth of the fantastic there are sudden unexpected turns—and see, one of these has suddenly
brought us back into their presence. For we have seen
why the supernatural is always injured by artistic treatment, why therefore the confused images evoked in our
mind by the mere threadbare tale of Faustus and Helena
are superior in imaginative power to the picture carefully
elaborated and shown us by Goethe. We can now
understand why under his hand the infinite charm of the
weird meeting of antiquity and the Middle Ages has
evaporated. We can explain why the strange fancy of
the classic Walpürgis-night, in the second part of *Faust*,
at once stimulates the imagination and gives it nothing.
If we let our mind dwell on that mysterious Pharsalian
plain, with its glimmering fires and flamelets alone breaking the darkness, where Faust and Mephistopheles wandering about meet the spectres of antiquity, shadowy in
the gloom—the sphinxes crouching, the sirens, the dryads
and oreads, the griffons and cranes flapping their

unseen wings overhead; where Faust springs on the
back of Chiron, and as he is borne along sickens for sudden joy when the centaur tells him that Helen has been
carried on that back, has clasped that neck ; when we let
our mind work on all this, we are charmed by the weird
meetings, the mysterious shapes which elbow us ; but let
us take up the volume and we return to barren prose,
without colour or perfume.   Yet Goethe felt the supernatural as we feel it, as it can be felt only in days of dis-
belief, when the more logical we become in our ideas,
the more we view nature as a prosaic machine constructed
by no one in particular, the more poignantly, on the
other hand, do we feel the delight of the transient belief in
the vague and the impossible; the greater the distinctness
with which we see and understand all around us, the
greater the longing for a momentary half-light in which
forms may appear stranger, grander, vaguer than they
are.   We moderns seek in the world of the supernatural
a renewal of the delightful semi-obscurity of vision and
keenness of fancy of our childhood ; when a glimpse into
fairyland was still possible, when things appeared in
false lights, brighter, more important, more magnificent
than now.   Art indeed can afford us calm and clear
enjoyment of the beautiful—enjoyment serious, self-
possessed, wide-awake, such as befits mature intellects ;
but no picture, no symphony, no poem, can give us that
delight, that delusory, imaginative pleasure which we
received as children from a tawdry engraving or a
hideous doll ; for around that doll there was an atmosphere of glory.   In certain words, in certain sights, in
certain snatches of melody, words, sights, and sounds
which we now recognise as trivial, commonplace, and

vulgar, there was an ineffable meaning; they were spells which opened doors into realms of wonder; they were precious in proportion as they were misappreciated. We now appreciate and despise; we see, we no longer imagine. And it is to replace this uncertainty of vision, this liberty of seeing in things much more than there is, which belongs to man and to mankind in this childhood, which compensated the Middle Ages for starvation and pestilence, and compensates the child for blows and lessons, it is to replace this that we crave after the supernatural, the ghostly—no longer believed, but still felt. It was from this sickness of the prosaic, this turning away from logical certainty, that the men of the end of the eighteenth and the beginning of this century, the men who had finally destroyed belief in the religious supernatural, who were bringing light with new sciences of economy, philology, and history—Schiller, Goethe, Herder, Coleridge—left the lecture-room and the laboratory, and set gravely to work on ghostly tales and ballads. It was from this rebellion against the tyranny of the possible that Goethe was charmed with that culmination of all impossibilities, that most daring of ghost stories, the story of Faustus and Helena. He felt the seduction of the supernatural, he tried to embody it— and he failed.

The case was different with Marlowe. The bringing together of Faustus and Helena had no special meaning for the man of the sixteenth century, too far from antiquity and too near the Middle Ages to perceive as we do the strange difference between them; and the supernatural had no fascination in a time when it was all permeating and everywhere mixed with prose. The whole

G

play of *Dr. Faustus* is conceived in a thoroughly realistic fashion; it is tragic, but not ghostly. To Marlowe's audience, and probably to Marlowe himself, despite his atheistic reputation, the story of Faustus's wonders and final damnation was quite within the realm of the possible; the intensity of the belief in the tale is shown by the total absence of any attempt to give it dignity or weirdness. Faustus evokes Lucifer with a pedantic semi-biblical Latin speech; he goes about playing the most trumpery conjuror's tricks—snatching with invisible hands the food from people's lips, clapping horns and tails on to courtiers for the Emperor's amusement, letting his legs be pulled off like boots, selling wisps of straw as horses, doing and saying things which could appear tragic and important, nay, even serious, only to people who took every second cat for a witch, who burned their neighbours for vomiting pins, who suspected devils at every turn, as the great witch-expert Sprenger shows them in his horribly matter-of-fact manual. We moderns, disbelieving in devilries, would require the most elaborately romantic and poetic accessories—a splendid lurid back-ground, a magnificent Byronian invocation of the fiend. The Mephistophilis of Marlowe, in those days when devils still dwelt in people, required none of Goethe's wit or poetry; the mere fact of his being a devil, with the very real association of flame and brimstone in this world and the next, was sufficient to inspire interest in him; whereas in 1800, with Voltaire's novels and Hume's treatises on the table, a dull devil was no more endurable than any other sort of bore. The very superiority of Marlowe is due to this absence of weirdness, to this complete realism; the last scene of the English play is infinitely above the end of the second part of *Faust* in tragic grandeur, just because Goethe made abortive attempts, after a conscious and artificial supernatural, while Marlowe was satisfied with perfect reality of situation. The position of Faustus, when the years of his pact have expired, and he awaits midnight, which will give him over to Lucifer, is as thoroughly natural in the eyes of Marlowe as is in the eyes of Shelley the position of Beatrice Cenci awaiting the moment of execution. The conversation between Faustus and the scholars, after he has made his will, is terribly life-like: they disbelieve at first, pooh-pooh his danger; then, half-convinced, beg that a priest may be fetched; but Faustus cannot deal with priests. He bids them, in agony, go pray in the next room. "Aye, pray for me, pray for me, and what noise soever you hear, come not unto me, for nothing can save me. . . . Gentlemen, farewell; if I live till morning, I'll visit you; if not, Faustus is gone to hell." Faustus remains alone for the one hour which separates him from his doom; he clutches at the passing time, he cries to the hours to stop with no rhetorical figure of speech, but with a terrible reality of agony:

> Let this hour be but
> A year, a month, a week, a natural day,
> That Faustus may repent and save his soul.

Time to repent, time to recoil from the horrible gulf into which he is being sucked; Christ, will Christ's blood not save him? He would leap up to heaven and cling fast, but Lucifer drags him down. He would seek annihilation in nature, be sucked into its senseless, feelingless mass . . . and, meanwhile, the time is passing, the interval of respite is shrinking and dwindling. Would that he were a soulless brute and might perish, or that at least eternal hell were finite—a thousand, a hundred thousand years let him suffer, but not for ever and without end! Midnight begins striking. With convulsive agony he exclaims as the rain patters against the window:

> O soul, be changed into small water-drops,
> And fall into the ocean, ne'er be found.

But the twelfth stroke sounds; Lucifer and his crew enter; and when next morning the students, frightened by the horrible tempest and ghastly noises of the night, enter his study, they find Faustus lying dead, torn and mangled by the demon. All this is not supernatural in our sense; such scenes as this were real for Marlowe and his audience. Such cases were surely not unfrequent; more than one man certainly watched through such a night in hopeless agony, conscious, like Faustus, of pact with the fiend—awaiting, with earth and heaven shut and bolted against him, eternal hell.

In this story of Doctor Faustus, which, to Marlowe and his contemporaries, was not a romance but a reality, the episode of the evoking of Helen is extremely secondary in interest. To raise a dead woman was not more wonderful than to turn wisps of straw into horses, and it was perhaps considered the easier of the two miracles; the sense of the ordinary ghostly is absent, and the sense that Helen is the ghost of a whole long-dead civilisation, that sense which is for us the whole charm of the tale, could not exist in the sixteenth century. Goethe's Faust feels for Helen as Goethe himself might have felt, as Winckelmann felt for a lost antique statue, as Schiller felt for the dead Olympus : a passion intensely imaginative and poetic, born of deep appreciation of antiquity, the essentially modern, passionate, nostalgic craving for the past. In Marlowe's play, on the contrary, Faustus and the students evoke Helen from a confused pedantic impression that an ancient lady must be as much superior to a modern lady as an ancient poem, be it even by Statius or Claudian, must be superior to a modern poem—it is a humanistic fancy of the days of the revival of letters. But, by a strange phenomenon, Marlowe, once realising what Helen means, that she is the fairest of women, forgets the scholarly interest in her. Faustus, once in presence of the wonderful woman, forgets that he had summoned her up to gratify his and his friends' pedantry ; he sees her, loves her, and bursts out into the splendid tirade full of passionate fancy :

> Was this the face that launched a thousand ships,
> And burnt the topless towers of Ilium ?
> Sweet Helen, make me immortal with a kiss !
> Her lips suck forth my soul ! See, where it flies !
> Come, Helen, come, give me my soul again.
> Here will I dwell, for Heaven is in these lips,
> And all is dross that is not Helena.
> I will be Paris, and for love of thee,
> Instead of Troy shall Wittenberg be sacked ;
> And I will combat with weak Menelaus,
> And wear thy colours on my plumed crest ;
> Yea, I will wound Achilles in the heel,
> And then return to Helen for a kiss.
> Oh ! thou art fairer than the evening air
> Clad in the beauty of a thousand stars ;
> Brighter art thou than flaming Jupiter
> When he appeared to hapless Semele ;

More lovely than the monarch of the sky
In wanton Arethusa's azure arms ;
And none but thou shalt be my paramour.

This is real passion for a real woman, a woman very
different from the splendid semi-vivified statue of
Goethe, the Helen with only the cold, bloodless, intellectual life which could be infused by enthusiastic
studies of ancient literature and art, gleaming bright
like marble or a spectre. This Helena of Marlowe
is no antique ; the Elizabethan dramatist, like the
painter of the fifteenth century, could not conceive the
purely antique, despite all the translating of ancient
writers, and all the drawing from ancient marbles. One
of the prose versions of the story of Faustus, contains a
quaint account of Helen, which sheds much light on
Marlowe's conception :

This lady appeared before them in a most rich gowne of purple
velvet, costly imbrodered ; her haire hanged downe loose, as faire
as the beaten gold, and of such length that it reached downe to
her hammes ; having most amorous cole-black eyes, a sweet and
pleasant round face, with lips as red as a cherry ; her cheeks of a
rose colour, her mouth small, her neck white like a swan ; tall and
slender of personage ; in summe, there was no imperfect place in
her ; she looked around about with a rolling hawk's eye, a smiling
and wanton countenance, which neerehand inflamed the hearts
of all the students, but that they persuaded themselves she was a
spirit, which make them lightly passe away such fancies.

This fair dame in the velvet embroidered gown, with
the long, hanging hair, this Helen of the original
Faustus legend, is antique only in name ; she belongs to
the race of mediæval and modern women—the Lauras,
Fiammettas, and Simonettas of Petrarch, Boccaccio,

and Lorenzo dei Medici ; she is the sister of that slily sentimental coquette, the Monna Lisa of Leonardo. The strong and simple women of Homer, and even of Euripides, majestic and matronly even in shame, would repudiate this slender, smiling, ogling beauty ; Briseis, though the captive of Achilles' spear, would turn with scorn from her. The antique woman has a dignity due to her very inferiority and restrictedness of position.; she has the simplicity, the completeness, the absence of everything suggestive of degradation, like that of some stately animal, pure in its animal nature. The modern woman, with more freedom and more ideal, rarely approaches to this character ; she is too complex to be perfect, she is frail because she has an ideal, she is dubious because she is free, she may fall because she may rise. Helen deserted Menelaus and brought ruin upon Troy, therefore, in the eyes of Antiquity, she was the victim of fate, she might be unruffled, spotless, majestic ; but to the man of the sixteenth century she was merely frail and false. The rolling hawk's eye and the wanton smile of the old legend-monger would have perplexed Homer, but they were necessary for Marlowe; his Helen was essentially modern, he had probably no inkling that an antique Helen as distinguished from a modern could exist. In the paramour of Faustus he saw merely the most beautiful woman, some fair and wanton creature, dressed not in chaste and majestic antique drapery, but in fantastic garments of lawn, like those of Hero in his own poem :

> The lining purple silk, with gilt stars drawn ;
> Her wide sleeves green, and bordered with a grove
> Where Venus, in her naked glory strove

To please the careless and disdainful eyes .
Of proud Adonis, that before her lies ;
Her kirtle blue . . . .
Upon her head she wore a myrtle wreath
From whence her veil reached to the ground beneath ;
Her veil was artificial flowers and leaves
Whose workmanship both man and beast deceives.

Some slim and dainty goddess of Botticelli, very mortal withal, long and sinuous, tightly clad in brocaded garments and clinging cobweb veils, beautiful with the delicate, diaphanous beauty, rather emaciated and hectic, of high rank, and the conscious, elaborate fascination of a woman of fashion—a creature whom, like the Gioconda, Leonardo might have spent years in decking and painting, ever changing the ornaments and ever altering the portrait; to whom courtly poets like Bembo and Castiglione might have written scores of sonnets and canzoni to her hands, her eyes, her hair, her lips, a fanciful inventory to which she listened languidly under the cypresses of Florentine gardens. Some such being, even rarer and more dubious for being an exotic in the England of Elizabeth, was Marlowe's Helen; such, and not a ghostly figure, descended from a pedestal, white and marble-like in her unruffled drapery, walking with solid step and unswerving, placid glance through the study, crammed with books, and vials, and strange instruments, of the mediæval wizard of Wittenberg. Marlowe deluded himself as well as Faustus, and palmed off on to him a mere modern lady. To raise a real spectre of the antique is a craving of our own century; Goethe attempted to do it and failed, for what reasons we have seen; but we have all of us the charm wherewith to evoke for ourselves a real Helena, on condition that, unlike Faustus and unlike Goethe, we seek not to show her to others, and remain satisfied if the weird and glorious figure haunt only our own imagination.

CHAPELMASTER KREISLER.

A STUDY OF MUSICAL ROMANTICISTS.

THERE is nothing stranger in the world than music : it exists only as sound, is born of silence and dies away into silence, issuing from nothing and relapsing into nothing; it is our own creation, yet it is foreign to ourselves ; we draw it from out of the silent wood and the silent metal, it lives in our own breath, yet it seems to come to us from a distant land which we shall never see, and to tell us of things we shall never know. It is for ever striving to tell us something, for ever imploring us to listen and to understand ; we listen, we strain, we try to take in its vague meaning ; it is telling us sweet and mighty secrets, letting drop precious talismanic words ; we guess, but do not understand. And shall we never understand ? May we never know wherefore the joy, wherefore the sadness ? Can we not subtilise our minds, go forth with our heart and fancy as interpreters, and distinguish in the wreathing melodies and entangled chords some words of superhuman emotion, even as the men of other ages distinguished in the sighing oak woods and the rustling reeds the words of the great gods of nature ?

To us music is no longer what it was to our grandfathers, a mere pleasing woof of meaningless pattern; we have left those times far behind, times whose great

masters were prophets uttering mere empty sounds to
their contemporaries; we have shaken off the dust of
the schools of counterpoint, we have thrown aside the
mechanical teachings of the art; for us music has become
an audible, quivering fata morgana of life, the embodiment of the intangible, the expression of the inexplicable,
the realisation of the impossible. And it has become a
riddle, a something we would fain understand but cannot, a spell of our own devising which we cannot
decipher; we sit listening to it as we sit looking into
the deep, dreamy eyes of an animal, full of some mute
language, which we vainly strive to comprehend.

The animal seems as though it could say much if only
it could speak; so also music would seem to contain far
deeper meanings than any spoken word, to be fraught
with emotion deeper than we can feel : it could confide
so much if we could understand. Yet the animal is but
an animal, with some of our virtues and some of our
vices, infinitely more ignorant than we are; dumb, not
because we cannot understand, but because he cannot
speak. And may it not be the same with music? May
not music be intellectually inscrutable because it is intellectually meaningless?

The idea is one from which we shrink; but are we
right in shrinking from it? Cannot music be noble in
itself apart from any meaning it conveys? Cannot we
be satisfied with what it certainly is, without thinking of
what it may be? It would seem to be so; it is the
spirit of our culture to strain restlessly after the unknown,
for ever to seek after the hidden, to reject the visible and
tangible. We yearn to penetrate through the blue of
the summer evening, to thread our way among the sun-

gilded clouds; yet the blue heaven, if we rise into it, is
mere tintless air; the clouds, if we can touch them, are
mere dull vapour. And so also we would fain seek a
meaning in those fair sounds which are fairer than any
meaning they could contain; we would break down in
rude analysis the splendours of *Don Giovanni* only to
discover beneath them the story of a punished Lovelace;
we would tear to shreds a glorious fugue of Bach for the
satisfaction of hearing the Jews yelling for Barabbas.

This is our tendency, this our way of enjoying the
great art of other days : to care not for itself, but for
what it suggests, nay, most often for the suggestion of
the mere name of the work of art, for there is no punished Lovelace in Mozart's melodies, no Barabbas in
Bach's fugues, there is nothing but beautiful forms made
out of sounds. The old prosaic masters of the past,
who worked at a picture or a statue or an opera as a
cobbler works at a pair of shoes, never thought of suggesting anything to us : they gave something substantial,
something intrinsically valuable, a well-shaped figure, a
richly tinted canvas, a boldly modulated piece of music;
to produce that and no more had been their object, it
was all they could give, and their contemporaries were
satisfied with it. Their art was their trade, pursued
conscientiously, diligently, intelligently, sometimes with
that superior degree of intelligence we call genius, but it
was their trade and no more. They themselves were
as prosaic as any artisan, and no more saw vague poetry
in their works, though these were the *Olympic Jove*, the
School of Athens, or the *Messiah*, than does the potter in
his pot or the smith in his iron; all they saw was that
their works were beautiful, as the potter sees that his pot

is round and smooth, and the smith that his blade is bright and sharp. For the rest they were terribly prosaic, terribly given up to the mechanical interests of their art and the material interests of their lives, as you may see them in Vasari, in the lives of Handel, of Bach, of Haydn, of Mozart, of the last of true, unpoetic musicians, Rossini, and as you would doubtless see the unknown sculptors of antiquity if you could see them at all.

But the time came when the world, which had lived off prose most heartily ever since the Middle Ages, grew sick of such coarse mental food, and longed for unsubstantial poetic ambrosia; the fact is, it was morally sick, and took its strong intellectual food in disgust, and fancied and yearned for impossible things, as sick men do. And in its loathing for the common, the simple, the healthy, the world took to eating the intellectual opium of romanticism; it enjoyed and was plunged for awhile in ineffable delights, such as only weakness can feel and poison afford ; the universe seemed to expand, the imagination to grow colossal, the feelings to become supernaturally subtle; all limits were removed, all impossibilities became possibilities; the fancy roamed over endless and ever varying tracts, and soared up into the clouds of the unintelligible, and dived into the bottomless abyss of chaos : all things quivered with a strange new life, with a life in other lives, with an unceasing, ever changing life ; everything was not only itself but something else :———all was greater, higher, deeper, brighter, darker, sweeter, bitterer, more ineffable than itself ; it was a paradise of Mahomet, of Buddha, of Dante ; it was enjoyment keen, subtle, intoxicating, which made the fancy swim, the senses ache, and the soul faint. Then came the reaction, the inevitable after-effect of the drug—depression, langour, palsy, convulsion.

About seventy years ago a great humourist, who frittered away a quaint and fantastic genius in etching grimacing caricatures, and scribbling gaunt ghost stories, the once popular, now almost forgotten, Hoffmann, looked on at this crisis in musical history, at this first in-toxication of romanticism ; sympathised with its poetry, its ludicrousness, and its sadness ; embodied them all in one grotesque, pathetic figure, and for the first and last time in his life produced a masterpiece. The master-piece is his poor, half-mad musician, Johannes Kreisler, " chapelmaster and cracked *musicus* par excellence," as he signs his letters, the artist of incomplete genius, of broken career, of poetic dreams and crazy fancies, who used to go about dressed in a coat the colour of C sharp minor, with an E major coloured collar. And of all the glimpses Hoffmann has given us of Chapelmaster Kreisler, none is so weirdly suggestive as that in which we see him improvising on the piano at his club of friends. The friends had met one evening expressly to hear Kreisler's extemporary performance, and he was just on the point of sitting down to the instrument, when one of the company recollected that a lever had on a previous occasion refused to do its duty. He took up a light, and began his search for the refractory lever ; when suddenly, as he leaned over the interior of the piano a heavy pair of brass snuffers crashed down from the candlestick on to the strings, of which half a dozen in-stantly snapped. The company began to exclaim at this unlucky accident, which would deprive them of the promised performance; but Chapelmaster Kreisler bade them be of good cheer, for they should still hear what was in his mind, as the bass strings remained intact.

Kreisler put on his little red skull cap and his Chinese dressing-gown, and sat down to the piano, while a trusty friend extinguished all the lights, so that the room remained in utter darkness. Then, with the muffling pedal down, Kreisler struck the full chord of A flat major, and spoke:

"What is it that murmurs so strangely, so sweetly, around me? Invisible wings seem to be heaving up and down. I am swimming in perfume laden air. But the perfume shines forth in flaming, mysteriously linked circles. Lovely spirits are moving their golden pinions in ineffably splendid sounds and harmonies."

Chord of A flat minor (mezzo forte). "Ah, they are bearing me off into the land of eternal desire, but even as they carry me, pain awakes in my heart, and tries to escape, tearing my bosom with violence."

Chord of E major (third), forte. "They have given me a splendid crown, but that which sparkles and lightens in its diamonds are the thousand tears which I shed; and in the gold shine the flames which are devouring me. Valour and power, strength and faith, for him who is called on to reign in the kingdom of spirits."

.   .   .   .

B major (accentuato). "What a gay life in field and woodland in the sweet springtide! All the flutes and pipes, which have lain frozen to death in dusty corners throughout the winter, have now awakened and remembered their best beloved melodies, which they trill cheerfully like the birds in the air."

B major with the diminished seventh (smanioso). "A warm west wind comes sullenly complaining, like some mysterious secret, through the wood, and wherever it brushes past, the fir trees murmur, the beeches murmur to each other: "Wherefore has our friend grown so sad?"'

E flat major (forte). "Follow him, follow him! His dress is green like the dark wood—sweet sounds of horns are his sighing words. Hearest him murmuring behind the bushes? Hearest

thou the sound?   The sound of horns, full of delight and sadness?
'Tis he ! up and meet him."

D third, fourth, sixth, chord (*piano*).   "Life plays its mocking
game in all manner of fashions.   Wherefore desire?   Wherefore
hope?   Wherefore demand?"

C major (third) chord (*fortissimo*).   "Let us rather dance over
the open graves in wild rejoicing.   Let us shout for joy, those beneath cannot hear it.   Hurrah, hurrah !   Dance and jollity ; the
devil is riding in with drums and trumpets."

C minor chords (*ff. in rapid succession*).   "Knowest thou him
not?   Knowest thou him not?   See, he stretches forth his burning
claw to my heart !   He masks himself in all sorts of absurd grimaces
—as a free huntsman, as a concert director, tapeworm doctor, *ricco
mercante*; he pitches snuffers into the strings to prevent my playing!
Kreisler, Kreisler, shake thyself up?   Seest thou it hiding, the pale
ghost with the red burning eyes, stretching out its clawy, bony hand
from beneath its torn mantle—shaking the crown of straw on its
smooth bald skull?   It is Madness !   Johannes, be brave !   Mad, mad,
witch-revelry of life, wherefore shakest thou me so in thy whirling
dance?   Can I not escape?   Is there no grain of dust in the universe
on which, diminished to a fly, I can save myself from thee, horrible
torturing phantom?   Desist, Desist !   I will behave.   My manners
shall be the very best.   *Hony soit qui mal y pense.*   Only let me
believe the devil to be a *galantuomo !*   I curse song and music ; I
lick thy feet like the drunken Caliban; free me only from my torments!
Aï ! Aï ! abominable one !   Thou hast trodden down all my flowers:
not a blade of grass still greens in the terrible desert—

Dead !   Dead !   Dead ! . . . ."

When Chapelmaster Kreisler ended, all were silent ;
poetry, passionate, weird, and grotesque, had poured
from their friend's lips ; a strange nightmare pageant
had swept by them, beautiful and ghastly, like a mad
Brocken medley of the triumph of Dionysos and the
dance of Death.

They were all silent—all save one, and that one said :
"This is all very fine, but I was told we were to have

music ; a good, sensible sonata of Haydn's—would have been much more the thing than all this." He was a Philistine, no doubt, but he was right; a good, sensible sonata of Haydn's—nay, the stiffest, driest, most wooden fugue ever written by the most crabbed professor of counterpoint would have been far more satisfactory for people who expected music. A most fantastic rhapsody they had indeed heard, but it had been a spoken one, and the best strings of the piano had remained hanging snapped and silent during the performance.

Poor Chapelmaster Kreisler ! He has long been forgotten by the world in general, and even those few that still are acquainted with his weird portrait, smile at it as at a relic of a far distant time, when life and art and all other things looked strangely different from how they look now. Yet the crazy musician of Hoffmann is but the elder brother of all our modern composers. With the great masters of the last century, Haydn, Mozart, Cimarosa, who were scarcely in their graves when he improvised his great word fantasia, he has no longer any connection with our own musicians, born half a century after his end, he is closely linked, for, like him, they are romanticists. They do not indeed wear C sharp minor coloured coats, nor do they improvise in the dark on pianos with broken strings ; they are perfectly sane and conscious of all their doings ; yet, all the same, they are but Kreisler's younger brothers. Like the poor chapelmaster of Hoffmann, music itself has a fantastic madness in it ; like him, it has been crazed by disappointment, by jealousy, by impotent rage at finding that it cannot now do what it once did, and cannot yet do what will never be done ; like Kreisler it deals no longer with

H

mere sequences of melody and harmony, but with
thoughts, feelings, and images, hopes and fears and despair, with wild chaotic visions of splendour and of
ghastliness.   But the position of our music differs from
that of Kreisler in this much, that no friendly pair of
snuffers crashes on to the strings and makes them fly
asunder ; that, while Kreisler spoke, our music can only
play its fancies and whimsies ; and that, instead of hearing intelligible spoken words, we hear only musical
sounds which are gibberish and chaos.

For the time when men sought in music only for
music's own loveliness is gone by ; and the time has
come when all the arts trespass on each other's ground,
and, worst of all, when the arts which can give and show
envy, poetry, the art which can neither give nor show
but only suggest, and when, for the sake of such suggestion, they would cheat us of all the real gifts—gifts
of noble forms of line and colour, and sweet woofs of
melody and harmony which they once gave us.   The
composer now wishes to make you see and feel all that
he sees and feels in his imagination, the woods and seas,
the joys and sorrows, all the confused day-dreams, sweet
and drowsy, all the nightmare orgies which may pass
through his brain ; the sound has become the mere
vehicle for this, the weak, vague language which he can
only stammer and we can only divine ; the artist breaks
violently against the restraint of form, thinking to attain
the unattainable beyond its limits, and sinks down
baffled and impotent amidst ruin.

We are apt to think of music as of a sort of speech
until, on examination, we find it has no defined meaning
either for the speaker or for the listener.   In reality,

music and speech are as different and as separate as
architecture and painting, as wholly opposed to each
other as only those two things can be which, having
started from the same point, have travelled in completely opposite directions, like the two great rivers
which, originating on the same alp, flow respectively to
the north, and to the south, each acquiring a separate
character on its way—the one as the blue river of Ger-
many, ending amidst the tide-torn sandbanks of the
North Sea ; the other as the green river of Provence,
dying amidst the stagnant pools and fever-haunted
marshes of the Mediterranean. As long as the Rhine
and the Rhone are not yet Rhine and Rhone, but merely
pools of snow-water among the glaciers, so long are they
indistinguishable ; but as soon as separated into distinct
streams, their dissimilarity grows with every mile of
their diverging course. So as to speech and music : as
long as both exist only in embryo in the confused cries
and rude imitations of the child or of the primitive
people, they cannot be distinguished; but as soon as
they can be called either speech or music, they become
unlike and increase in dissimilarity in proportion as
they develop. The cry and the imitative sound become,
on the one hand, a word which, however rude, begins to
have an arbitrary meaning, and, on the other hand, a
song which, however uncouth, has no positive meaning ;
the word, as it develops, acquires a more precise and
abstract signification, becomes more and more of a
symbol; the song, as it develops, loses definite meaning,
becomes more and more a complete unsymbolical form,
until at length the word, having become a thing for use,
a mere means of communication, ceases to require vocal

utterance, and turns into a written sign ; while the song,
having become an object of mere pleasure, requires more
and more musical development, and is transported from
the lips of man to the strings of an instrument.   But
while speech and music are thus diverging, while the one
is becoming more and more of an arbitrary symbol conveying an abstract idea, and the other is growing more
and more into an artistic form conveying no idea, but
pleasing the mind merely by its concrete form—while
this divergence is taking place, a corresponding movement accompanies it which removes both speech and
music farther and farther from their common origin : the
cry of passion and the imitative sound.   The Rhone
and the Rhine are becoming not only less like each
other, but as the one becomes green and the other blue,
so also are both losing all trace of the original dull white
of the snow water.   In the word, the cry and the imitation are being effaced by arbitrary, symbolical use, by
that phonetic change which shows how little a word as
it exists for us retains of its original character ; in the
song they are being subdued by constant attempts at
obtaining a more distinct and symmetrical shape, by the
development of the single sounds and their arrangement
with a view to pleasing the ear and mind.   Yet both
retain the power of resuming to a limited extent their
original nature ; but in proportion as the word or the
song resumes the characteristics of the cry or of the
imitation does each lose its own slowly elaborated value,
the word as a suggester of thought, the song as a pre-
senter of form.   Now, in so far as the word is a word, or
the song a song, its effect on the emotions is comparatively small : the word can awaken emotion only as

a symbol, that is, indirectly and merely suggestively; the song can awaken emotion only inasmuch as it yet partakes of the nature of the brute cry or rude imitation. Thus, while language owes its emotional effects to the ideas arbitrarily connected with it, music owes its power over the heart to its sensuous elements as given by nature. But music exists as an art, that is to say, as an elaboration of the human mind, only inasmuch as those sensuous brute elements are held in check and measure, are made the slaves of an intellectual conception. The very first step in the formation of the art is the subjection of the emotional cry or the spontaneous imitation to a process of acoustic mensuration, by which the irregular sound becomes the regular, definite *note ;* the second step is the subjection of this already artificial sound to mensuration of time, by which it is made rhythmical; the third step is the subjection of this rhythmical sound to a comparative mensuration with other sounds, by which we obtain harmony; the last step is adjustment of this artificially obtained note and rhythm and harmony into that symmetrical and intellectually appreciable form which constitutes the work of art, for art begins only where the physical elements are subjected to an intellectual process, and it exists completely only where they abdicate their independence and become subservient to an intellectual design.

Music is made up of two elements : the intellectual and the sensuous on the one hand, of that which is conceived by the mind and perceived by the mind (for our ears perceive only the separate constituent sounds of a tune, but not the tune itself); on the other hand, of that which is produced by the merely physical and appreci-

ated by the merely physical, by the nerves of hearing,
through which it may, but only indirectly, affect the
mind.   Now if, from an artistic point of view, we must
protest against any degradation of the merely sensuous
part, it is because such a degradation would involve a
corresponding one in the intellectual part, because the
physical basis must be intact and solid before we can
build on it an intellectual structure, because the physical
element through which mentality is perceived must be
perfect in order that the mental manifestation be equally
so; but the physical must always remain a mere basis,
a mere vehicle for the mental.   The enjoyment obtainable from the purely physical part may indeed be very
great and very valuable, but it is a mere physical enjoyment; and the pleasure we derive from a fine voice, as
distinguished from a fine piece or a fine interpretation,
is as wholly unartistic as that which we receive from a ripe
peach or a cool breeze : it is a purely sensuous pleasure,
given us ready-made by nature, to give or to perceive
which requires no mentality, in which there is no human
intention, and consequently no art.   Now, the effect of
the cry or of the imitation, and that of certain other
manifestations of sound, such as tone, pitch, volume,
rhythm, major or minor intervals, which are cognate with,
but independent of, the cry or the imitation—the effect
of all this is an entirely sensuous one, an effect of unin-
telligent matter on the nerves, not of calculating intelligence on the mind, and it is to these physical effects, and
not to the mentally elaborated form, that music owes
its peculiar power of awaking or even of suggesting
emotion.

   That this is the case is shown by various circumstances. The ancients, who, as is now proved beyond dispute, possessed very little of the intellectual part of music, little of what we should deem its form, enjoyed its emotional effects to a far higher degree than could we in our present musical condition; the stories of Timotheus, Terpander, and other similar ones, being at least founded on fact, as is evident from the continual allusions of Greek writers to the moral or immoral effect of the art, and their violent denunciations of people whose only social crime was to have added a string to a lyre or a hole to a flute. We ourselves have constant opportunities of remarking the intense emotional effects due to mere pitch, tone, and rhythm; that is to say, to the merely physical qualities of number, nature, and re-petition of musical vibrations. We have all been cheered by the trumpet and depressed by the hautboy; we have felt a wistful melancholy steal over us while listening to the drone of the bagpipe and the quaver of the flute of the pifferari at the shrine; we have felt our heart beat and our breath halt on catching the first notes of an organ as we lifted the entrance curtain of some great cathedral; we have known nothing more utterly harrow-ing than a hurdy-gurdy playing a cheerful tune, or a common accordion singing out a waltz or a polka. Nay, it is worthy of remark that the instruments capable of the greatest artistic development are just those which possess least this power over the nerves: the whole violin and harpsichord tribe, the human voice when sound and natural—saying least themselves, are capable of saying most for others; whereas the trumpet, the accordion, the harp, the zither, are condemned by their very expressive-ness to a hopeless inferiority; they produce an effect spontaneously by their mere tone; the artist can produce on them but that effect, and can scarcely heighten even it. A musical critic of the beginning of this century, Giuseppe Carpani, wishing to defend Rossini from the accusation of being unemotional, boldly laid down the principle that it never is the composer who makes people cry, but the author of the words and the singer. As to the composer, he can only please, but not move.

Never (he says) were people more moved than by a certain scene in Metastasio's *Araserse*, set by Mortellari, and sung by the famous Pacchierotti (about 1780); and do you think perhaps that it was Mortellari, who made them cry? Mortellari, the stupidest mediocrity, *Dio l'abbia in gloria!* No, it was Metastasio and Pacchierotti, the verse and the voice.

This was a mere absurd exaggeration, and a mere captious plea for Rossini, who, had he only had Metastasio to write the words and Pacchierotti to sing, would doubtless have moved the whole universe to tears, with "Di tanti palpiti." Yet in this exaggeration, an important truth has been struck out. This truth is that the writer of the libretto, having at his disposal the clear, idea-suggesting word, can bring up a pathetic situation before the mind; that the singer, having at his command the physical apparatus for producing an effect on the nerves, can sensuously awaken emotion; while the composer, possessing neither the arbitrary idea-suggesting word, nor the nerve-moving sound, but only the artistic form, can please to the utmost, but move only to a limited degree.

Thus, there is a once popular but now deservedly forgotten air in the *Romeo e Giulietta* of Zingarelli, which some seventy years ago possessed the most miraculous power over what people called the heart, and especially over the not too sensitive one of Napoleon, who, whenever it was sung by his favourite Crescentini, invariably burst into tears. The extraordinary part of the matter is that this air happens to be peculiarly insipid, without any very definite expression, but, on the whole, of a sort of feeble cheerfulness, and certainly is the last piece that we should judge capable of such deeply emotional effects. But the situation of Romeo is an intensely pathetic one, and it is probable that the singer's voice may have possessed some strange power over the nerves, something of the purely sensuous pathos of an accordion or a zither, especially in the long, gradually diminished notes, "fine by degrees and beautifully less," which move like an Æolian harp. But, if the pathetic effect of "Ombra adorata" could not be ascribed to the composition neither could it be ascribed to the interpretation. For this sensuous pathos, though enhanced by the singer's intellectual qualities, in no way depends upon them; the intellect can make him graduate and improve the form of a piece, all that which is perceived by the mind, but it has no influence on the nerves; Crescentini's musical intelligence may have enabled him to make "Ombra adorata" a beautiful song, but only his physical powers of voice could have enabled him to make it a pathetic one.

As these physical elements are the material out of which artistic forms are moulded by the musician, he necessarily deals with and disposes of those powers over the nerves which are inherent in them. When he creates a musical form out of minor intervals, he necessarily gives that form something of the melancholy effect of such intervals; when he composes a piece with the peculiar rhythm of a march, he necessarily gives his piece some of the inspiriting power of that rhythm; when he employs a hautboy or a trumpet, he necessarily lends his work some of the depressing quality of the hautboy or some of the cheering quality of the trumpet. Thus the intellectually conceived and perceived forms are invested with the power over the nerves peculiar to certain of the physical elements of music; but it is in those component physical elements, and not in the forms into which they are disposed, that lies the emotional force of the art. Nor is this all: the physical elements, inasmuch as they are subdued and regulated and neutralized by one another in the intellectual form, are inevitably deprived of the full vigour of their emotional power; the artistic form has tamed and curbed them, has forbidden their freely influencing the nerves, while at the same time it —the form—has exerted its full sway over the mind. The mountains have been hewn into terraces, the forests have been clipped into gardens, the waves have been constrained into fountains, the thunder has been tuned down into musical notes ; nature has submitted to man, and has abdicated her power into his hands. The stormy reign of instinctive feeling has come to an end ; the serene reign of art has begun.

In order to see these sensuous elements of music in their unmixed purity, in their unbridled strength, we must descend to the lowest stages of the art, compared with whose emotional effects those of modern music are as nothing, and least of all in the classic periods of the art ; but even in modern music, what really strong emotional effects there may be are due to a momentary suspension of artistic activity, to a momentary return to the formless, physically touching music of early ages. The most emotional thing ever written by Mozart is the exclamation of Donna Elvira, when, after leaving Don Giovanni at his ill-omened supper, she is met on the staircase by the statue of the commander ; this exclamation is but one high, detached note, formless, meaningless, which pierces the nerves like a blade ; submit even this one note to artistic action, bid the singer gradually swell and diminish it, and you at once rob it of its terrible power. This is Mozart's most emotional stroke ; but was a Mozart, nay, was any musician, necessary for its conception ? Would not that cry have been the same if surrounded by true music ? A contrary example, but to the same effect, is afforded by Gluck in his great scene of Orpheus at the gate of Hades, which may have moved our great-grandfathers, accustomed to fugues and minuets and *rigaudons*, but which seems coldly beautiful as some white antique group to us, accustomed as we are to romantic art. The *No !* of the Furies loses all its effects by being worked into a definite musical form, by being locked into the phrase begun by Orpheus; it is merely a constituent note and no more, until after some time it is repeated detached, and without any reference to the main melody sung by Orpheus : at first it is part of a work of art, later it becomes a mere brute shout, and then, and then only, does it obtain a really moving character.

When these potent physical elements are held in subjection by artistic form, emotion may be suggested, more or less vaguely, but only suggested : we perceive them in the fabric which imprisons them, and we perceive their

power, but it is as we should perceive the power of a tiger
chained up behind a grating : we remember and imagine
what it has been and might be, but we no longer feel it ;
for us to again feel it, the artistic form must be torn down ;
the physical elements unchained, and then, and then
only, shall we tremble once more before them.   Mozart
may be on his door-step as a regiment passes : he may
feel the inspiring, courage-awakening effect of its rough
rhythm and discordant, screeching trumpets : he may go
upstairs, sit down to his piano, make use of all those
sensuous elements, of the rhythm and of the wind instruments, which have stirred him in that regimental
music : he may use them in a piece professedly suggested
by that music ; the piece will be " Non più andrai," and
a masterpiece.   We shall be reminded of military music
by it, and we shall be aware of the fact that its rhythm
and accompaniment are martial ; we shall even call it a
martial piece ; but will it stir us, will it make us step out
and feel soldier-like as would the coarsest regimental
trumpets?   Jommelli may enter a cathedral as the bells
are tolling to mass, and all seems undulating and heaving
beneath their swing ; he may feel the awful effect of those
simple, shapeless sounds : he may listen to their suggestion and frame the opening of his Mass for the Dead
on that deep monotonous sway ; he will produce a
masterpiece, the wondrous *Introitus* of his Requiem, in
which we shall indeed recognize something of the solemn
rhythm of the bells, something that will awaken in us
the recollection of that moment when the cathedral
towers seemed to rock to their movement, and the aisles
re-echoed their roar, and when even miles away in the
open country the clear deep toll floated across the silent

fields; but that effect itself we shall never hear in the music. The artist has used the already existing emotional elements for his own purposes, but those purposes are artistic ones ; they aim at delighting the mind, not at tickling the nerves.

The composer, therefore, inasmuch as he deprives the emotional elements of music of their freedom and force of action, cannot possibly produce an effect on the emotions at all to be compared with that spontaneously afforded by nature ; he can imitate the rush of waters or the sob of despair only so distantly and feebly that the effect of either is well-nigh lost, and even for such an imitation he must endanger the artistic value of his work, which is safe only when it is the artist's sole aim and object. The most that the composer can legitimately do is to suggest a given emotion by employing in his intellectual structure such among the physical elements of his art as would in a state of complete freedom awaken that given emotion ; he may choose such sensuous elements as would inspire melancholy, or joy, or serenity ; he may reject any contrary element or any incongruous effect, and he may thus produce what we shall call a pathetic piece, or a cheerful piece, or a solemn piece.

But this pathetic, cheerful, or solemn character depends not upon the intellectual forms imagined by the composer, but upon the sensuous elements afforded by nature; and the artistic activity of the composer consists in the conception of those forms, not in the selection of those physical elements. When, therefore, a composer is said to express the words which he is setting, he does so by means not of the creation of artistic forms, but by the selection of sensuous materials; the suggestion of an emotion analogous to that conveyed by the words is due not to the piece itself, but to its physical constituents; wherefore the artistic value of the composition in no way depends upon its adaptation to the words with which it is linked. There is no more common mistake, nor one which more degrades artistic criticism, than the supposition that the merit of " He was despised and rejected of men," or of " Fin ch'an del vino," depends upon their respective suitableness to the words : the most inferior musician would perceive that such and such physical elements were required to suggest a mental condition in harmony with either of these verbal expressions of feeling; the most inferior musician could have given us a piece as melancholy as " He was despised," or as cheerful as " Fin ch'an del vino," but—and here lies the unique test of artistic worth—only Handel could have given us so beautiful a melancholy piece as the one, and only Mozart so beautiful a cheerful piece as the other. As it is with the praise, so likewise is it with the blame : a composer who sets a cheerful piece to dismal words, or a dismal piece to cheerful words, may be reprehensible for not reflecting that the mind thus receives together two contrary impressions, and he may be condemned for want of logic and good sense; but not a word can be said against his artistic merit, any more than we could say a word against the artistic merit of the great iron-worker of the Renaissance, who closed the holy place where lies the Virgin's sacred girdle with a screen of passion flowers, in whose petals hide goats and ducks, on whose tendrils are balanced pecking cranes, and in the curling leaves of which little naked winged Cupids are drawing their bows and sharpening their arrows even

as in the bas-reliefs of a pagan sarcophagus. In the free
and spontaneous activity of musical conception, the
composer may forget the words he is setting, as the
painter may forget the subject he is painting in the
fervour of plastic imagination ; for the musician conceives not emotions, but modulations ; and the painter
conceives not actions, but gestures and attitudes.
Thence it comes that Mozart has made regicide Romans
storm and weep as he would have made Zerlina and
Cherubino laugh, just as Titian made Magdalen smite
her breast in the wilderness with the smile of Flora on
her feast-day ; hence that confusion in all save form,
that indifference to all save beauty, which characterises
all the great epochs of art, that sublime jumble of times
and peoples, of tragic and comic, that motley crowding
together of satyrs and anchorites, of Saracens and ancient Romans, of antique warriors and mediæval burghers,
of Gothic tracery and Grecian arabesque, of Theseus and
Titania, of Puck and Bottom, that great masquerade of
art which we, poor critics, would fain reduce to law and
rule, to chronological and ethnological propriety.

Those times are gone by : we wish to make every
form correspond with an idea ; we wish to be told a story
by the statue, by the picture, most of all by that which can
least tell it—by music. We forget that music is neither
a symbol which can convey an abstract thought, nor a
brute cry which can express an instinctive feeling ; we
wish to barter the power of leaving in the mind an in-
delible image of beauty for the miserable privilege of
awakening the momentary recollection of one of nature's
sounds, or the yet more miserable one of sending a
momentary tremor through the body ; we would rather

compare than enjoy, and rather weep than admire. Therefore we try to force music to talk a language which it does not speak and which we do not understand; and succeed only in making it babble like a child or rave like a madman, obtaining nothing but unintelligible and incoherent forms in our anxiety to obtain intelligible and logical thoughts. We forget that great fact, forever overlooked by romanticism, that poetry and music are essentially distinct in their nature; that Chapelmaster Kreisler's improvisation was not played but spoken; and that had not the snuffers fallen into the piano, had not the strings snapped asunder, Hoffmann would have had to record, not a grandly grotesque series of images, but a succession of formless and meaningless chords.

CHERUBINO.

A PSYCHOLOGICAL ART FANCY.

IT is a strange and beautiful fact that whatsoever is touched by genius, no matter how humble in itself, becomes precious and immortal. This wrinkled old woman is merely one of thousands like herself, who have sat and will sit by the great porcelain stove of the Dutch backshop, their knitting or their bible on their knees. There is nothing to make her recollected; yet we know her after two centuries, even as if we had seen her alive, because, with a few blurred lines and shadows hastily scratched on his etching plate, it pleased the whim of Master Rembrandt to pourtray her. And this little commonplace Frankfurt shopkeeper's maiden, in her stiff little cap and starched frill, who should remember her? Yet she is familiar to us all, because she struck the boyish fancy of Goethe. For even as the fact of its once having sparkled on the waiscoat of Mozart makes us treasure up a tarnished brass button; and as the notion of their having been planted by the hand of Michael Angelo made us mourn the cutting down of a clump of sear and rusty old cypresses, so also the fact of having been noticed, noted down by genius, with brush, or pen, or chisel, makes into relics men and things which would else have been forgotten; because the stroke of that pen, or brush, or chisel removes them

1

from the perishable world of reality to the deathless world of fancy. Nay, even the beautiful things, the perfect, physically or morally, of the world, those which called forth admiration and love as long as they existed: Antinous and Monna Lisa, Beatrice and Laura, would now be but a handful of nameless dust, were it not for the artists and poets who have made them live again and for ever: the deeds and sufferings of the Siegfrieds and Cids, of the Desdemonas and Francescas, would have died away had they not been filched out of the world of reality into the world of fiction. And even as the perishable, the humble, the insignificant reality becomes enduring and valuable by the touch of genius; so also in the very world of fiction itself the intellectual creations of one man may be raised to infinitely higher regions by the hand of another, may be transported into the kingdom of another and nobler art, and there be seen more universally and surrounded by a newly acquired radiance. In this manner the tale of Romeo and Juliet, graciously and tenderly narrated by the old Italian story-teller, was transfigured by Shakespeare and enshrined in all the splendours of Elizabethan poetry; the figure of Psyche, delicately graceful in the little romance of Apuleius, re-appeared, enlarged and glorified by the hand of Raphael, on the walls of the Farnesina; and thus also our Cherubino, the fanciful and brilliant creature of Beaumarchais, is known to most of us far less in his original shape than in the vague form woven out of subtle melodies to which Mozart has given the page's name. Mozart has, as it were, taken away Cherubino from Beaumarchais; he has, for the world at large, substituted for the page of the comedy the page of the opera. Beaumarchais could

give us clear-spoken words, dialogue and action, a visible
and tangible creature; and Mozart could give only a
certain arrangement of notes, a certain amount of rhythm
and harmony, a vague, speechless, shapeless thing; yet
much more than the written words do those notes represent to our fancy the strange and fascinating little
figure, the wayward, the amorous, the prankish, the
incarnation of childishness, of gallantry, of grace, of fun,
and of mischief, the archetype of pages—the page
Cherubino. What could music do for Cherubino? of
what means could it dispose to reproduce this type,
this figure? and how did, how should music have disposed of those means? About this fantastic and
brilliant little jackanapes of a page centres a curious
question of artistic anomaly, of artistic power, and of
artistic duty.

The part of Cherubino: the waywardness, the love, the
levity, the audacity, the timidity, the maturity and
immaturity of the page's feelings, are all concentrated
by the admirable ingenuity of the Venetian D'Aponte,
who arranged Beaumarchais's play for Mozart's music,
into one air, the air sung by Cherubino in that very
equivocal interview with the Countess and Susanna, so
rudely to be broken by the thundering rap of the Count
at the door. The air is "Voi che sapete"—Cherubino's
description, half to the noble and sentimental lady, half
to the flippant and laughing waiting-maid, of the curious
symptoms, the mysterious hankerings and attractions
which the boy has of late begun to experience—symptoms of which he is half ashamed, as calculated to
bring down laughter and boxes on the ear, and half
proud, mischievously conscious that they make him a

personage for all this womankind. Every one has heard
"Voi che sapete" sung a hundred times by dozens of
singers in dozens of fashions, till it has become in the
recollection a sort of typical jumble of all these various
readings; but we once chanced to hear a reading of
"Voi che sapete" which has remained strangely distinct
and separate in our remembrance; which made that
performance of the hackneyed piece remain isolated in
our mind, almost as if the air had never before or never
since been heard by us. The scene of the performance
has remained in our memory as a whole, because the
look, the attitude, the face of the performer seemed to
form a whole, a unity of expression and character, with the
inflexions of the voice and the accentuation of the words.
She was standing by the piano: a Spanish Creole, but,
instead of the precocious, overblown magnificence of
tropical natures, with a something almost childlike
despite seriousness, something inflexible, unexpanded,
unripe about her; quite small, slender, infinitely slight
and delicate; standing perfectly straight and motionless
in her long, tight dress of ashy rose colour; her little
dark head with its tight coils of ebony hair perfectly
erect; her great dark violet-circled eyes, with their perfect ellipse of curved eyebrow meeting curved eyelash,
black and clear against the pale, ivory-tinted cheek,
looking straight before her; self-unconscious, concentrated, earnest, dignified, with only a faint fluttering
smile, to herself, not to the audience, about the mouth.
She sang the page's song in a strange voice, sweet and
crisp, like a Cremonese violin, with a bloom of youth,
scarcely mature yet perfect, like the honey dust of the
vine-flower; sang the piece with an unruffled serenity,

with passion, no limpness or languor, but passion restrained, or rather undeveloped ; with at most a scarcely perceptible hesitation and reticence of accent, as of budding youthful emotion ; her voice seeming in some unaccountable manner to move in a higher, subtler stratum of atmosphere, as it dextrously marked, rounded off, kissed away each delicate little phrase. When she had done, she gave a slight bow with her proud little head, half modestly and half contemptuously, as, with her rapid, quiet movement, she resumed her seat; she probably felt that despite the applause, her performance did not really please. No one criticised, for there was something that forbade criticism in this solemn little creature ; and every one applauded, for every one felt that her singing had been admirable. But there was no warmth of admiration, no complete satisfaction : she had sung with wonderful delicacy and taste and feeling; her performance had been exquisitely finished, perfect ; but something familiar, something essential had been missing. She had left out Cherubino: she had completely forgotten and passed over the page.

How was it? How could it be that the something which we felt was the nature of the page, the something which even the coarsest, poorest performers had brought out in this piece, had completely disappeared in this wonderfully perfect rendering by this subtle little singer? Perhaps the rendering had been only materially perfect : perhaps it was merely the exquisite tone of the voice, the wonderful neatness of execution which had given it an appearance of completeness ; perhaps the real meaning of the music had escaped her ; perhaps there was behind all this perfection of execution only a stolid

dulness of nature, to which the genius of Mozart was
not perceptible.   None of all these possibilities and probabilities : the chief characteristic of the performance
was exactly the sense of perfect musical intuition, of
subtle appreciation of every little intonation, the sense
that this docile and exquisite physical instrument was
being played upon by a keen and unflinching artistic
intelligence.   The more you thought over it, the more
you compared this performance with any other performance of the piece, the more also did you feel convinced that this was the right, the only right reading of
the piece ; that this strange, serious little dark creature
had given you the whole, the perfection of Mozart's conception ; no, there could be no doubt of it, this and this
alone was Mozart's idea of "Voi che sapete."   Mozart's
idea ? the whole of Mozart's conception ? here, in this
delicate, dignified, idyllic performance ?   The whole ?
Why then, where, if this was the whole of Mozart's conception, where was Cherubino, where was the page ?
Why, nowhere.   Now that the song had been presented
to us in its untampered perfection, that the thought of
the composer was clear to us—now that we could begin
to analyse the difference between this performance and
the performances of other singers—we began to see,
vaguely at first and not without doubts of our powers of
sight, but to see, and more and more distinctly the
longer we looked, that Cherubino was not in Mozart's
work, but merely in Beaumarchais.   A very singular
conclusion to arrive at, but one not to be shirked :
Cherubino had passed into the words of Mozart's Italian
libretto, he had passed into the dress, the face, the
feature, the action of the thousands of performers who

had sung the "Marriage of Figaro" on the stage; but
he had not passed into Mozart's notes; and because he
had not entered into those notes, that subtle and serious
little Spaniard, who had seen and understood so well the
meaning and beauty of Mozart's music, had known
nothing of Cherubino.

Now, after all this discussion respecting his presence
and his absence, let us stay awhile and examine into the
being of this Cherubino, so familiar and so immediately
missed by us; let us look at the page, whom the clever
playwright D'Aponte transported, with extraordinary
success, out of the French comedy into the Italian opera
text. Very familiar to all of us, yet, like the things
most familiar, rather vaguely; seen often and in various
lights, fluctuating consequently in our memory, as distinguished from the distinct and steadfast image of
things seen only once and printed off at a stroke on to
our mind. At the first glance, when we see him sitting
at the feet of the Countess, singing her his love songs, he
seems a delicate poetic exotic, whose presence takes us
quite aback in the midst of the rouged and pigtailed
philosophy, the stucco and tinsel sentimentality of the
French eighteenth century. In these rooms, all deco-
rated by Boucher and Fragonard, in this society redolent
with the theories of Diderot and the jests of Voltaire, this
page, this boy who is almost a girl, with his ribbons and
his ballads, his blushes, his guitar, and his rapier, appears
like a thing of long past days, or of far distant countries;
a belated brother of Shakspeare's Cesario and Fletcher's
Bellario, a straggler from the Spain of Lope de Vega,
who has followed M. Caron de Beaumarchais, ex-watch-
maker and ex-musicmaster to Mesdames the daughters

of Louis XV., from Madrid, and leaped suddenly on to
the planks of the Comédie Française . . . a ghost of
some mediæval boy page, some little Jehan de Saintré
killed crusading with his lady's name on his lips.   Or is
not Cherubino rather a solitary forerunner of romanticism, stumbled untimely into this France of Marie An-
toinette; some elder brother of Goethe's Mignon . . .
nay, perhaps Mignon herself, disguised as or metamor-
phosed into a boy. . . .   But let us look well at him :
let him finish his song and raise his audacious eyes ; let
him rise and be pulled to and fro, bashful with false
bashfulness half covering his mischievous, monkish im-
pudence, while Susanna is mumming him up in petti-
coats and kerchiefs ; let us look at him again now, and
we shall see that he is no Jehan de Saintré, no male
Mignon, no Viola in boy's clothes, no sweetly pure little
romantic figure, but an impertinent, precocious little
Lovelace, a serio-comic little jackanapes, sighing and
weeping only to giggle and pirouette on his heels the
next moment.   From the Countess he will run to the
gardener's daughter, from her to the waiting-maid, to
the duenna, to all womankind ; he is a professed lady-
killer and woman-teaser of thirteen.   There is indeed
something graceful and romantic in the idea of this
pretty child consoling, with his poetical, absurd love, the
poor, neglected, ill-used lady.   But then he has been
smuggled in by that dubious Abigail, Susanna ; the
sentimental, melancholy Countess is amused by dressing
him up in women's clothes ; and when, in the midst of
the masquerade, the voice of the Count is heard without,
the page is huddled away into a closet, his presence is
violently denied, and the Countess admits her adored

though fickle lord with a curious, conscious, half-guilty
embarrassment. We feel vaguely that Shakspeare would
never have introduced his boy Ganymede or his page
Cesario into that dressing-room of the Countess Alma-
viva; that the archly jesting Maria would never have
dreamed of amusing the Lady Olivia with such mum-
mings; we miss in this proudly sentimental lady, in this
sly waiting-woman, in this calf-loving dressed-up boy
the frank and boisterous merriment of Portia and Nerissa
in their escapades and mystifications; there is in all this
too much locking of doors and drawing of curtains, too
much whispered giggling, too little audible laughter;
there hangs an indefinable sense of impropriety about
the whole scene. No, no, this is no delicate and gracious
young creature of the stock of Elizabethan pages, no
sweet exotic in the France of 1780; this Cherubino is
merely a graceful, coquettish little Greuze figure, with
an equivocal simplicity, an ogling *naïveté*, a smirking
bashfulness, a hidden audacity of corruption; a creature
of Sterne or Marivaux, tricked out in imitation Mediæval
garb, with the stolen conscious wink of the eye, the
would-be childlike smile, tinged with leer, of eighteenth
century gallantry. He is an impertinent, effeminate,
fondled, cynical little jackanapes; the youngest, childish,
monkeyish example, at present merely comic and con-
temptible, of the miserable type of young lovers given
to France by the eighteenth century; the *enfant du
siècle*, externally a splendid, brilliant, triumphant success,
internally a miserable, broken, unmanned failure; the
child initiated into life by cynicism, the youth educated
to love by adultery; corrupt unripeness; the most
miserable type of demoralisation ever brought into

literature, the type of Fortunio and Perdican, and of
their author Alfred de Musset ; a type which the Eliza-
bethans, with their Claudios and Giovannis, could not
have conceived; which the Spaniards, with their Don
Juans and Ludovic Enios, would have despised, they
who had brought on to the stage profligacy which
bearded death and hell, turning with contempt from
profligacy which could be chastised only with the birch.
Cherubino is this : his love is no poetic and silly passion
for a woman much older than himself, before whom he
sinks on his knees as before a goddess ; it is the instinct
of the lady-killer, the instinct of adventures, the consciousness in this boy of thirteen that all womankind is
his destined prey, his game, his quarry. And womankind instinctively understands and makes the Lovelace
of thirteen its darling, its toy, its kitten, its pet monkey,
all whose grimacings and coaxings and impertinences
may be endured, enjoyed, encouraged.   He is the graceful, brilliant, apish Ariel or Puck of the society whose
Mirandas and Titanias are Julie and Manon Lescaut ;
he is the page of the French eighteenth century.

Such is, when we analyse him, the page Cherubino ;
looking at him carelessly, with the carelessness of familiarity, these various peculiarities escape our notice ; they
merge into each other and into the whole figure.   But
although we do not perceive them consciously and in
detail, we take in, vaguely and unconsciously, their total
effect : we do not analyse Cherubino and classify his
qualities, we merely take him in as a general type.   And
it is this confused and familiar entity which we call the
page, and which we expect to have brought home to us
as soon as we hear the first notes, as we see the title of

"Voi che sapete." It is this entity, this character thus vaguely conceived, which forms for us an essential part of Mozart's music ; and whose absence from that music made us feel as if, despite the greatest musical perfection, Mozart's idea were not completely given to us. Yet, in reality, this psychological combination called Cherubino does not exist in the work of Mozart. It exists only by the side of it. We speak of the " Marriage of Figaro " as Mozart's work ; we are accustomed to think of the Countess, of Figaro, of Susanna, of Cherubino as belonging to Mozart ; but in reality only one half of the thing we call the " Marriage of Figaro " belongs to Mozart—that half which consists in melodies and harmonies ; and as it happens, it is not in that, but in the other half belonging to Beaumarchais and D'Aponte, the half consisting of words and their suggestions of character, of expression and of movement, that really exists, either the Countess, or Figaro, or Susanna, or Cherubino. Those notes, which alone are Mozart's and which are nothing more than notes, have been heard by us in the mouths of many women dressed and acting as Beaumarchais's characters ; they have been heard by us associated to the words of Beaumarchais ; they have been heard delivered with the dramatic inflections suggested not by themselves but by those words ; and thus, by mere force of association, of slovenly thought and active fancy, we are accustomed to consider all these characters as existing in the music of Mozart, as being part and parcel of Mozart's conception ; and when we are presented with those notes, which, to the musician Mozart, were merely notes without those dramatic inflections suggested solely by Beaumarchais's words, when

we hear in " Voi che sapete " only Mozart's half of the
work, we are disappointed and indignant, and cry out
that the composer's idea has been imperfectly rendered.

Cherubino, we say, is not in Mozart's half of the work;
he is in the words, not in the music.   Is this a fault or a
merit? is it impotence in the art or indifference in the
artist?   Could Mozart have given us Cherubino? and if
able, ought he to have given him?   The question is
double ; a question of artistic dynamics, and a question
of artistic ethics : the question what can art do ; and the
question what art ought to do.   The first has been
answered by the scientific investigations of our own
scientific times ; the second has been · answered by the
artistic practice of the truly artistic days of music.   The
questions are strangely linked together, and yet strangely
separate ; and woe betide us if we receive the answer to
the one question as the answer to the other ; if we let
the knowledge of what things are serve us instead of the
instinct of what things should do ; if we let scientific
analysis step into the place of ethical or æsthetical judgment; and if, in the domain of art or of morals we think
to substitute a system of alembics and microscopes for
that strange intangible mechanism which science tells us
does not exist, and which indeed science can never see
or clutch, our soul.   For science has a singular contempt
for all that is without its domain ; it seeks for truth, but
when truth baffles and eludes it, science will turn towards
falsehood ; it will deny what it cannot prove, and call
God himself a brain-phantom because he cannot be
vivisected.   So, when logic, which can solve only logical
propositions, remains without explanation before the
dicta of the moral and æsthetic parts of us, it simply

denies the existence of such dicta and replaces them by
its own formulæ ; if we ask for the aim of things and
actions, it tells us their origin ; if we trustingly ask when
we should admire beauty and love virtue, it drops the
rainbow into its crucible to discover its chemical com-
ponents, and dissects the brain of a saint to examine the
shape of its convolutions ; it meets admiration and love
with experiment and analysis, and, where we are required to judge, tells us we can only examine. Thus, as
in ethics, so also in æsthetics, modern philosophy has
given us the means instead of the aim, the analysis instead of the judgment ; let us therefore ask it only how
much of human character and emotion music *can* express ; the question how much of it music *ought* to
express must be answered by something else : by that
artistic instinct whose composition and mechanism and
origin scientific psychology may perhaps some day explain, but whose unformulated, inarticulate, half-unconscious dicta all the scientific and logical formulæ in
the world can never replace. As yet, however, we have·
to deal only with the question how much of human
character and emotion music can express, and by what
means it does so ; and here modern psychology, or
rather the genius of Herbert Spencer, is able to answer
us. Why does dance music cheer us, and military music
inspirit us, and sacred music make us solemn ? A
vague sense of the truth made æstheticians answer, for
well-nigh two centuries, "by the force of association." Dance music cheers us because we are accustomed to hear it in connection with laughing and quips
and cranks ; military music inspirits us because we are
accustomed to hear it in connection with martial move-

ments and martial sights; sacred music depresses us
because we are accustomed to hear it at moments when
we are contemplating our weakness and mortality;
'tis a mere matter of association. To this easy-going
way of disposing of the problem there was an evident
and irrefutable objection: but why should we be accustomed to hear a given sort of music in connection with
these various conditions of mind? Why should dance
music, and martial music, and sacred music all have
a perfectly distinct character, which forbade, from the
very first, their being exchangeable? If it is a matter
of association of ideas, tell us why such characters
could have been kept distinct before the association
of ideas could have begun to exist? To this objection there was no reply; the explanation of musical
expression by means of association of ideas seemed
utterly hollow; yet the confused idea of such an association persisted. For it was, after all, the true explanation. If we ask modern psychology the reason of the
specific characters of the various sorts of music, we
shall again be answered: it is owing to the association
of ideas. But the two answers, though apparently
identical, are in fact radically different. The habit
of association existed, according to the old theory,
between various mental conditions and various sorts of
music, because the two were usually found in connection; hence no explanation why, before habit had created
the association, there should have been any connection,
and, there being no connection, no explanation why the
habit and consequently the mental association should
ever have been formed. According to the modern
theory, on the contrary, the habit of association is not

between the various mental conditions and the various
styles of music ; but between specific mental conditions
and specific sounds and movements, which sounds and
movements, being employed as the constituent elements
of music, give to the musical forms into which they have
been artistically arranged that inevitable suggestion of a
given mental condition which is due to memory, and
become, by repetition during thousands of years, an instinct ingrained in the race and inborn in the individual,
a recognition rapid and unconscious, that certain audible
movements are the inevitable concomitants of certain
moral conditions. The half-unconscious memory become
part and parcel of the human mind, that, just as certain
mental conditions induce a movement in the muscles
which brings tears into the eye or a knot into the throat,
so also certain audible movements are due to the muscular tension resulting from mental buoyancy, and certain others to the muscular relaxation due to mental
depression, this half-unconscious memory, this instinct,
this inevitable association of ideas, generated long before
music existed even in the most rudimentary condition,
carried with the various elements of pitch, movement,
sonority, and proportion into the musical forms constructed out of these elements, this unconscious association of ideas, this integrated recollection of the inevitable
connection between certain sounds and certain passions
is the one main cause and explanation of the expressiveness of music. And when to it we have added the conscious perception, due to actual comparison, of the
resemblance between certain modes of musical delivery
and certain modes of ordinary speaking accentuation,
between certain musical movements and certain move-

ments of the body in gesticulation ; when we have completed the instinctive recognition of passion, which makes
us cry or jump, we know not why, by the rapidly
reasoned recognition of resemblance between the utterance of the art and the utterance of human life, which,
when we listen for instance to a recitative, makes us say,
"This sentence is absolutely correct in expression," or,
"No human being ever said such a thing in such a
manner ;" when we have the instinctive perception of
passion, and the conscious perception of imitation ; and
we have added to these two the power of tone and harmony, neither of them connected in any way with the
expression of emotion, but both rendering us, by their
nervous stimulant, infinitely more sensitive to its expression ; when we have all this, we have all the elements which the musician can employ to bring home to
us a definite state of mind ; all the mysterious unspoken,
unwritten words by means of which Mozart can describe
to us what Beaumarchais has described in clear, logical,
spoken, written words—the page Cherubino.

Now let us see how much of Cherubino can be shown
us by these mere musical means. Cherubino is childish,
coquettish, sentimental, amorous, timid, audacious, fickle ;
he is self-conscious and self-unconscious, passionately
troubled in mind, impudently cool in manner ; he is
brazen, calm, shy, fluttered ; all these things together.
Sometimes in rapid alternation, sometimes all together
in the same moment ; and in all this he is perfectly con-
sistent, he is always one and the same creature. How
does the playwright contrive to make us see all this ?
By means of combinations of words expressing one or
more of these various characteristics, by subtle phrases

woven out of different shades of feeling, which glance in
irridescent hues like a shot silk, which are both one thing
and another; by means also of various emotions cunningly adapted to the exact situation, from the timid
sentimentality before the countess, down to the audacious
love-making with the waiting-maid; by means, in short,
of a hundred tiny strokes, of words spoken by the page
and of the page, by means of dexterously combined
views of the boy himself, and of the reflection of the boy
in the feelings of those who surround him. Thus far the
mere words in the book; but these words in the book
suggest a thousand little inflections of voice, looks, gestures, movements, manners of standing and walking,
flutter of lips and sparkle of eyes, which exist clear
though imaginary in the mind of the reader, and become
clearer, visible, audible in the concrete representation of
the actor.

Thus Cherubino comes to exist. A phantom of the
fancy, a little figure from out of the shadow land of
imagination, but present to our mind as is this floor upon
which we tread, alive as is this pulse throbbing within
us. Ask the musician to give us all this with his mere
pitch, and rhythm and harmony and sonority; bid him
describe all this in his language. Alas! in the presence
of such a piece of work the musician is a mere dumb
cripple, stammering unintelligible sounds, tottering
through abortive gestures, pointing we know not whither,
asking we know not for what. Passionate music? And
is not Othello passionate? Coquettish music? and is
not Susanna coquettish? Tender music? and is not
Orpheus tender? Cool music? and is not Judas Maccabæus cool? Impudent music? And is not the snatch

K

of dance tune of a Parisian grisette impudent? And
which of these sorts of music shall fit our Cherubino, be
our page? Shall we fuse, in wonderful nameless abomination of nonsense, all these different styles, these different suggestions, or shall, as in a masquerade, this dubious
Cherubino never seen with his own face and habit, appear successively in the musical trappings of Othello, of
Orpheus, of Susanna, of Judas Maccabæus, and of the
Grisette? Shall we, by means of this fusion, or this
succession of musical incongruities, have got one inch
nearer to Cherubino? Shall we, in listening to the mere
wordless combination of sounds, be able to say, as we
should with the book or the actors before us, this is
Cherubino? What, then, can music give us, with all its
powers of suggestion and feeling, if it cannot give us
this? It can give us one thing, not another: it can give
us emotion, but it cannot give us the individual whom
the emotion possesses. With its determined relations
between the audible movement and the psychical movement, it can give us only musical gesture, but never
musical portrait; the gesture of composure or of violence,
the solemn tread of self-possessed melody, the scuffling
of frantically rushing up and down, of throbbing, quivering, gasping, passion-broken musical phrases; it can give
us the rhythm which prances and tosses in victory, and
the rhythm which droops, and languishes, and barely
drags itself along for utter despair. All this it can give
us, even as the painter can give the ecstatic bound-for-
wards of Signorelli's "Calling of the Blessed," or the
weary, dreary enfolding in gloomy thought of Michael
Angelo's "Jeremiah:" this much, which we can only
call gesture, and which expresses only one thing, a mood.

Let the hopeful heroes of Signorelli, stretching forth impetuous arms towards Paradise, only lose sight of the stately viol-playing angels who guide them, let them suddenly see above them the awful sword of the corsleted Angel of Judgment, and they will sink, and grovel, and writhe, and their now up-turned faces will be draggled in the dust; let the trumpet of warfare and triumph shrill in the ear of Michael Angelo's "Jeremiah," and the dreary dream will be shaken off; he will leap up, and the compressed hand-gagged mouth will open with the yell of battle; let only the emotion change, and the whole gesture, the attitude, plastic or musical, must change also; the already existing, finite, definite work will no longer suffice; we must have a new picture, or statue, or piece of music. And in these inexplicit arts of mere suggestion, we cannot say, as in the explicit art of poetry, this grovelling wretch is a proud and hopeful spirit; this violent soldier is a vague dreamer; this Othello, who springs on Desdemona like a wild beast, loves her as tenderly as a mother does her child. Unliterary art, plastic or musical, is inexorable: the man who grovels is no proud man; the man who fells down to the right and left, is no dreamer; the man whose whole soul is wrath and destruction, is no lover; the mood is the mood; art can give only it; and the general character, the connection between moods, the homogeneous something which pervades every phase of passion, however various, escapes the powers of all save the art which can speak and explain. How then obtain our Cherubino, our shiftiest and most fickle of pages? How? Why, by selecting just one of his very many moods, the one which is nearest allied to fickleness and volubility; the mood which must most commonly be the underlying, the connecting one, the mood into which all his swagger and sentiment sooner or later resolve ; the tone of voice into which his sobs will quickest be lost, the attitude which will soonest replace the defiant strut ; the frame of mind which, though one and indivisible itself, is the nearest to instability : levity.

Let Cherubino sing words of tenderness and passion, of audacity and shyness, to only one sort of music, to light and careless music ; let the jackanapes be for ever before us, giggling and pirouetting in melody and rhythm ; it will not be Cherubino, the whole Cherubino ; it will be only a miserable fragmentary indication of him, but it will be the right indication ; the psychological powers of music do not go far, but thus far they can go. Analysis of the nature of musical expression has shown us how much it may accomplish ; the choice of the artist alone can tell us how much it should accomplish ; the scientific investigation is at an end, the artistic judgment must begin. Chapelmaster Wolfgang Amadeus Mozart, here are your means of musical expression, and here is the thing to be expressed ; on careful examination it appears distinctly that the only way in which, with your melodies, rhythms, and harmonies, you can give us, not a copy, but a faint indicative sketch, something approaching the original as much as four lines traced in the alley sand of your Schloss Mirabell Gardens at Salzburg resemble the general aspect of the Mirabell Palace ; that the only way in which you can give us such a distantly approximative. . . . .

Signor Maestro Wolfgang Amadeus Mozart, Vice-Chapelmaster of His Most Reverend Highness the

Prince Archbishop of Salzburg, has meanwhile sat down at his table near his thin-legged spinet, with the bird-cage above and the half-emptied beer-glass at his side ; and his pen is going scratch, scratch, scratch as loud as possible.

"The only way in which you can possibly give us such a distantly approximative copy of the page Cherubino as shown " . . . (Scratch, scratch, scratch goes the pen on the rough music paper), " as shown in the words of Beaumarchais and of your librettist D'Aponte, is to compose music of the degree of levity required to express the temper *jackanapes.*"

The Chapelmaster Mozart's pen gives an additional triumphant creak as its point bends in the final flourish of the word *finis ;* Chapelmaster Mozart looks up—

"What was that you were saying about jackanapes ? Oh, yes, to be sure, you were saying that literary folks who try to prescribe to musicians are jackanapes, weren't you ? Now, do me the favour, when you go out, just take this to the theatre copyist ; they are waiting in a hurry for Cherubino's song. . . . Yes, that was all very interesting about the jackanapes and all the things music can express. . . . Who would have thought that musical expression is all that ? Lord, Lord, what a fine thing it is to have a reasoning head and know all about the fundamental moods of people's characters ! My dear sir, why don't you print a treatise on the musical interpretation of the jackanapes and send it to the University of Vienna for a prize ? that would be a treatise for you ! Only do be a good creature and take this song at once to the copyist. . . . I assure you I consider you the finest musical philosopher in Christendom."

The blotted, still half-wet sheet of note paper is handed across by Chapelmaster Wolfgang Amadeus Mozart.   It is the manuscript of " Voi che sapete."

" But dearest Chapelmaster Mozart, the air which you have just written appears to be not in the least degree light—it is even extremely sentimental.   How can you, with such phrases, express the Cherubino of Beaumarchais ? "

" And who, my dear Mr. Music Philosopher, who the deuce told you that I wanted to express the Cherubino of Beaumarchais ? "

Chapelmaster Mozart, rising from his table, walks up and down the room with his hands crossed beneath his snuff-coloured coat-tails, humming to himself—

> Voi che sapete che cosa è amor,
> Donne, vedete s' io l' ho nel cor,

and stops before the cage hanging in the window, and twitching the chickweed through the wires, says—

" Twee ! twee ! isn't that a fine air we have just composed, little canary-bird, eh ? "

" Twee ! twee ! " answers the canary.

Mozart has willed it so : there is no possible appeal against his decision ; his artistic sense would not listen to our logic ; our arguments could not attain him, for he simply shook from off his feet the dust of logic-land, and calmly laughed defiance from the region of artistic form, where he had it all his own way, and into which we poor wretches can never clamber.   So here is the page's song irrevocably sentimental ; and Mozart has been in his grave ninety years ; and we know not why, but we do shrink from calling in Offenbach or Lecocq to rewrite that air in true jackanapsian style. What can be done? There still remains another hope.

For the composer, as we have seen, could give us— as could the painter or the sculptor—only one mood at a time; for he could give us only one homogeneous artistic form. But this artistic form exists so far only in the abstract, in the composer's brain or on the paper. To render it audible we require the performer; on the performer depends the real, absolute presence of the work; or, rather, to the performer is given the task of creating a second work, of applying on to the abstract composition the living inflexions and accentuations of the voice. And here, again, the powers of musical expression, of awaking association by means of sounds or manner of giving out sounds such as we recognize, automatically or consciously, to accompany the emotion that is to be conveyed; here again these powers are given to the artist to do therewith what he choose. This second artist, this performer, is not so free indeed as the first artist, the composer; he can longer choose among the large means of expression the forms of melody and rhythm, the concatenation of musical phrases; but there are still left to him the minor modes of expression, the particular manner of setting forth these musical forms, of treating this rhythm; the notes are there, and their general relations to one another, but on him depends the choice of the relative stress on the notes, of the tightening or slackening of their relations; of the degree of importance to be given to the various phrases. The great outline cartoon is there, but the cunning lights and shades, transitions, abrupt or insensible, from tint to tint, still remain to be filled up. A second choice of

mood is left to the singer. And see! here arises a
strange complication : the composer having in his work
chosen one mood, and the singer another, we obtain in
the fusion or juxtaposition of the two works, of the two
moods, that very thing we desired, that very shimmer
and oscillation of character which the poet could give,
that dualism of nature required for Cherubino. What
is Cherubino ? A sentimental jackanapes. Mozart in
his notes has given us the sentiment, and now we can
get the levity from the performer—unthought-of combination, in which the very irrational, illogical choice
made by the composer will help us. Here are Mozart's
phrases, earnest, tender, noble—Mozart's love song fit
for a Bellario or a Romeo ; now let this be sung quickly,
lightly, with perverse musical head-tossing and tripping
and ogling, let this passion be gabbled out flippantly,
impudently—and then, in this perfect mixture of the
noble and ignoble, of emotion and levity, of poetry and
prose, we shall have, at last, the page of Beaumarchais.
A brilliant combination ; a combination which, thus
reasoned out, seems so difficult to conceive ; yet one
which the instinct of half, nay, of nearly all the performers in creation would suggest. A page ? A jackanapes ? Sing the music as befits him ; giggle and ogle,
and pirouette, and languish out Mozart's music : an
universal idea now become part and parcel of tradition :
the only new version possible being to give more or less
of the various elements of giggling, ogling, pirouetting,
and languishing ; to slightly vary the style of jackanapes.

But no, another version did remain possible : that
strange version given by that strange solemn little
Spanish singer, after whose singing of " Voi che sapete "

we all felt dissatisfied, and asked each other, " What has she done with the page ? " That wonderful reading of the piece in which every large outline was so grandly and delicately traced, every transition so subtly graduated or marked, every little ornament made to blossom out beneath the touch of the singular crisp, sweet voice : that reading which left out the page. Was it the blunder of an idealess vocal machine ? or the contradictory eccentricity of a seeker after impossible novelty ? Was it simply the dullness of a sullen, soulless little singer ? Surely not. She was neither an idealess vocal machine, nor a crotchetty seeker for new readings, nor a soulless sullen little creature ; she was a power in art. A power, alas ! wasted for ever, of little or no profit to others or herself ; a beautiful and delicate artistic plant uprooted just as it was bursting into blossom, and roughly thrown to wither in the sterile dust of common life, while all around the insolent weeds lift up their prosperous tawdry heads. Of this slender little dark creature, with the delicate stern face of the young Augustus, not a soul will ever remember the name. She will not even have enjoyed the cheap triumphs of her art, the applause which endures two seconds, and the stalkless flowers which wither in a day ; the clapping which interrupts the final flourish, the tight-packed nosegays which thump down before the feet, of every fiftieth-rate mediocrity. Yet the artistic power will have been there, though gone to waste in obscurity : and the singer will have sung, though only for a day, and for that day unnoticed. Nothing can alter that. And nothing can alter the fact that, while the logical heads of all the critics, and the soulless throats of all the singers in

Christendom have done their best, and ever will do their best to give us a real musical Cherubino, a real sentimental whipper-snapper of a page, this utterly unnoticed little singer did persist in leaving out the page most completely and entirely. Why? Had you asked her, she would have been the last person in the world capable of answering the question. Did she consider the expression of such a person as Cherubino a prostitution of the art? Had she some theory respecting the propriety of dramatic effects in music? Not in the very least; she considered nothing and theorised about nothing: she probably never had such a thing as a thought in the whole course of her existence. She had only an unswerving artistic instinct, a complete incapacity of conceiving the artistically wrong, an imperious unreasoning tendency to do the artistically right. She had read Mozart's air, understood its exquisite proportions, created it afresh in her appreciation, and she sang it in such a way as to make its beauty more real, more complete. She had unconsciously carried out the design of the composer, fulfilled all that could be fulfilled, perfected the mere music of Mozart's air. And as in Mozart's air there was and could be (inasmuch as it was purely beautiful) no page Cherubino, so also in her singing of the air there was none: Mozart had chosen, and she had abided by his choice.

Such is the little circle of fact and argument. We have seen what means the inherent nature of music afforded to composer and performer for the expression of Beaumarchais's Cherubino; and we have seen the composer, and the performer who was true to the composer, both choose, instead of expressing an equivocal jackanapes, to produce and complete a beautiful work of art. Were they right or were they wrong? Criticism, analysis, has said all it could, given all its explanations; artistic feeling only remains to judge, to condemn, or to praise: this one fact remains, that in the work of the great composer, we have found only certain lovely patterns made out of sounds; but in them, or behind them, not a vestige of the page Cherubino.

IN UMBRIA.

A STUDY OF ARTISTIC PERSONALITY.

> . . . . grande, austera, verde,
> Da le montagne digradanti in cerchio,
> L'Umbria guarda.—CARDUCCI.

THE autumn sun is declining over the fields and oak-
woods and vineyards of Umbria, where—in the wide
undulating valley, inclosed by high rounded hills, bleak
or dark with ilex, each with its strange terraced white
city, Assisi, Spello, Spoleto, Todi—the Tiber winds lazily
along, pale green, limpid, scarce rippled over its yellow
pebbles, screened by long rows of reeds, and thinned,
yellowing poplars, reflecting dimly the sky and trees, the
pointed mediæval bridges and the crenelated towers on
its banks; so clear and placid that you can scarcely
bring home to yourself that this can really be the Tiber
of Rome, the turbid mass of yellow water which eddies
sullen and mournful round the ship-shaped island, along
by Vesta's temple, beneath the cypressed Aventine, and
away into the desolate Campagna. Gradually, as the
sun sinks, the valley of the Tiber fills with golden light
moving along, little by little, travelling slowly up the
wooded hillocks; covering the bluish mountains of Somma
and Subasio with a purple flush, making the white towns
rosy on their flanks, and then dying away into the pale
amber horizon, rosy where it touches the hill, pearly,

then bluish where it merges imperceptibly into the upper sky. Bluer and bluer become the hills, deeper and deeper the at first faint amber ; the valley is filled with grey-blue mist ; the hills stand out dark blue, cold, and massive; the sky above becomes a livid rose colour; there is scarcely a filament of cloud, and only a streak of golden orange where the sun has disappeared. There is a sudden stillness, as when the last chords of a great symphony have died out. All the way up the hill on which stands Perugia we meet the teams of huge oxen, not merely white, but milky, with great, deep, long-lashed eyes, swaying from side to side with their load of wine-vats; and the peasants returning home from ploughing up the last corn stubble. All is peaceful and very solemn, more so than after sunset in other places, in this sweet and austere Umbria, the fit home of the Christian revival of the early Middle Ages. And it makes us think, this beautiful and solemn evening, of the little book which epitomises all the emotions of this new birth, of this charming new childhood of humanity, when the feelings of men seem to have somewhat of the dewy freshness of dawn. The book is the "Fioretti di San Francesco," a collection of legends and examples relating to the cycle of St. Francis of Assisi by some monk or monks of the end of the thirteenth century. Flowerets they may well be called—flowers such as might grow, green and white-starred and delicately pearled with gold, in the thick grass across which dance Angelico's groups of the Blessed. Yet with a certain humanness, a certain reality and naturalness of sweetness, such as the great paradise painter, with his fleshless madonnas, his glory of radiant, unearthly draperies and

golden skies, never could have conceived. A singular
charm of simplicty and lucidness in this little book ; no
fever visions or unhealthy glories; an earnestness not
without humour : there is nothing grim or absurd in the
credulity and asceticism of these Umbrian saints. The
asceticism is so gentle and tender, the credulity so
childish and poetical, that the ridiculous itself ceases to
be so. These monks, so far from being engrossed with
the care of their own souls, or weighed down by the
dread of hell, seemed to have awakened with perfect
hope and faith in celestial goodness, with perfect desire
to love all around them in the most literal sense : religion for them is love and reliance on love. The gentleness with which they admonish the sinning and back-
sliding, the confidence in the inner goodness of man,
from whose soiled surface all evil may be washed, ex-
tends in these men to the whole of creation, and makes
them fraternise with beasts and birds, as is shown, with
a delicate, slightly humorous grace, in the stories of St.
Francis and the turtle doves, and of the ferocious wolf
" Frate Lupo " of Gubbio, whom rather than kill, it
pleased the saint to bring round to harmlessness by fair
words, expostulations, and faithfully kept promises, ex-
pecting from the wolf fidelity to his word as much as
from a human being. There is in this little book a
vague, floating, permeating life of affection, of love un-
bounded by difference of species. Communion with all
men, with Christ, with angels, with doves, and with
wolves ; the force of love bringing down God and raising
up brutes to the level of these saints. And as we think
over the little book we feel in a way as if we, to whom
Francis and his companions are mere mortal men, and

the tales of the "Fioretti" mere beautiful fancies, hollow and sad for their very sweetness, were looking down upon a sort of holy land, as we look down in the white twilight upon the misty undulations of this solemn and beautiful Umbria.

A serene country, neither rugged and barren, nor flat and fertile, not the grey, sharp Florentine valley, whose thin soil must be irrigated and ploughed, and on whose hillsides the carefully nurtured olives are stunted with winter wind and summer scorchings, where every outline is clear and bone-like in that same hard, light atmosphere which, as Vasari says, makes all appear hard and clear and logical to the minds of the Florentines. Not the endless flatness and fruitfulness of Lombardy, where the mists steam up in the evening golden round the great misty golden descending sun-ball, and the buildings flush like the cheeks of Correggio's joy-drunken seraphs, and the thin, clear outline of the rows of poplars looks against the sky like the outshaken golden hair combed into minute filaments of one of Lionardo's women. Nor the dreary wastes of sere oakwoods and livid sandhills of Orvieto; nor the sea of lush vegetation gilded by the sun, merging into the vaporous damp blue sky of the plain of Lucca. None of these things is the Tiber valley, not harsh nor poor nor luxuriant; sober and restrained, without excess or scantness, an undulating country of pale and modest tints, and, save in the distant Apennine tops, of simple outline, with what glory of colours it may have, due mainly to sky and sunset of cloud, and even in that more chaste than other parts of Italy; neither poor nor rich; without the commerce of Lombardy or the industry of Tuscany, wholly without any intellectual

movement, rural, believing, with but little of the imported
influence of reviving Paganism, and still much of the
clinging moral atmosphere of Christian contemplation
and ecstacy of the days of St. Francis. Such is this
isolated Tiber valley, whose skies and whose legends are
so perfectly in harmony, and in it was born, of the
country and of the traditions, a special, isolated school
of art.

Is it a school or a man?—A school concentrated in
one man, or a man radiating into a school. There are a
great many men all about the one man Perugino, masters or pupils ; the first seem so many bungled attempts
to be what he is, the second so many disintegrations of
him. Even the more powerful individualities are lost in
his presence ; at Perugia we know nothing of the real
Pinturicchio, the bright, vain, thoughtless painters of the
pageant scenes, brilliant like pages of Boiardo's fairy
tales, on the walls of the Sienese Library. Raphael is
no separate individual, has no personal qualities before
he leaves Perugia. Everything is Perugino, in more or
less degree. The whole town, nay, the surrounding
country, is one vast studio in which his themes are being
developed, his works being copied, his tricks being imitated. A score of artists of talent, one or two like Lo
Spagna and the young Raphael, of first-rate powers, and
a host of mere mechanical drudges, give us, in all Perugia,
nothing new, nothing individual, no impression which we
can disentangle from the general, all-pervading impression given by the one man Perugino. The country,
physical and moral, has exhausted itself in this one
artistic manifestation. One not merely, but unique and
one-sided. What Perugino has done has been done by

no other master ; and what Perugino has done is only
one thing, and that to all eternity. The sense of complete absence of variety, of difference ; the impression of
all being reduced to the minimum of everything, the
vague consciousness that all here is one, isolated and
indivisible, which haunts us all through the churches and
galleries of Perugia, pursues us likewise through all the
works of the school, that is to say, of Perugino himself.
This unique school, consisting in reality of a single man,
possesses only one theme, one type, one idea, one feeling ; it does, it attempts but one thing, and that one
thing means isolation, concentration, elimination of all
but one single mood.

It is the painting of solitude ; of the isolated soul,
alone, unaffected by any other, unlinked in any work, or
feeling, or suffering, with any other soul, nay even with
any physical thing. The men and women of Perugino
are the most completely alone that any artist ever
painted, alone though in fours, or fives, or in crowds.
Their relations to each other are purely architectural : it
is a matter of mere symmetry, even as it is with the
mouldings or carvings of the frame which surrounds
them. Superficially, taken merely as so many columns,
or half-arches of the pinnacled whole of the composition,
they are, in his larger works, more rigorously related to
each other than are the figures of any other painter of
severely architectural groups ; compared with Perugino,
the figures in Bellini's or Mantegna's most solemn altarpieces are irrelevant to each other : one saint is turning
too much aside, another looking too much on his neighbour. Not so with Perugino : his figures are all in relation to one another. The scarf floating in strange

snakelike convolutions, from the shoulder of the one angel
flying, cutting across the pale blue air as a skater cuts
across the ice, floats and curls in distinct reference to the
ribbons which twist, like lilac or yellow scrolls, about the
head and neck of the other angel; the lute, with down-
turned bulb, of the one seraph, his shimmering purple or
ultramarine robe clinging in tight creases round his feet
in the breeze of heaven, is rigorously balanced by the viol,
upturned against the stooping head, of his fellow-seraph;
the white-bearded anchorite stretches forth his right foot
in harmony with the outstretched left foot of the scarlet-
robed cardinal; the dainty arch-angelic warrior drolly
designated as Scipio, or Cincinnatus on the wall of the
Money Changer's Hall turns his delicate, quaintly-
crested head, and raises his vague-looking eyes to match
the upturned plumed head of the other celestial knight.
All the figures are distinctly connected with each other;
but they are connected as are the pillarets, various, but
different, which balance each other in length and thick-
ness and character, a twisted with a twisted one, a twin,
strangely linked pair with another such, on the sym-
metrically sloping front of some Lombard cathedral; the
connection is purely outer, purely architectural; and the
solitude of each figure as a human being, as a body and
a mind, is only the more complete.   There is no grouping in these cunningly balanced altarpieces; there is no
common employment or movement, no action or reaction.   Angels and warriors and saints and sibyls
stand separate, the one never touching the other, apart,
each alone against the pale greenish background.   They
may look, the one towards the other, but they never see
each other.   They exist quite single and isolated, each

unconscious that there is any other.' Another—indeed, there is no other; in reality, every one is in complete solitude; it is only the canvas which makes them appear in the same place. They are not in the same place, or rather there is no place; the soft green field, the blue hills, darkening against the greenish evening sky, the spare, thinly leaved little trees, the white tower in the distance, this little piece of Umbrian country has nothing to do with any of them. They are nowhere; or rather each taken singly is nowhere. Place, like subject and action, has been eliminated; everything has, which possibly could. The very bodies seem reduced to the least possible: there is no interest in them: all is concentrated upon the delicate nervous hands, on the faces; in the faces, upon eyes and mouth, till the whole face seems scarcely more than tremulous lips, half parted, raised vividly to kiss, to suck in the impalpable; than dilating pupils, straining vaguely to seize, to absorb, to burn into themselves the invisible. It is the embodiment, with only as little body as is absolutely required, of a soul; and that soul simplified, rarefied into only one condition of being: beatitude of contemplation. As place and action have been eliminated, so also has time: they will for ever remain, alone, in the same attitude; they will never move, never change, never cease; there exists for them no other occupation or possibility. And as the bodies are separate, isolated from all physical objects, so is the soul: it touches no other human soul, touches no earthly interest: it is alone, motionless, space and time and change have ceased for it : contemplating, absorbing for all eternity that which the eye cannot see, nor the hand touch nor the will influence, the mysterious, the ineffable.

Are they really saints and angels, and prophets and
sibyls? Surely not—for all such act or suffer; for each
of these there is a local habitation, and a definite duty.
These strange creatures of Perugino's are not supernatural beings in the same sense as are those robed
in iridescent, impalpable glory of Angelico; or those
others, clothed in more than human muscle and sinew,
of the vault of the Sixtine. What are they? Not
visions become concrete, but the act of vision personified.
They are not the objects of religious feeling; they are
its most abstract, intense reality. Yes, they are reality.
They are no far-fetched fancies of the artist. They are
souls and soul-saturated, soul-moulded bodies which he
saw around him. For in that Umbria of the dying
fifteenth century—where the old cities, their old freedom
and industry and commerce well-nigh dwindled to
nothing, had shrunk each on its mountain-side into mere
huge barracks of mercenary troopers or strongholds of
military bandit nobles, continually besieged and sacked
and heaped with massacre by rival families and rival
factions; where in the open country, the villagers, pent-
up in fortified farms and barns, were burnt, women and
children, with the stored-up fodder, or slaughtered and
cast in heaps into the Tiber, and every year the tangled
brushwood of ilex and oak and briars encroached further
upon the devastated cornfields and oliveyards, and the
wolves and foxes roamed nearer and nearer to the cities—
in this terrible barbarous Umbria of the days of Cæsar
Borgia, the soul developed to strange unearthly perfection. It developed by the force of antagonism and
isolation. This city of Perugia, which was governed by
the most ferocious and treacherous little mercenary cap-

tains; whose dark precipitous streets were full of broil and
bloodshed, and whose palaces full of evil, forbidden lust
and family conspiracy, was one of the most pious in all
Italy. Wondrous miraculous preachers, inspired and
wild, were for ever preaching in the midst of the iniquity;
holy monks and nuns were for ever seeing visions and
curing the incurable ; churches and hospitals were being
erected throughout town and country ; novices crowded
the ever-increasing convents. Sensitive souls were
sickened by the surrounding wickedness, and terrified.
lest it should triumph over them ; resist it, bravely ex-
pose themselves to it, prevent or mitigate the evil of
others they dared not : a moral plague was thick in the
air, and those who would escape infection must needs
fly, take refuge in strange spiritual solitude, in isolated
heights where the moral air was rarefied and icy. Of
the perfectly human, sociable devotion of the days of St.
Francis, of the active benevolence and righteousness,
there was now no question : the wolves had become too
frightfully numerous and ravenous to be preached to like
that Brother Wolf of the *Flowerets of St. Francis*. Active
good there could now no longer be : the pure soul became inactive, passive, powerless over the evil around,
contemplating for ever a distant, ineffable excellence ;
aspiring, sterile, and meagre, at being absorbed into that
glory of perfect virtue at which it was for ever gazing.
This solitary and inactive devotion, raised far above this
world, is the feeling out of which are moulded those
scarce embodied souls of Perugino's. Those emaciated
hectic young faces, absorbed in one ineffable passion,
which in their weakness and intensity are so infinitely
feminine, are indeed mainly the faces of women—of those

noble and holy ladies like Atalanta Baglioni, living in
moral solitude among their turbulent clan of evil fathers
and brothers and husbands: the victims, or worse, the
passive spectators, the passive accomplices, of iniquity of
all sorts, whom the grand old chronicler, Matarazzo,
shows by glimpses, walking through the blood and lust-
soiled houses of the brilliant and horrible Gianpavolos
and Semonettos and Griffones of Perugia, pure and
patient like nuns, and as secluded in mind as in any
cloister. Theirs are these faces, and at the same time
the faces which vaguely, confusedly looked down upon
them, glorified reflections of their own, from above.
These creatures of Perugino's are what every great
artist's works must be—at once the portrait of those for
whom he paints, and the portrait of their ideals, that is,
of their intenser selves. He is the painter of the city
where, in the Italian Renaissance, the unmixed devotional feeling, innate in the country of St. Francis, untroubled by Florentine scepticism or Lombard worldly
sense, thrust back and concentrated upon itself by surrounding brutal wickedness, existed most intense; he is
the painter of this kind of devotion. The very daintiness
of accessory, the delicate embroidered robes, the long
fringed scarves, the embossed armour, light and pliable
like silk, which cannot wound the tender young archangels, the carefully waved and curled hair—all this is
the religious luxuriousness of nuns and novices, the one
vent for all love of beauty and ease and costliness of the
poor delicate creatures, worn and galled by their shapeless hair cloth, living and sleeping in the dreary white-
washed cell. This is unmixed devotion, religious
contemplation and aspiration absolutely separated from

any other sort of moral feeling ; there is the destructive wrath of righteousness in the prophets of Michael Angelo, and the gentleness of candour and charity in the Florentine virgins of Raphael ; there is the serenity and solemnity of moral wisdom in Bellini, and the sweetness and' cordiality of domestic love in Titian ; there is even the half-animal motherly love in Correggio; there is, in almost all the schools of Italian painting, some character of human goodness; but in Perugino there is none of these things. Nothing but the one all-absorbing, abstract, devotional feeling—intense passive contemplation of the unattainable good ; souls purged of every human desire or will, isolated from all human affection and action, raised above the limits of time and space ; souls which havé long ceased to be human beings and can never become angels, hovering, half pained, half joyful, in a limbo of endless spiritual desire.

Such is the work. Let us seek the master. Pietro Vannucci, of Città della Pieve, surnamed Perugino, Petrus de Castro Plebis, as he signed himself, lived, as tradition has it, in a very good house in Via Deliziosa. Via Deliziosa is one of the many quiet little paved lanes of Perugia, steep and tortuous, looking up at whose rough scarred houses you forever see overgrown plants of white starred basil or grey marjoram bursting out of broken ewers and pipkins on the boards before the high windows, or trails of mottled red and green tomatos, or long crimson-tasselled sprays of carnation dangling along the broken, blackened masonry, crevassed and held together by iron clamps ; where, at every sudden turn, you get, through some black and oozy archway, a glimpse of green sun-gilded vineyard and distant hills, hazy and blue through the yellow summer air. Here, in the best part of the town, Perugino had his house and his workshop. In the house, full of precious stuffs and fine linen and plate and everything which a wealthy burgher could desire, lived the handsome wife of the master, for whom he was for ever designing and ordering new clothes, and whose beautiful hair he loved himself to dress in strange fantastic diadems and helmets of minute plaits and waves and curls, that she might go through the town as magnificent and quaintly attired as any noble lady of the Baglionis or Antinoris or Della Staffas. In the workshop was the master and a host of pupils : Giannicola Manni, Doni, the Alfani, Tiberio d'Assisi ; the exquisite anonymous stranger, of whom we know only as John the Spaniard, and perhaps that gentle fair feminine boy from Urbino, whom, in half-womanish gear and with wonderful delicate feathers and jewels in his hair, Perugino painted among the prophets in the Money Changer's Hall. A workshop indeed. Not merely the studio of a master and his pupils, but an enormous manufactory of works of devotional art; the themes of Perugino, the same saints, the same madonnas, the same angels, in the same groups, for ever repeated in large and small, some mere copies, others slightly varied or composed of various incoherent portions, by the pupil ; some half by the master, half by the pupil, some possibly touched up by him, one or two wholly from his own exquisite hand. Things of all degrees of merit and execrableness, to suit the richest and the poorest ; all could be had at that workshop, for Master Pietro had the monopoly of the art, good bad, or indifferent, of the country. You could order designs for wood carvings or silver ware ; you

could hire church banners, of which store was kept to be
let out for processions at so much the hour. You could
obtain men to set up triumphal arches of cardboard, and
invent moulds for ornamental sweetmeats, like those of
Astorre Baglioni's wedding ; patterns, doubtless also for
embroidery and armour embossing ; you could have a
young Raphael Santi set to repeating some Marriage of
the Virgin for a Sforza or a Baglioni, or some tattered
smearer to copy a copy of some madonna for a village
church ; or you could commission the master himself to
go to Rome and paint a wall of Pope Sixtus's Chapel.
For there never was a manufactory of art carried on
more methodically or satisfactorily than this one. There
never was a commercial speculator who knew so well
how much good and bad he could afford and venture to
give ; who knew his public so thoroughly. He had, in
his youth and poverty, invented, discovered (which shall
we call it ?) the perfection of devotional painting, that
which perfectly satisfied his whole pious Umbria, and
every pious man or woman of more distant parts : a
certain number of types, a certain expression, a certain
mode of grouping, a certain manner of colouring which
constituted a perfect whole ; a conception to embody
which most completely he had in his youth worked like a
slave, seeking, perfecting all that which belonged to the
style : the clear, delicate colour, the exquisite, never excessive finish, the infinitely delicate modelling of finger
and wrist, of eyelid and lip, the diaphanous sheen of
light, soft, scarcely coloured hair on brow and temple and
cheek ; he had coolly turned away from everything else.
The problems of anatomy, of perspective, of light and
shade, and of grouping, at which in Florence he had seen

men like Pollaiolo, Ghirlandaio, Filippino, Lionardo
wasting their youth, he never even glanced at. No real
bodies were required for his saints as long as he could give
them the right, wistful faces; no tangible background,
no well-defined composition. All this was unnecessary;
and he wanted only the necessary. When he had got
the amount and sort of skill required for this narrow
style, he stopped ; when he had invented the three or
four types of faces, attitude, and composition, he ceased
inventing. He had the means of making a fortune.
All that remained was to organise his mechanism, to
arrange that splendid system of repeating, arranging,
altering, copying, on the part of himself and his scholars,
by which he could, without further enlarging style or
ideas, furnish Umbria and Italy with the pure devotional
painting it required, in whatever amount and of whatever degree of excellence it might wish. He succeeded.
True, other artists sneered at him, like that young Buo-
narroti, who had called him a blunderer; true, the
Florentines complained that when he painted their fresco
for them at S. Maria Maddalena dei Pazzi, he had
cheated them, giving mere copies of works they had had
from him twenty years before. About the judgment of
other painters he cared not a fig ; success was the only
test; to the Florentines he calmly answered that as
those figures had pleased them twenty years before, they
ought to please them now; that he at least was not going
to seek anything new as long as the old sufficed. For
men who grew old in constant attempts after new styles,
new muscles, new draperies, like Signorelli yonder labour-
ing solitary on the rock of Orvieto, spending years in
cramming new figures into spaces which he, Perugino,

would have finished in a month with six isolated saints
and a bit of blue sky; or frittered away time in endless
sketches, endless cooking of new paints and trying of
new washes, like Lionardo da Vinci: or who ruined
themselves buying bits of old marble to copy, like crazy
Mantegna at Mantua ; for all such men as these Perugino
must have had a supreme contempt. As long as money
came in, all was right; new ideas, improvements, all
such things were mere rubbish. Thus he probably
preached to his pupils, and kept them carefully to their
task of multiplying his own works, till his school became
sterile and imbecile ; and the young Raphael, in disgust,
left him and begged the Lady Giovanna della Rovere
for a letter to the Gonfaloniere Soderini, which should
open to him the doors of the Florentine schools. With
what contempt must not Master Perugino have looked
after this departing young Raphael ; with what cynical
amusement he must have heard how the young fool,
once successful, kept for ever altering his style, wearing
his frail life out, meditating and working himself into
the hectic broken creature whom Marc-Antonio has
etched, seated, fagged and emaciated on the steps before
his work. We can imagine how Perugino descanted on all
this folly to the other young men in his workshop. For he
was a cynical man as well as a grasping: he saw no wisdom
beyond the desire for money and comfort. He had begun life almost a beggar, sleeping on a chest, going without food, in tatters, giving himself no respite from drudgery,
sustained by one idea, one wish !—to be rich. And rich
he had become; he had built houses on speculation at
Florence, to let them out ; and had farms at Città della
Pieve, and land near Perugia. He had obtained all he

had ever desired or could conceive desirable : safety from poverty. In other things he did not believe: not in an after life, nor in God, nor in good ; all these ideas, says Vasari, could never enter into his porphyry hard brain, " This Peter placed all his hopes in the good things of fortune, and for money would have made any evil bargain."

This is how Vasari has shown us Perugino. The unique painter of archangels and seraphs appears a base commercial speculator, a cynic, an atheist : the sort of man whom you could imagine transfigured into a shabby pettifogging Faustus, triumphing over the fiend by making over to him, in return for solid ducats, a bond mortgaging a soul which he knew himself never to have possessed. Some people may say, as learned folk are forever saying now-a-days, that all this is pure slander on the part of Vasari; and indeed, what satisfactory historical villain shall we soon possess, at the rate of present learned rehabilitations ? Be this as it may, there remains for the present the typical contrast between this man and his works ; and looking at it, other contrasts between noble art and grovelling artists vaguely occur to us, and we ask ourselves, Can it be ? Can a pure and exquisite work be produced by a base nature ? Can such anomaly exist—must the mental product not be stained by the vileness of the mind which has conceived it ? Must we, together with a precious and noble gift taken from a hand we should shrink from touching, accept the disheartening, the debasing conclusion, that in art purity may spring from foulness, and the excellent be born of the base ? It is a conclusion from which we instinctively shrink, feeling, rather than absolutely understanding, that it seems to strip the holiness from art, the worthiness, nay, almost the innocence, from our enjoyment. We feel towards any beautiful work of art something akin to love : a sort of desire to absorb it into our soul, to raise ourselves to it, to be with it in some manner united ; and thus the mere thought that all this may be sprung from out of unworthiness, that this noble century-enduring work may be the sister of who knows how many long dead base thoughts and desires and resolves born together with it in the nature of its maker—this idea of contamination of origin, makes us shudder and suspect. . . . Alas, how many of us, of the better and nobler of us, have not often sickened for a moment as the thought quivered across their mind of the foulness out of which the noblest of our art has arisen. But instinctively we have struck down the half-formulated idea as we dash away any suspicion against that which we love, and which our love tells us must be good. And thus, as a rule, we have persuaded ourselves that, though by a horrible fatality our greatest art—in sculpture, and painting, and music, and poetry, has oftenest belonged not to a simple and austere state of society, to the strong manly days of Greece or Rome, to the first times of Christian abnegation and martyrdom, to the childlike angelic revival of mediæval Christianity, to the solemn self-concentration of Huguenot France or Puritan England, that it has not sprung out of the straightforward purity of periods of moral regeneration, but rather from out of the ferment, nay, the putrescence, of many-sided, perplexed, anomalous times of social dissolution. That although our greatest art seems thus undeniably to have arisen in corrupt times, yet the individuals to whom

we proximately owe have been the nobler and purer of
their day. Nay, we almost persuade ourselves that in
those dubious times of doubt and dissolution, the spotless, the unshaken were in a way divinely selected, like
so many vestal virgins, to cherish in isolation the holy
fire of art. And we call up to our minds men noble and
pure, like Michael Angelo and Beethoven: we eagerly
treasure up like relics anecdotes showing the gentleness
and generosity of men like Lionardo and Mozart: trifling
tales of caged-birds let loose, or of poor fellow-workers
assisted, which, in our desire to trace art back to a noble
origin, seem to shed so much light upon the production
of a great picture or great symphony. And yet, even as
the words leave our lips, words so sincerely consoling,
we seem to catch in our voice an unintentional inflexion
of deriding scepticism. So much light! these tales of
mere ordinary goodness, such as we might hear (did we
care) of so many a dull and blundering artisan, or vacant
idler, these tales shed so much light upon the production of great works of art! A sort of reasoning devil
seems to possess us, to twitch our little morsels of un-
reasoned consolation, of sanctifying, mystical half-
reasoning away from our peace-hungry souls. And he
says: "What of Perugino? What of so many un-
deniable realities which this Perugino of ours, even if the
purest myth, so completely typifies? How did this
cynic, this atheist, come to paint these saints? You say
that he was no cynic, no atheist, that it is all vile slander."
Well, I won't dispute that: perhaps he *was* a saint after
all. I will even grant that he was. But in return
for the concession, let us examine whether the saints
could not have been equally well painted by the tradi-

tional, unrehabilitated Perugino, Vasari's Perugino—not
the real one, oh no, I will admit not the real one—by
the typical Perugino ; the man "of exceeding little religion, who could never be got to believe in the soul's
immortality; nay, with arguments suited to his porphyry
intellect, obstinately refused all good paths ; who placed
all his hopes in the goods of fortune and for money
would have consented to any evil compact." Nay, even
by a Perugino a good deal worse.

An ugly, impertinent little reasoning fiend within us ;
but now-a-days we have lost the formula of exorcism for
this kind of devil, and listen we must ; indignantly, and
with mind well made up to find all his arguments completely false. Think over the matter, now that idea is
once started, we can no longer help. So let us discuss it
with ourselves, within ourselves, the place where most
discussion must ever go on. Let us sit here on the low-
broken brick parapet, which seems to prevent all this
rough, black Perugia from precipitating itself, a mass of
huddled, strangled lanes, into the ravine below ; sit with
the grey, berry-laden olives, and twisted sere-leaved fig-
trees with their little brown bursting fruit, pushing their
branches up from the orchard on the steep below, where
the women dawdle under the low evening sun, sickle in
hand, mowing up the long juicy grass, tearing out
wreath after wreath, of vine and clematis, spray after
spray of feathery bluish fennel, till their wheel-shaped
crammed baskets look as if destined for some sylvan
god's altar, rather than to be emptied out into the
sweltering darkness before the cows mewed up in the
thatched hut yonder by the straw-stack and the laven-
der and rose-hedged tank.

The question which, we scarcely know how, has thus been started within us, and which, (like all similar questions) develops itself almost automatically in our mind, without much volition and merely a vague feeling of discomfort, until it have finally taken shape and left our consciousness for the limbo of decided points, this question is simply : What are the relations between the character of the work of art and the character of the artist who creates it? To what extent may we infer from the peculiar nature of the one the peculiar nature of the other? Such, if we formulate it, is the question, and the answer thereunto seems obvious : that as the peculiarity of the fruit depends, *cæteris paribus*, upon the peculiarity of the tree (itself due in part to soil and temperature and similar external circumstances), so also must the peculiarity of the spiritual product be due to the peculiarities of the spiritual whole of which it is born. And thus, in inverted order of ideas, the definite character of the fruit proves the character of the tree, the result argues the origin : there must exist a necessary relation between the product and that which has produced. If then we find a definite quality in the works of an artist, we have a right to suppose that corresponding qualities existed in the artist himself: if the picture, or symphony, or poem be noble, and noble moreover with a special sort of nobility, then noble also, and noble with that special sort of nobility must be the artistic organism, the artist, by whom it was painted, or composed of written. And this once granted (which we cannot help granting), we must inevitably conclude that the man Perugino, who painted those wonderful intense types of complete renunciation of the world, could not in reality have been the worldly, unconscientious atheist described by Vasari. So, at least, it would seem. But tarry awhile. We have decided on analogy, and by a sort of instinct of cause and effect, that the work must correspond in its main qualities with the main qualities of the artist, of the artistic organism by which it is produced. Mark what we have said: of the artist, or artistic organism. Now what is this artistic organism, this artist? An individual, a man, surely? Yes, and no. The artist and the man are not the same : the artist is only part of the man ; how much of him, depends upon the art in which he is a worker. The work is produced by the man, but not by the whole of him ; only by that portion which we call the artist ; and how much that portion is, what relation it bears to the whole man, we can ascertain by asking ourselves what faculties are required for the production of a work of art. And thus we soon get to a new question. The faculties required for the production of a work of art may be divided into two classes; those which directly and absolutely produce it, and those which are required to enable the production to take place without interference from contrary parts of the individual nature. These secondary qualities, merely protective as it were, are the moral qualities common, in greater or less degree, to all workers : concentration, patience, determination, desire of improvement ; they are not artistic in themselves, and are not more requisite to the artist than to the thinker, or statesman, or merchant, or soldier, to preserve his very different mental powers from the disturbing influence of laziness, or fickleness, or any more positive tendencies, vices or virtues, which might interfere with the development of his talents.

M

And of these purely protective qualities only so much
need exist as the relative strength of the artistic faculty
and of the unartistic tendencies of the individual require
in order that the former be protected from the latter;
and thus it comes that where the artistic endowment has
been out of all proportion large, as in the case of such a
man as Rossini, it has been able to produce the most
excellent work without much of what we should call
moral fibre : the man was lazy and voluptuous, but he
was, above all, musical ; it was easier for him to be musi-
cally active than to be merely dissipated and inactive:
the artistic instincts were the strongest, and were passively
followed. When these moral qualities, merely protective
and secondary in art, are developed beyond the degree
requisite for mere protection of the artistic faculties (a
degree small in proportion to the magnitude of the artistic instinct), they become ruling characteristics of the
whole individual nature, and influence all the actions of
the man as distinguished from the artist : they make
him as inflexible in the pursuit of the non-artistic aims
of life as in that of mere excellence in his own art. The
timorous and slothful Andrea del Sarto is quite as
complete an artist as the eager and inquisitive Lionardo
da Vinci ; but, whereas Andrea's activity stops short at
the limits of his powers of painting, the increasing
laboriousness and never satisfied curiosity of Lionardo
extend, on the contrary, to all manner of subjects quite
disconnected with his real art. When once the glorious
fresco of the Virgin, seated like a happier Niobe, by
the mealsack, has been properly finished in the cloister
of the Servites, Andrea goes home and crouches beneath
the violence of his wife, or to the tavern to seek feeble

consolation. But when, after never-ending alterations and additional touches, Lionardo at length permits Paolo Giocondo to carry home the portrait of his dubious, fascinating wife, he sets about mathematical problems or chemical experiments, offers to build fortresses for Cæsar Borgia, manufactures a wondrous musical instrument like the fleshless skull of a horse and learns to play thereon, or writes treatises on anatomy : there is in him a desire, a capacity for work greater than even his subtle and fantasticating style of art can ever fully employ. Such are the non-artistic qualities required, merely as protectors from interference, for the production of a work of art : the same these, whatever the art, as they are the same if, instead of art, we consider science, or commerce, or any other employment. The artistic, the really directly productive qualities, differ of course according to the art to which the work belongs, differ not only in nature but also in number. For there are some arts in which the work is produced by a very small number of faculties ; others where it requires a very complex machine, which we call a whole individuality : and here we find ourselves back again before our original question, to what extent the personality of an artist influences the character of his work. We have got back to the anomaly typified by Perugino ; back to it, and as completely without an answer to the problem as we were on starting. We have been losing our time, going round and round a question merely to find ourselves at our original starting-point. Not so : going round the question indeed, but in constantly narrowing circles, which will dwindle, let us hope, till we find ourselves on the only indivisible centre, which is the solution of the problem. For there are many

questions which are like the towns of this same Umbria
of Perugino : built upon the brink of a precipice, walled
round with a wall of unhewn rock, seeming so near if we
look up at them from the ravine below, and see every
roof, and cypress-tree, and pillared balcony; but which
we cannot approach by scaling the unscalable, sheer
precipice, but must slowly wind round from below,
circling up and down endless undulations of vineyard and
oakwood, coming for ever upon a tantalising glimpse of
towers and walls, for ever seemingly close above us, and
yet forever equally distant; till at last, by a sharp turn
of the gradually ascending road, we find ourselves before
the unexpected gates of the city.   And thus we have
approached a little nearer to the solution of the question.
We have, in our wanderings, left behind one part of the
ground.   We have admitted that the work of art is produced not by the man, but merely by that portion of
him which we call the artist; we have even dimly
foreseen that the case may be that in one art the
artist, that is to say, the art-producing organism,
comprises nearly the whole of the mere individual :
that the artistic part is very nearly the complete human
whole.   Now, in order to approach nearer our final
conclusion, namely, whether the man Perugino could
have painted those saints and those angels had he
really been the mercenary atheist of Vasari, we must set
afresh to examine what, in the various arts, are the
portions of an individual necessary to constitute the
mere artist, that is to say, the producer of a work of art.

But stop again. Are we quite sure that we know what
we mean when we say " a work of art ? " Are we quite
sure that we may not, without knowing it, be talking of

two things under one name? Surely not: when we apply the word to one of Perugino's archangels, we certainly refer to one whole object. So far, certainly, we mean (let us put it in the crudest way) a certain amount of colour laid on to a canvas in such a manner, and with such arrangements of tints and shadows, that it presents to our eyes and mind a certain form, a form which we define, from its resemblance to other forms made out of flesh and bone, the face and body of a young man; a form which, owing to certain constitutional peculiarities and engrained habits of our mind, we also declare to a given extent beautiful. This form, moreover, distinctly recalls to our mind real forms which experience has taught us to associate with the idea of moral purity, self-forgetfulness, piety; simply because we have noticed or been told since our infancy that persons with such bodily aspects are usually pure, self-forgetful and pious; because, without our knowing it, thousands of painters have accustomed us by giving us such forms as the portraits of saints to consider this physical type as distinctly saintly. This perception, that the form into which the colours on Perugino's canvas have been combined is such as we are accustomed to think of in connection with saintliness, immediately awakens in our mind a whole train of associations: we not merely see with our physical eyes the combination of colours and lines constituting the form, but with our mental eyes we rapidly and half unconsciously glance over all the occupations, aspirations, habits of such a creature as we conceive this form to belong to. We not merely see the delicate, thin, pale lips, thrown back head and neck, and the wide-opened, dilated, greyish eyes; we imagine in our mind

the vague delights after which those lips are thirsting as
the half-closed pale flowers thirst for the rain-drops, the
ecstasy of fulfilled hope which makes the veins of the
neck pulse and the head fall back in weariness of inner
quivering; the confused glory of heaven after which
those wide-opened eyes are straining; while our bodily
sight is resting on the mere coloured surface of Perugino's
picture, our mental sight is wandering across all the past
and future of this strange being whose bodily semblance
the artist has suddenly thrust upon us.   All this is what
we vaguely think of when we speak of a work of art.
Perhaps we can so little disentangle our impressions and
our fancies that their combination may thus be treated
as a unity.   But this unity is a dualism : the mere colour
arrangement constituting the form which we see with
our bodily eyes, and with our bodily eyes find beautiful,
is one half; and the whole moral apparition, conjured
up by association and imagination, is the other.   And,
as far as so infinitely interwoven a dualism can be divided, coarsely, and leaving or taking too much on one
side or the other, we can divide this dual existence into
that which has been given to us by the artist, the visible,
material form ; and that which association, recollection,
fancy, has been added by ourselves to the artist's work.
Of this dualism, therefore, of impression and fancy, only
that portion of the work of art which is absolutely visible
and concrete; the form, whether it exist in combined
colour and shadow, or marble mass, as in the plastic arts,
or in partially combined and partially successive sounds,
as in music, only this form is really given by the artist,
is that which, with reference to his productive power, we
can call the work of art.   He may, it is true, have de-

liberately chosen that form which should lead us to such
associations of ideas, but in so far he has been acting not
as the artist, but as a sort of foreshadowed spectator or
listener ; he has, before taking up his own work with the
mere material, visible, tangible, audible realities of the
art, stepped into the place to be occupied by ourselves,
and foreseen, by his knowledge of the effects which he
can produce, by his experience of what associations are
awakened by each of his various forms, the imaginative
activities which his yet unfinished work will call for in
those who see or hear it. But he will, in so doing, be
deliberately or unconsciously leaving his own work, fore-
stalling ours : nay, the artist who says to himself, " Now
I will paint a soul in a condition of ecstasy," is in reality
transforming himself into the customer who would enter
his workshop and say, " Paint me a figure such as your
experience tells you suggests to beholders the idea of
religious enthusiasm ; copy the features of any religious
enthusiast of your acquaintance, or put together such
dispersed features as seem to you indicative of that
temper of mind." All this, while the real artistic work
has not begun ; for that begins when the artist first
places before his easel the model for his archangel :
either the delicate, hectic, little girlish novice-boy, or the
distinct outline of the armed young angel existing in his
mind and requiring only to be printed off into concrete
existence. Thus, in our examination of the amount of
an artist's personality which can go into his work, we
must remember that this work is merely the externally
existing, definite, finite form, and not the ideas of emotions which, by the power of association, that form may
awaken in ourselves. What the artist gives is merely

the arrangement of lines and colours in a given manner, which may, as in painting, resemble an already existing natural object ; or, as in architecture and pattern decoration, resemble no already existing natural object ; the arrangement of sounds which may, as in a dramatic air, recall the inflexions proper to a given emotion, or, as in a formal fugue, recall no emotional inflexions whatever. This, and not any train of thoughts awakened by this possibly but not necessarily existing resemblance to an already known natural object, or to an already known sort of emotional voice inflexion, is what is given by the artist, and this is artistic form, the absolutely, objectively existing work of art. And now we may examine what mental faculties, in the various arts, are required for the production of this work : what portions of the whole individual man are included or excluded in that smaller, more limited individual whom we call the artist. Let us investigate the point by a sort of experiment: by stripping away, one by one, those qualities of an ideal individual which are not necessary for the production of the various kinds of artistic work ; let us separate and afterwards, if need be, select and reunite the qualities which are required and those which are not required to make up a poet, a painter, a sculptor, or a musician.

And first we must create our ideal man, who contains within him the stuff of every kind of artist, the faculties of producing every kind of artistic work. First, a word about this ideal man, and about the manner in which he differs from other men. He differs in completeness, in balance, in intensity. For almost every one of us has some mental faculty so imperfectly developed that we

may say that it does not exist: it exists indeed, and
perhaps not without a certain necessary effect, but as
with a single solitary instrument in a powerful orchestra
of dozens of every other kind of instruments, this effect
is not consciously perceived. And the faculties which
we do possess are rarely of very remarkable strength and
intensity: we have enough of them for our ordinary
wants of life, but not necessarily more. Our sense of
hearing is sufficient to distinguish the voice of one friend
from another, but not always sufficient to be able to enjoy music, still less often to perform, least often of all to
compose. And similarly with every other mental
faculty: most men can follow a simple argument, some
a more complex one, but few can reason out unaided a
complicated proposition. Now the creative degree in
any faculty is the most intense in its development. The
painter is the man who receives the largest number of
most delicately complete visional impressions ; the musician the man who receives the largest number of most
delicately complete audible impressions : to the painter
everything is a shape, a colour ; to the musician everything is a sound ; the whole universe, to the thinker, is
but a concatenation of logical propositions. Thus, our
ideal man must, at starting, possess every higher faculty,
developed to the most intense degree, and every one of
them developed equally : for out of him is to be made
every kind of artist. Here, then, we have our ideal man:
he possesses in the highest degree, and in the most perfect balance, all the emotional, logical, and perceptive
powers of the mind ; he is, if you choose, the abstract
creature (never existing, and never, alas! to exist), the
all beautiful, all powerful, perfect fiction, which we call

humanity ; and with him is our work. He is perfectly balanced, he is a mere abstraction : for these two reasons he is, so far, inactive; we cannot, with the best will in the world, imagine his doing anything as long as he can do everything: he will, in all probability, merely passively enjoy. Before he can create, we must alter him. And he is to create, remember, not as a statesman or a handi-craftsman, but as an artist : he is to deal not with realities, but with fictions; he is not to touch our material interests, he is merely to evoke for us a series of phantom sights or sounds, of phantom men and women. Therefore, our first act must be to diminish, by at least a half, all the practical sides of his nature, so that no practical activities divert him from his purely ideal field. So that it be for him infinitely more natural to think, to feel, to imitate, to combine impressions, than to be of any immediate use in the world ; so that the mere employment of his powers be his furthest aim, without thinking what effect that employment will have upon the real condition of himself or of others. This much we have done : we have obtained a creature whose interest is never purely practical. But this will not suffice. We must diminish by at least a quarter his mere logical powers, thus rendering him far more inclined to view things as concrete, living manifestations, than as logical abstractions. This has served to prevent his being diverted into metaphysic or scientific speculations: there is now no longer any fear of his becoming a psychologist instead of a poet, a mathematician or physicist instead of a painter or a composer : things now interest him no longer for their practical bearing, nor for their abstract meaning : he cares for them not as forces, nor as ideas, but as forms,

as visions. And this time we have, as it were, rough-
hewn our artist. But what artist? He is, it is true,
mainly attracted by the mere contemplation of things
apart from practical or scientific interests, but he is
equally attracted by all sorts of visions: he receives
every kind of impression. This time, again, he will, from
perfect balance, remain inactive. We must throw his
faculties a little into disorder, we must, at random, diminish here in order (relatively) to increase there: let us,
for instance, diminish by a trifle his faculty for manipu-
lating colours or masses of stone, his faculty for conceiving sounds in succession and in combination ; let us, in
short, make it a little difficult for him to be a painter or
sculptor or musician.

What will he be, this first made artist of ours? this
creature, clipped in all the mere practically scientific instincts, only that his whole intense personality may be
given more completely, more absolutely to the world of
artistic phantoms? Before breaking up this huge psychological snow-man, this ungainly monster roughly
moulded into caricature shape by awkward removing of
material here and adding on there, before dashing it back
into the limbo of used up and unformed similes, let us
ask ourselves what artist he vaguely resembles : what is
the artist thus formed, it would seem, of a mere intense
human being ; of all the faculties of our nature, only
more subtle and powerful, and working not in the world
of practical realities, nor of abstract truths, but in that of
imaginary forms? The answer comes instinctively, un-
hesitatingly to all of us : this universal artist, this artistic
organism which contains the whole intensified individual,
is the poet. Nay: why call him poet? why reserve this

supreme place of artist not of colours or sounds, but of
spoken emotion, and perception, and action, for the man
whose words are grouped into metrical shape? Is it this
metrical shape, this mere enveloping form perceived
merely by the ear, this monotonous, rudimentary music,
so paltry by the side of the musician's real music, is it
this which requires for its production that wondrous
combination of faculties, that whole intensified human
individuality? For those same faculties, that same intensified individuality, will act and bear fruit in the man
who lets his words drift on, unmetrical, in mere spoken
manner. And yet he shall be accounted less, and shall
cede to the other, who can measure his words into verses,
and couple them into rhyme. Surely there is injustice
in this. Wherefore, I pray you, should you, my friend,
my beloved little child poet, with the keen eyes and
eager lips of Keats, who sit (in fancy at least) here by
my side on the rough wall overlooking the orchard ravine
at Perugia, drowsily listening (as poets listen to prose)
to our discussion, wherefore should you, the poet, be
worth more than I, the prose writer, merely inasmuch as
you are the one and I am the other? Why be surrounded, even in my eyes, by a sort of ideal halo; why
pointed out by my own secret instinct as the artist? All
this must be mere folly, prejudice, dried old forms of
thought handed down from the days when poets were
priests and lawgivers and prophets, when their very
credit depended upon their not being solely what you
modern poets are; all this is a mere historic myth, in
which the world continues foolishly to believe, letting
itself be told from generation to generation, till the idea
has become engrained in its mode of thinking, that the

poet is a special creature, a thing of finer mould, in whose
life, and movements, and feelings it expects something
different from the rest of humanity ; in whose eyes it
seeks a dim reflection, in whose voice a distant echo of
the colours and sounds of that fairyland out of which he
has come as a changeling into the world of realities.
Infatuation and injustice. But no ! mankind at large is
right in its ideas, but as it usually is, without knowing
why it has them : right in giving instinctively this place
of artist of the merely suggested, as distinguished from
the absolutely seen or heard forms of other arts, to the
poet alone. For the poet is, in the kingdom of words,
the real, complete artist. The artistic external form
which he gives to his creations removes them out of the
domain of the practically useful, or the scientifically interesting. This metrical setting enables the poet to
show a part, to make perfect the tiniest thing ; to give
complete significance, complete beauty, and eternal life
to a perception, an emotion, an image which cannot be
expanded beyond the fourteen lines of a sonnet ; while
the poor prose writer, reduced to being a mere smith or
mechanist, can do nothing with any stray gem he may
cut, knows not how to set it, and is forced in despair to
stick it clumsily into some unwieldy utensil or imple-
ment, some pot out of which to drink knowledge, or
some shield to ward off disaster. The prose writer is
for ever being driven to seek employment outside
the land of pure art. Therefore, the poet is truly the
exclusive artist in words ; or rather the exclusive artist
in words must needs become the poet ; if the man
feel that he cannot hammer wearily at some clumsy
ornamented piece of furniture, some bastard of artistic

uselessness and practical utility, that he cannot write histories, or ethical disquisitions or psychological studies (waxworks of spiritual pathology, technically called novels), in order to bury in them the delicate artistic fragments which he spontaneously produces ; then that man will assuredly learn the manner of making metrical settings ; that man, that word artist will infallibly become a poet : nay, he is one.   Thus, the poet is in reality the artist who suggests emotions, and actions, and sights, and sounds, as the painter is the artist who shows coloured shapes, and the musician the artist who creates forms made of sounds.   The poet, therefore, is the artist into whose work there enters, or can enter, the greatest number of fragments of his whole personality : for his works are made up of all that which his nature perceives and evolves and desires : of the forests and fields, and sea and skies which have printed their likenesses on his mind ; of the faces and movements of the men and women whom he has known, nay, of whom once perhaps, only once in his life, he has caught a never forgotten glimpse ; of the events which have taken place before his eyes, or of which he has been told ; of the emotions and passions which he has felt hidden in himself or seen burst out in others ; of all that he can see, feel, hear, conceive, imagine.   He is the man who assimilates most, initiates most, perceives most of all that passes within and without him, and unites it all in a homogeneous outer shape : nothing for him is waste : not the hard, scaly first shoot of the reed, pale green, which catches his feet as he walks on the riverside, across the grass, half sere, half renovated by spring ; not the scent of first raindrops on the upturned mould of the fields ;

not the sentence read at random in a book opened by
accident; not the sudden, never-recurring look in the
eyes of one beloved; not the base appetite which he has
hidden away, trampled back out of sight of his own consciousness; not the preposterous ideal which his vanity
may have shown him for one second; not anything,
however small or however large, however common or
however rare, not anything inanimate or feeling, not
anything in life or in death, not anything which can be
seen, or heard, or felt, or understood, which may not be
moulded by the poet into some form which will have
meaning and charm, and eternal value for all men.
The poet is the man who receives a greater number of
more intense impressions than any other man; he is, of
all creatures, the most sensitive in the whole of his
being; for the whole of his being is at once the raw
material, and the forming mechanism of the work of art.
This is the ideal, the universal poet, the type: of him
every individual poet represents a limited portion, and
is a fresh repartition of faculties, a fresh combination
and proportion of material and mechanism, due to the
accident of race, of time, of birth, of education. The
typical poet assimilates and reproduces everything; and
each fragment of this type, each individual, differs from
every other individual in that which is assimilated and
reproduced by him: the one feels more, the other sees
more, the third imagines more; and each feels, sees, and
imagines, according to what external things have been
put within reach of his feelings, his sight, his fancy.
As, therefore, the typical poet is the whole type of
humanity affording material and acting as manipulative
apparatus to produce the work of art, so also the in-

dividual poet is the individual man, moulding into shape
all the qualities which are strongest in his nature. All
the qualities, let us however mark, which are indisputedly
dominant ; often, therefore, only the better, and in only
the lowest tempers the worst. For, remembering what
we noticed about moral faculties of will which protect
the artistic workings from the interference of other parts
of our nature, we may see that it must often happen that
a noble spirit may be able to keep out of his mere abstract creations those baser instincts (which though recognized with shame) he is unable to subdue in practise ;
his works show him as he would desire himself to be, as
he, alas ! has not the strength to be in reality ; let us not,
therefore, complain of those who are unable to live up to
their conceptions, for they have given to us their better
part, and kept for themselves, with bitterness and shame,
their worse.

The poet, therefore, is the artist into whose work
there enters the greatest proportion of his individual
nature ; if he be flippant in temper his works cannot be
earnest ; if he be impure his writings cannot be actively
pure ; the distinctive features of his nature must be reflected in his work, since his work is made out of and by
his nature. Now let us proceed. We had constructed
a sort of typical giant, promising all the powers and
qualities of all humanity ; and this, by the gradually
stripping away of some of these human powers, we had
reduced to the condition of typical poet. Now let us
continue our work. Of course there are kinds of poetry
which form links with other intellectual work ; and to
obtain these we must remove such faculties as do not
enter into them : separate from the artist those qualities

which belong only to the man. There is first of all that great poetical anomaly the drama, for which, it would seem, that less of the writer's own personality is required than for any other form; for the dramatist stands half way between the artist and the psychologist; he can obtain innumerable varieties of character and feeling merely by his reasoning powers, not by any personal experience. He is a sort of synthetic metaphysician, who can construct the saint, the villain, the simpleton, the knave, not out of anything within himself, but out of the very elements of these characters which he has obtained by analysis; hence it is that, while we can from their works reconstruct the character of poets like Milton, or Wordsworth, or Leopardi, or Musset, we remain wholly ignorant of the personality of Shakespeare; he cannot be all that he shows us, and in the doubt he remains none of it at all. Let us put aside therefore this anomalous artist, and continue stripping away some of the purely emotional characters of our typical colossus. We shall soon meet the last and simplest form of poet—the mere describer; of his aspirations and emotions we know but little; we know only of his tastes, his preferences for certain sights and sounds. He cares for the sea, or the woods, or the fields, or the skies; he is very near being a mere thing of eyes and ears. Yet not wholly; for he perceives not only the colour and movement of the waves, but their sound, their briny scent; he perceives not only the green and tawny tints of leaves and moss, he hears the crackling of the brushwood, the rustling of the boughs, the confused hum of bees, the faint murmur of waters; nay, in the waves and in the woods he perceives something more, vague resemblances to other things; vague expressions of mood and feeling which, when the waters rush in, make his heart leap; when the grey light steals in among the branches, sends a sadness throughout him. Nay, in this artist, in this simplest, least human sort of poet, there remains yet an infinite amount of the human individuality, of its passions and desires. Let us tear away, throw aside this last amount of human feeling, reduce our typical artist to mere intense powers of seeing. Shall we still have wherewith to obtain any work at all? will this rarified, simplified mentality be much above a mere feelingless optic machine? Let us see. Here we have a creature out of which we have removed as much as possible of all human qualities: a creature which can perceive with infinite keenness and reproduce with the most perfect exactitude, every little subtle line and tint and shadow which escapes other men; a creature whose delicate perception vibrates with delight at every harmonious combination, and writhes, as if it would shatter to atoms, at every displeasing mixture of lines or colours. A living and most sensitive organism which feels, thinks everything as form and colour, fostered with the utmost care by other such organisms, themselves nurtured into intensity more intense than that with which they were born; for ever put in contact with the visual objects which are, let us remember, the air it breathes, the food it assimilates until this visual organism becomes beyond compare perfect in its power of perceiving and reproducing. Then, imagine this abstract being, this quivering thing of sight, placed in the midst of a country of austere, delicate lines, and solemn yet diaphanous tints; among the undulating fields and oakwoods, beneath the pearly

sky of Umbria ; imagine that before it are placed, as the
creatures most precious and lovely, the creatures whose
likeness must for ever be copied in all its intensity,
youths, young women, old men, delicate and emaciate
with solitude and maceration, with eyes grown dilated
and bright from straining to see the glorious visions, the
celestial day-dreams which flit across their mind ; with
lips grown tremulous and eager with passionate longing
for constantly expected, never-coming bliss ; always
alone, inactive, with listless limbs and workless hands, in
the bare, unadorned cell or oratory ; or if, coming forth,
walking through the streets, passing through the crowd
(giving way with awe), erect, self-engrossed, seeing and
hearing nothing around, like one entranced. Let us
imagine this organism, thus perfect for perceiving and
reproducing all that it sees, for ever in the presence of
such lines and colours, such faces and figures as these ;
and then let us ask ourselves what this quite abstract,
unhuman power will produce, what this artist, who is
completely divested of all that which belongs merely to
the man, would paint. What would that be, that work
thus produced ? What save those delicate, wan angels
and saints and apostles, standing in solitary contemplation and ecstasy, those scarcely embodied souls, raised
beyond the bounds of time and space, concentrated, absorbed in longing for heavenly perfection ? And if this
subtle visual organism, nurtured among these sights,
should happen to be lodged in the same body with a
sordid, base, cynical temper, can it be altered thereby ?
Surely not. The eye has seen, the hand has reproduced
—seen and reproduced that which surrounds them—and
inevitably, fatally, although eye and hand belonged to

the man "who placed all his hopes in the good things of
fortune, into whose porphyry brain no idea of good could
enter, who for money would have concluded any evil
bargain," the work thus produced by this commonplace,
grasping atheist, Peter Perugino, must be the ideal of all
purely devotional art.   He was an atheist and a cynic,
but he was a great painter, and lived in Umbria, in the
country of sweet and austere hills and valleys, in the
country whose moral air was still scented by the
" flowerets of St. Francis."

This is the end of our long wandering up and down,
round and round, the question of artistic personality,
even as we must wander up and down, round and round,
before we can reach any of these strange Umbrian towns.
And, as after long journeying, when we enter the city,
and find that that which seemed a castle, a grand,
princely town, all walled and towered and battlemented,
is in reality only a large, rough village, with blackened
houses and fissured church steeples, a place containing
nothing of any interest : so also in this case, when we
have finally reached our paltry conclusion that this
painter of saints was no saint himself, we must admit to
ourselves that to arrive at this conclusion was scarcely
our real object ; even as while travelling through this
country of Perugino we make our guide confess that
what, in all this expedition, we were meant to see and
enjoy, was not the paltry, deceptive hill-top village, but
the sere-brown oakwoods, tinged russet by the sun, the
grey olive hills through which we have slowly ascended,
and the glimpses of undulating grey-green country and
distant wave-blue mountains which we have had at every
new turn of our long and up-hill road.

RUSKINISM.

THE WOULD-BE STUDY OF A CONSCIENCE

I GIVE a place to the following pages, because, for all the difference of form, this essay is of the same sort, has had the same kind of origin, as the so seemingly incongruous studies with which it is bound up. For this also is the rough putting together of notes made at various times and in various phases of study ; it is a series of self-questionings and answers, of problems, perhaps only half-formulated and half-solved, which have arisen round one man, one artist, one art philosophy, even as in the adjoining essays they have arisen around some one statue, or song, or picture ; self-questionings and problems, these present ones, not of æsthetic right and wrong suggested by a given work of art, but of moral fitness and unfitness suggested by the doubts, the divisions, the mistakes, by the comprehension (or, if you prefer, the misapprehension) of the conscience of perhaps the greatest and strangest artist of our days.

JOHN RUSKIN stands quite isolated among writers on art. His truths and his errors are alike of a far higher sort than the truths and errors of his fellow-workers : they are truths and errors not of mere fact, nor of mere reasoning, but of tendency, of moral attitude ; and his philosophy is of far greater importance than any

other system of æsthetics, because it is not the philosophy of the genius, evolution or meaning of any art
or of all art, but the philosophy of the legitimacy or
illegitimacy of all and every art. In the case of every
other writer on art the evils due to a false system are,
in proportion to the great interests of our lives and of
the life around, but very paltry evils : the evils of mis-
conceiving the relations between various masters and
various schools, and the causes of various artistic phenomena ; the evils of misappreciating a work or a form of
art, of preferring an inferior picture, or statue or piece of
music, to a superior one ; the evils of buying fluttering
St. Theresas of Bernini rather than noble goddesses of
Scopas; of ornamenting our houses with plaster dragons,
grimacing toothless masks, and meagre lines of lintel and
clumsy agglomerations of columns, rather than with the
leaf and flower moulding, the noble arches and dainty
cornices of mediæval art ; the evils in short of not understanding quite well or of not appreciating quite correctly.
Very important evils within the limited sphere of our
artistic interests, and which we must not neglect to
eradicate ; but evils such as cannot deeply trouble our
whole nature, or seriously damage our whole lives.
Such is the case with the æsthetic systems, with the
truths and errors of men like Winckelmann, Lessing,
Hegel, or Taine ; but it is not so with the æsthetic system of Ruskin. For the theories of all other writers on
art deal only with the meaning and value of one work or
school of art compared with another work or school ;
they deal only with the question how much of our liking
or disliking should we give to this art or to that ; they
are all true or false within the region allotted to art.

But the theories of Ruskin deal with the comparative importance of artistic concerns and the other concerns of our lives : they deal with the problem, how much of our thoughts and our energies we have a right to give to art, and for what reasons we may give any portion of them : it deals with the question of the legitimacy not of one kind of artistic enjoyment more than another, but of the enjoyment of art at all.

The question may at first sight seem futile from its very magnitude: unnecessary because it has so long been answered. In the first moment many of us may answer with contempt that the thinking men and women of to-day are not ascetics of the Middle Ages, nor utilitarians of the 18th century, nor Scotch Calvinists, that they should require to be taught that beauty is neither sinful nor useless, that enjoyment of art is not foul self-indulgence nor childish pastime. And so at first it seems. The thinking men and women of our day are not any of these things, and do not require to be answered these questions. But though these scruples and doubts no longer trouble us, we, in our nineteenth century, are yet not entirely at peace in our hearts. For, just in proportion as the old religious faith is dying out, we are feeling the necessity to create a new ; as the old vocations of belief are becoming fewer and further between, the new vocations of duty are becoming commoner ; as the old restrictions of the written law are melting away, so there appears the new restriction of the unwritten law, the law of our emancipated conscience; and the less we go to our priests, the more do we go to our own inner selves to know what we may do and what we should sacrifice : with our daily growing liberty, grows and must grow, to

all the nobler among us, our responsibility. Nay, the
more we realise that we have but this one brief life
wherein to act and to expiate, the more earnestly do we
ask ourselves to what use we should put the little that is
vouchsafed us. And thus it comes to pass that there
exist among us many who, seeing the evil around them,
seeing the infinitude of falsehood which requires to be
dispelled and of pain which requires to be alleviated, and
of injustice which requires to be destroyed, must occasionally pause and ask themselves what right they have
to give all, or any, of their limited time and thought and
energy to the mere enjoyment of the beautiful, when
there exists on all sides evil which it seems to require
unlimited effort to quell. Many there must be, and every
day more, who are harried by their love of art and their
sense of duty, who daily ask themselves the question
which first arose, nearly forty years ago, in the mind of
John Ruskin ; and which, settled by false answers, has re-
curred to him ever and anon, and has shaken and
shattered the very system which was intended to answer
it for ever.

John Ruskin has been endowed as have been very few
men as an artist, a critic, and a moralist ; in the immense
chaotic mass, the constantly altered and constantly prop-
ped up ruins of an impossible system, which constitute
the bulk of his writings, he has taught us more of the
subtle reasons of art, he has reproduced with his pen
more of the beauty of physical nature, and he has made
us feel more profoundly the beauty of moral nature, than
has, perhaps, been done separately by any critic, or
artist, or moralist of his day. He has possessed within
himself two very perfect characters, has been fitted out

for two very noble missions :—the creation of beauty and the destruction of evil ; and of these two halves each has been warped ; of these two missions each has been hampered ; warped and hampered by the very nobility of the man's nature : by his obstinate refusal to compromise with the reality of things, by his perpetual resistance to the evidence of his reason, by his heroic and lamentable clinging to his own belief in harmony where there is discord, in perfection where there is imperfection. There are natures which cannot be coldly or resignedly reasonable, which, despite all possible demonstration, cannot accept evil as a necessity and injustice as a fact ; which must believe their own heart rather than their own reason ; and when we meet such natures, we in our cold wisdom must look upon them with pity, perhaps, and regret, but with admiration and awe and envy. Such a nature is that of John Ruskin. He belongs, it is true, to a generation which is rapidly passing away ; he is the almost isolated champion of creeds and ideas which have ceased even to be discussed among the thinking part of our nation ; he is a believer not only in Good and in God, but in Christianity, in the Bible, in Protestantism ; he is, in many respects, a man left far behind by the current of modern thought, but he is, nevertheless, and unconsciously, perhaps, to himself, the greatest representative of the highly developed and conflicting ethical and æsthetical nature which is becoming more common in proportion as men are taking to think and feel for themselves ; his is the greatest example of the strange battles and compromises which are daily taking place between our moral and our artistic halves ; and the history of his aspirations and his errors is the type of the inner history of many a humbler thinker and humbler artist around us.

When, nearly forty years ago, Ruskin first came before the world with the wonderful book—wonderful in sustained argument and description, and in obscure, half crazy, half prophetic utterances—called *Modern Painters*, it was felt that a totally new power had entered the region of artistic analysis. It was not the subtle sympathy with line and curve, with leaf and moulding, nor the wondrous power of reproducing with mere words the depths of sky and sea, the radiancies of light and the flame and smoulder of cloud; it was not his critical insight nor his artistic faculty which drew to him at once the souls of a public so different, in its universality, from the small eclectic bands which surround other æstheticians ; it was the feeling, in all who read his books, that this man was giving a soul to the skies and seas ; that he was breathing human feeling into every carved stone and painted canvas ; that he was bidding capital and mosaic, nay, every rudest ornament hewn by the humblest workman, to speak to men with the voice of their own heart ; that for the first time there had been brought into the serene and egotistic world of art the passion, the love, and the wrath of righteousness. He came into it as an apostle and a reformer, but as an apostle and a reformer strangely different from Winckelmann and Schlegel, from Lessing and Goethe. For, while attacking the architecture of Palladio and the painting of Salvator Rosa ; while expounding the landscapes of Turner and the churches of Verona, he was not merely demolishing false classicism and false realism, not merely vindicating a neglected artist or a wronged school : he was come to sweep usurping evil out of the kingdom of art, and to reinstate as its sole sovereign no human craftsman, but God himself.

God or Good : for to Ruskin the two words have but one meaning. God and Good must receive the whole domain of art; it must become the holy of holies, the temple and citadel of righteousness. To do this was the avowed mission of this strange successor, haughty and humble, and tender and wrathful, of the pagan Winckelmann, of the coldly serene Goethe. How came John Ruskin by this mission, or why should his mission differ so completely from that of all his fellows ? Why should he insist upon the necessity of morally sanctifying art, instead of merely æsthetically reforming it ? Why was it not enough for him that artistic pleasure should be innocent, without trying to make it holy ? Because, for Ruskin's nature, compounded of artist and moralist, artistic engagement was a moral danger, a distraction from his duty—for Ruskin was not the mere artist, who, powerless outside his art, may, because he can only, give his whole energies to it ; he was not the mere moralist who, indifferent to art, can give it a passing glance without interrupting for a moment his work of good ; he felt himself endowed to struggle for righteousness and bound to do so, and he felt himself also irresistibly attracted by mere beauty. To the moral nature of the man this mere beauty, which threatened to absorb his existence, became positively sinful ; while he knew that evil was raging without requiring all his energies to quell it, every minute, every thought diverted from the cause of good was so much gain for the cause of evil ; innocence, mere negative good, there could not be, as long as there remained positive evil. Thus it appeared to Ruskin. This strange knight-errant of righteousness, conscious of his heaven-endowed strength, felt that during every half-hour of delay in the Armida's garden of art, new rootlets were being put forth, new leaves were being unfolded by the enchanted forest of error which overshadowed and poisoned the earth, and which it was his work to hew and burn down ; that every moment of reluctant farewell from the weird witch of beauty meant a fresh outrage, an additional defiling of the holy of holies to rescue which he had received his strong muscle and his sharp weapons. Thus, refusing to divide his time and thoughts between his moral work and his artistic, Ruskin must absolutely and completely abandon the latter; if art seemed to him not merely a waste of power, but an absolute danger for his nobler side, there evidently was no alternative but to abjure it for ever. But a man cannot thus abandon his own field, abjure the work for which he is specially fitted ; he may mortify, and mutilate and imprison his body, but he cannot mortify or mutilate his mind, he cannot imprison his thoughts. John Ruskin was drawn irresistibly towards art because he was specially organised for it. The impossible cannot be done : nature must find a vent, and the artistic half of Ruskin's mind found its way of eluding the apparently insoluble difficulty : his desire reasoned, and his desire was persuaded. A revelation came to him : he was neither to compromise with sin nor to renounce his own nature. For it struck him suddenly that this irresistible craving for the beautiful, which he would have silenced as a temptation of evil, was in reality the call to his mission ; that this domain of art, which he had felt bound to abandon, was in reality the destined field for his moral combats, the realm which he must reconquer for God and for Good. Ruskin had considered art as sinful as long as it was only negatively innocent: by the strange logic of desire he made it positively righteous, actively holy ; what he had been afraid to touch, he suddenly perceived that he was commanded to handle. He had sought for a solution of his own doubts, and the solution was the very gospel which he was to preach to others ; the truth which had saved him was the truth which he must proclaim. And that truth, which had ended Ruskin's own scruples, was that the basis of art is moral ; that art cannot be merely pleasant or unpleasant, but must be lawful or unlawful, that every legitimate artistic enjoyment is due to the perception of moral propriety, that every artistic excellence is a moral virtue, every artistic fault is a moral vice ; that noble art can spring only from noble feeling, that the whole system of the beautiful is a system of moral emotions, moral selections, and moral appreciation ; and that the aim and end of art is the expression of man's obedience to God's will, and of his recognition of God's goodness.

Such was the solution of Ruskin's scruples respecting his right of giving to art the time and energies he might have given to moral improvement ; and such the æsthetical creed which he felt bound, by conviction and by the necessity of self-justification, to develop into a system and to apply to every single case. The notion of making beauty not merely a vague emanation from the divinity, as in the old platonic philosophies, but a direct result, an infallible concomitant of moral excellence ; of making the physical the mere reflexion of the moral, is indeed a very beautiful and noble idea; but it is a false idea. For—and this is one of the points which Ruskin will not admit—the true state of things is by no means always the noblest or the most beautiful; our longing for ineffable harmony is no proof that such harmony exists: the phantom of perfection which hovers before us is often not the mirage of some distant reality, but a mere vain shadow projected by our own desires, which we must follow, but may never obtain. In the soul of all of us exists, oftenest fragmentary and blurred, a plan of harmony and perfection which must serve us as guide in our workings, in our altering and rebuilding of things; but we must not expect that with this plan should coincide the actual arrangements of nature; we must beware lest we use as a map of the earth into which we have been created the map of the heaven which we seek to create; for we shall find that the ways are different, we shall go astray bewildered and in bitterness, we shall sit down in despair in this country which is evil where it should have been good, arid where it should have been fruitful, and we shall uselessly weep or rage until all the time for our journeyings and workings is over, and death has come to ask how much we have done. Sin and Pain and Injustice are realities, and what is worse, they are necessities: they are not despite Nature, but through Nature; destructive forces perhaps, but which Nature requires for her endless work of construction; punished perhaps in the individual wretch devoted to them, but ordered nevertheless by that same punishing power which requires them. And worse still, evil and good are not opponents, they are not for ever destroying each other's work, for ever marshalled in battle against each other;

they are combined though hostile, used in the same great work of action and reaction: together they build and destroy, together they are knit in closest and most twisted bonds of cause and effect ; bonds so close, so inextricably crossed and recrossed that severing one of them, tearing and cutting them asunder, it seems as if the whole universe would crash down upon us. In this world of reality where evil leads to good and life to death; where harmonies are imperfect, there is no unvarying correspondence between things, no necessary genesis of good from good, and evil from evil. There is much conflict and much isolation. And thus the world of the physically beautiful is isolated from the world of the morally excellent: there is sometimes correspondence between them, and sometimes conflict, but both accidental and due to no inner affinity, but only to exterior causes : most often there is no relation at all. For the qualities of right and wrong, and of beautiful and ugly, and our perceptions of them, belong to different parts of our being, even as to a yet different part of our being belong our perception of true and false, that is, of existing and non-existing. A true thing need by no means be a good or a beautiful thing : that generations of men are doomed to sin and misery is no good fact ; that millions of putrifying bodies lie beneath the ground is no beautiful fact, but both are nevertheless true facts, true with that truth of which science, had it perception of good and of beauty as well as mere perception of truth, should say, " I recognize, but I shudder "—And thus also is it with the good and the beautiful : they have no connection except that, each in its kingdom, is the best, the desirable, that for which we should all strive, that for which

the whole of nature, despite its inextricable evils, seems
to crave and to struggle. A pure state of soul is like a
pure state of body: a morbid craving is like a disease; a
noble moral attitude is like a noble physical attitude:
moral excellence and physical beauty are both the
healthy, the perfect; but they are the healthy, the perfect,
in two totally different halves of nature, and we perceive and judge them by totally different organisms.
Whence our moral instincts have come, or how they
ever entered into the scheme of a world in which •there
is so much to shock them ; how the preference for the
good of others was ever evolved out of the preference for
the good of self is a question most speedily solved by the
men of science who seek the reasons why Christ is good
and the thinned gold-leaved poplars by the river are beautiful, in the living nerves of ripped-up beasts ; this much is
evident that moral instinct judges that part of actions
which is neither to be felt with our hands, nor to be
seen with our eyes, nor to be tasted or heard or smelt :
it judges and finds good or evil certain qualities or combinations of qualities which do not materially exist :
things which though they have as real an existence as
anything which can be tasted or sniffed or fingered, have
yet a purely intellectual existence, can be found only by
those mysterious senses which, even as touch and hearing, and smell and taste and sight, put us in communication with the physical world outside us, put us far more
wonderfully in communication with the moral world
within us. The qualities constituting physical beauty,
on the other hand, are, to a large extent at least, perceived by our physical senses : there is indeed a point
where the mere nerve sensations no longer serve to ex-

plain æsthetical likings or dislikings, where, on the other
hand, the addition of mere logical considerations of fitness seem insufficient to account for phenomena, where,
in short, we are forced to have recourse to a very confused and at present untenable idea of inherited habits and
love of proportion, but it nevertheless remains evident
that physical beauty is a thing perceived through the
physical senses and concretely extant in the world
around us. We say that a character is morally good because certain actions or words reveal to us the existence of
certain tendencies and habits of feeling which (no matter
how instituted) satisfy and delight our moral nature,
because there is between these tendencies of feeling and
our moral nature a mysterious affinity, which may depend on nerve cells or on logical arguments, but does
not in the least resemble either. But when we say that
a tree is beautiful, it is because, in the first instance, its
mere sensation-giving qualities, taken separately, affect
us agreeably in our various physical parts : the colour
stimulating or soothing our colour nerves, the size, en-
abling our visual nerves to take in its shape agreeably;
its shadyness, which even as a mere suggestion, pleases
our tactile nerves, its rustle, which pleasantly moves our
nerves of hearing ; and even if we admit that the perception that the tree as a whole is beautiful, as distinguished from certain of its qualities being agreeable, depends upon something higher and more recondite than
mere nerve tickle, even then it remains that whatever
abstract instinct of beauty we may possess, it is only
through physical sensations that this instinct is reached;
and that a man born blind cannot perceive beauty of
colours nor a man born deaf beauty of sounds, simply

because the physical receptive organs of sight and sound are wanting. Thus, in short, beauty is a physical quality, as goodness is a moral quality: and if they are in a way equivalents, beauty being physical goodness, and goodness moral beauty, it is exactly because each has a separate sphere in which each respectively, represents the best. That beauty is in itself physical, is a point which few have denied : that beautiful curves and harmonies are moral qualities very few have asserted. But few have as yet been willing to admit that beauty is a quality independent of goodness, independent sometimes to the extent of hostility : that it is as independent of moral excellence as is logical correctness. Yet thus it is ; and thus all of us must vaguely feel ; all those who think, must closely perceive it to be. There is no justice, no charity, no moral excellence in physical beauty. It is a negative thing. If it refuses to associate with evil, to dwell in the putrid corpse or in the face of the murderer, it is because physical beauty is a concomitant of physical purity and health, and decaying corpses are always unhealthy, while evil souls nearly always leave ugly marks on the bodies : but the putrescent corpse and the murderer's face are both ugly because they are physically wrong, not because they are morally abominable. Beauty, in itself, is neither morally good nor morally bad: it is æsthetically good, even as virtue is neither æsthetically good nor æsthetically bad, but morally good. Beauty is pure, complete, egotistic: it has no other value than its being beautiful. This is a bitter thing to say, a cruel confession on the part of one whose love and whose chief interest is the beautiful, to make to himself : this that his beloved and much studied Beautiful, which is his happiness and his study, has no moral value : that above this superb and fascinating thing, there are things which are better, nobler, more necessary, and for whose sake, in case of conflict, this adored quality must be trampled under foot. A bitter confession ; but the truth is the truth, and must be admitted ; to ourselves first of all. It is, as we have said, one of the wicked anomalies of this world that the true, the existing, is at variance with that which we should wish to exist : we cannot replace with impunity the ugly, the cruel, the mean truth by the charming, the generous fancy ; if we do so, we must be prepared to break with all truth, or to compromise with all falsehood : we shall create an evil a hundredfold worse than the one we wished to avoid. We are afraid of a truth which jars upon our sense of the morally desirable : we invent and accept a lie, plausible and noble ; and behold ! in a moment we are surrounded by a logical work of falsehood, which must be for ever torn and for ever patched up if any portion of truth is to enter.

Such has been the case with John Ruskin ; he shrank from owning to himself what we have just recognized, with reluctance, indeed, and sorrow, that the beautiful to whose study and creation he was so irresistibly drawn, had no moral value; that in the great battle between good and evil, beauty remained neutral, passive, serenely egotistic. It was necessary for him that beauty should be more than passively innocent: he must make it actively holy. Only a moral meaning could make art noble ; and as, in the deep-rooted convictions of Ruskin, art was noble, a moral meaning must be found. The whole of the philosophy of art must be remodelled upon an ethical basis ; a moral value must everywhere sanc-

tion the artistic attraction. And thus Ruskin came to
construct a strange system of falsehood, in which moral
motives applied to purely physical actions, moral meanings given to the merely æsthetically significant, moral
consequences drawn from absolutely unethical decisions;
even the merest coincidences in historical and artistic
phenomena, nay, even in the mere growth of various
sorts of plants, nay, even the most ludicrously applied
biblical texts, were all dragged forward and combined
into a wondrous legal summing-up for the beatification
of art; the sense of the impossibility of rationally referring certain æsthetical phenomena to ethical causes
producing in this lucid and noble thinker a sort of
frenzy, a wild impulse to solve irrational questions by
direct appeals for an oracular judgment of God, to be
sought for in the most trumpery coincidences of accidents; so that the man who has understood most of
the subtle reasons of artistic beauty, who has grasped
most completely the psychological causes of great art
and poor art, is often reduced to answer his perplexities
by a sort of æsthetico-moral key and bible divination, or
heads-win tails-lose, toss-up decision. The main pivots
of Ruskin's system are, however, but few: first, the assertion that all legitimate artistic action is governed by
moral considerations, is the direct putting in practise of
the commandments of God; and secondly, that all
pleasure in the beautiful is the act of appreciating the
goodness and wisdom of God. These two main theories
completely balance one another; between them, and
with the occasional addition of mystic symbolism, they
must explain the whole question of artistic right and
wrong. Now for Ruskin artistic right and wrong is not

only a very complex, but, in many respects, a very fluctuating question; in order to see how complex and how
fluctuating, we must remember what Ruskin is, and what
are his aims. Ruskin is no ordinary æsthetician, interested in art only inasmuch as it is a subject for
thought, untroubled in the framing of histories, psychological systems of art philosophy by any personal likings
and dislikings ; Ruskin is essentially an artist, he thinks
about art because he feels about art, and his sole object
is morally to justify his artistic sympathies and aver-
sions, morally to justify his caring about art at all. With
him the instinctive likings and dislikings are the original
motor, the system is there only for their sake. He cannot, therefore, like Lessing, or Hegel, or Taine, quietly
shove aside any phenomenon of artistic preference which
does not happen to fit into his system ; he could, like
Hegel, assign an inferior rank to painting, because painting has to fall into the category assigned to romantic,
that is to say, imperfect art; he could not, like Taine,
deliberately stigmatise music as a morbid art because it
had arisen, according to his theory, in a morbid state of
society; with Ruskin everything must finally yield to
the testimony of his artistic sense: everything which he
likes must be legitimated, everything which he dislikes
must be condemned ; and for this purpose the system of
artistic morality must for ever be altered, annotated, provided with endless saving-clauses, and special cases.
And all this the more especially as, in the course of his
studies, Ruskin frequently perceives that things which
on superficial acquaintance displeased him, are in reality
delightful, in consequence of which discovery a new
legislation is required to annul their previous condemna-

tion and provide for their due honour. Thus, having conceived a perhaps exaggerated aversion (due, in great part, to the injustice of his adversaries) to the manner of representing the nature of certain Dutch painters of the 17th century, Ruskin immediately formulated a theory that minute imitation of nature was base and sinful; and when he conceived a perhaps equally exaggerated admiration for the works of certain extremely careful and even servile English painters of our own times, he was forced to formulate an explanatory theory that minuteness of work was conscientious, appreciative, and distinctly holy. Had he been satisfied with mere artistic value, he need only have said that the Dutch pictures were ugly, and the English pictures beautiful; but having once established all artistic judgment upon an ethical basis, it became urgent that he should invent a more or or less casuistic reason, something not unlike the *distinguo* by means of which the Jesuit moralists rendered innocent in their powerful penitents what they had declared sinful in less privileged people, to explain that, under certain circumstances, minute imitation was the result of insolence and apathy, and in other cases the sign of humility and appreciation. Again, having been instinctively impressed by the coldness and insipidity of the schools of art which ostensibly refused to copy individual nature, and professed to reproduce only the more important and essential character of things, Ruskin annihilated these idealistic conventionalists by a charge of impious contempt for the details of individual peculiarities which God had been pleased to put into his work; and when, on the other hand, his growing love for mediæval art and for mysticism began to draw him towards the Giottesque and even the pre-Giottesque artists, who left out of their work all except the absolutely essential and typical traits, Ruskin sanctified their conventionalism as the result of preference for the merely spiritual and morally interesting portion of the subject. The fact that the over refinement of the idealists of the 16th century ended in insipidity because it was due to a general organic decline in the art, and that the rudeness of the conventional artists of the 14th century possessed a certain nobility because it was merely a momentary incapacity in a rapidly progressing art ; this fact, and with it the knowledge that the development and decline of every art is due to certain necessities of general change, all that explains the life of any and every art, completely escapes Ruskin on account of his explanation by moral motives. In this way Ruskin has constructed a whole system of artistic ethics, extremely contradictory and, as we have remarked, bearing as great a resemblance to the text book, full of *distinguos* and *directions of the intention* of one of Pascal's Jesuits as a very morally pure and noble work can bear to a very base and depraved one. And throughout this system scattered fragmentarily throughout his various books, every artistic merit or demerit is disposed of as a virtuous action or a crime ; the moral principle established for the explanation of one case naturally involving the prejudgment of another case ; and the whole system explaining by moral delinquencies the artistic inferiority of a given time or people, and, on the other hand, attributing the moral and social ruin of a century or a nation to the artistic abominations it had perpetrated. The arrangements of lintels and columns, the amount of

incrustation of coloured marble on to brick, the degree
to which window traceries may be legitimately attenu-
ated and curled, the value of Greek honeysuckle patterns
as compared with Gothic hedge-rose ornaments, all these
and a thousand other questions of mere excellence of
artistic effect, are discussed on the score of their morality
or baseness, of their truthfulness, or justice, or humility;
and Ruskin's madness against any kind of cheating or
deception goes to the length, in one memorable passage
in the *Seven Lamps of Architecture*, of condemning Correggio's ceiling of St. Paolo at Parma because, as real
children might be climbing in a real vine trellise above
our heads, there is possibility of deception and of sin ;
whereas, as none of us expect to see the heavens open
above us, there is no possibility of deception, and consequently no sin in Correggio's glory of angels in the
Parma Cathedral ; thus absolving on the score of
morality a rather confused and sprawling composition,
and condemning as immoral one of the most graceful
and childlike works of the Renaissance. The result of
this system of explaining all artistic phenomena by
ethical causes is, as we have remarked, that the real
cause of any phenomenon, the explanation afforded us
by history, is entirely overlooked or even ignominiously
rejected. Thus Ruskin attributes the decay of Gothic
architecture to "one endeavour to assume, in excessive
flimsiness of tracery, the semblance of what it was not "
—to its having "sacrificed a single truth." Now the
violation of the nature and possibilities of the material,
what Ruskin in ethical language calls the endeavour to
trick, was not the cause but the effect of a gradual decline in the art. The lace work of 15th century Gothic

is not a *lie*, it is an effete form. The perfect forms had
been obtained, and as the growth of the art could not
be checked, imperfect ones naturally succeeded them ;
the workman had hewn enough, had diminished the
stone surfaces sufficiently, had carved the leafage as
much as was compatible with beauty ; the succeeding
generations of workmen continued to work, and what
happened ? They hewed away too much, they diminished
the stone surface too much, they carved the leafage too
deep, each generation cutting away more and more, until the whole fabric had reached such a degree of flimsiness that, had not the Renaissance swept its cobwebs
away, they would have been torn to shreds by the Gothic
artists themselves. An art corrupts and dies of its own
vital principles, as does every other living and changing
thing, as a flower withers of its own life : you begin by
chipping, you end, as in Gothic architecture, by chipping
into nothingness. You begin with grouping : you end
with grouping, like Michelangiolo and Parmegianno,
into knots and lumps ; you begin by raising your figures
out of the background : you end, like Ghiberti, by tying
them on with the narrowest slip of bronze ; you begin
with modulating : you end, like Raff, Brahms, and other
Wagnerists, by modulating into chaos. Art, if it lives,
must grow, and if it grows it must grow old and die.
And this fact gradually, though instinctively, beginning
to be felt by all thinkers on art, Ruskin, with his theory
of moral æsthetics, could never recognize. For him the
corruption of the art is due to the moral corruption of
the artist : if the artist remained truthfully modest, the
perfection of the art would continue indefinitely.

Again, the necessity of referring all good art to moral-

ity and all bad art to immorality, obliges Ruskin to
postulate that every period which has produced bad art
has been a period of moral decay. The artistic habits
which displease him must be a direct result of a vicious
way of feeling and acting in all things : the decay of
Venetian architecture and sculpture must be distinctly
referable to the decay of Venetian morality in the 15th
century; and the final corruption and ruin of the state
must be traced to the moral obliquity which caused
Venetians to adopt pseudo-classic forms in the Riva façade
of the Ducal palace; moral degradation and artistic
degradation, acting and re-acting on each other, bring
about, according to Ruskin, political ruin ; the iniquities
of the men who became apostates to Gothic architecture
are visited upon their distant descendants, upon the
Venetians of the days of Campo Formio. Now here
again the ethical basis induces a complete historical
misconception, a misconception not only in the history
of art, but also in the history of civilization. For, just
as his system of moral sin and artistic punishment blinds
Ruskin to the necessities of change and decay in art, so,
also, it prevents his seeing the inevitable necessity of
political growth and decline. Ruskin seeks the cause of
the fall of Venice in moral corruption manifested, or
supposed to be manifested, in art ; but the cause of the
fall of Venice must be sought elsewhere. Look at this
lagoon, this Adriatic, this Mediterranean : in the 14th
century they are the source of the greatness of the Zenos
and Pisanis ; three or four hundred years later they will
be the cause of the pettiness of the Morosinis and
Emos. In the present, in this time of Dandolo, into
which Ruskin has led us, it is to them that Venice owes

the humiliation of Barbarossa in the porch of St. Mark's ; to them in the future will be owed the triumph of Bonaparte and the tricolour waving from the flagstaff of the square. For in the middle ages the sea means the Mediterranean and the Baltic, the two great navigable, wealth-yielding lakes, and around them arises prosperity : Amalfi, Pisa, Genoa, Venice, Lübeck, Dantzig, Brehmen ; the men who live on the shores of the Mediterranean take the riches of the East and of India, and conquer Greece and the islands, and grow rich ; and on this strip of marshland keep armies which can cope with the united forces of Europe. Such is the sea of the middle ages. But the sea of modern times is the ocean ; give the means of navigating that, give to the barbarians who in-habit its coasts just enough civilization to build a ship and steer it, and those barbarians, yes, the boors of Frisia, the savages of England, and of Normandy, and of Portugal, will become the masters of the world, and Venetians and Genoese shall be their puppets, and the Mediterranean their pond. Since to the commerce of the Mediterranean they will oppose the commerce of the ocean, to the riches of Greece, of Asia Minor, Persia, and Egypt, the riches of Mexico and Peru, of India and of China, which will flow into the banks of London, of Lisbon, of Antwerp, and which will create armies to sweep all Italy out of the field. The Ocean has super-seded the Mediterranean, the boundless the bounded ; this is the explanation of the fall of Venice, of her political torpor and her consequent vices. It is a law of nature that the small and sheltered spots shall suffice while civilization is small, but that as it grows it will seek a wider field, and its original homes be abandoned.

A small country, a small sea, made Greece and Italy
greatest in antiquity and the middle ages; a small
country, a narrow sea, make them smallest in modern
times.   And when the first galley of Prince Henry, the
first pinnace of Amsterdam or London, nay, the first
little Norman craft set sail for St. Brandan's Isle, the
fate of Venice was sealed ; Lodovico Manin, and Casa-
nova, and Bonaparte, and Campo Formio, all that in
Venetian history can mean corruption and disgrace, all
was irrevocably fixed ; the geographical chance which
had raised the palaces of Venice has also caused them
to moulder ; time which made has also unmade, for life
is movement and movement is change.   That immorality
is not the cause but the effect of political decline is as
little conceived by Ruskin as that neither the one nor
the other can be produced by artistic degradation; in
his system which makes artistic inferiority the visible expression of moral corruption, and national misfortune its
direct punishment, there can be no room for any of the
great laws of development and decay which historical
science is now beginning to perceive.   All things must
be carried on upon the miraculous system of Sunday
school books, where planks of bridges give way from
the cogent mechanical reason that the little boys passing
over them have just been telling lies or stealing apples ;
God is for ever busy unbolting trapdoors beneath the
feet of the iniquitous and rolling stones down on the
heads of blasphemers.   And this same necessity of condemning morally a period whose artistic work in any
particular line is æsthetically worthless in Ruskin's judgment, not only leads him into the most absurd misap-
preciation of the moral value of a time, but entirely

forbids his recognizing the fact that the decay of one art, is frequently coincident with, and in some measure due to, the efflorescence of another. The independent development of painting required the decay of the architecture of the middle ages, whose symbolical, purely decorative tendency condemned painting to be a sort of allegorical or narrative Arabesque ; whose well defined arches might not be broken through by daring perspective, whose delicate cornices might not enclose more than a mere rigid and simply tinted mosaic, or mosaic-like fresco. When, therefore, painting arose mature in the 16th century, architecture was necessarily crumbling. But to Ruskin the 16th century, being the century of bad architecture, is hopelessly immoral, and being immoral, its painting, Raphael, Michel Angelo, Correggio, all except a few privileged Venetians, must needs be swept away as so much rubbish ; while the very imperfect painting of the Giottesques, because it belongs to a time whose morality must be high since its architecture is good, is considered as the ideal of pictorial art. Again, Ruskin perceives that the whole plastic art of the 18th century, architecture, sculpture, and painting, are as bad as bad can be ; the cause must necessarily be found not in the inevitable decline of all plastic art since the Renaissance, but in the fiendish wickedness of the 18th century, that abominable age which first taught men the meaning of justice as distinguished from mercy, of humanity as distinguished from charity : which first taught us not to shrink from evil but to combat it. And thus, because the 18th century is proved by its smirking furbelowed goddesses and handkerchief-cravatted urns to be utterly, morally, abominable, the one great art which flourished in this period, the glorious music of Bach, and Gluck, and Marcello, and Mozart, must necessarily be silently carted off to the dust heap of artistic baseness.

Thus the radical falsehood of the ethical system of æsthetics warps the whole of Ruskin's view of the genius and evolution of art, of its relations with national morality and political supremacy. But it does more than this. It warps also Ruskin's view of art itself; its sophisms force him to contradict, to stifle his own artistic instincts. For if, as Ruskin has established, we are not permitted to love the beautiful for its own sake, but only because it is supposed to represent a certain moral excellence, that moral excellence must be the sole valuable portion, and equally artistically valuable when separated from the beautiful; while the beautiful must in itself be worthless, and consequently dangerous. The absolutely ugly must, if it awaken virtuous emotion, have a greater artistic value than the beautiful if it awaken none; the macerated hermits, the lepers and cripples of the middle ages must be artistically preferable to the healthy and beautiful athletes of antiquity; compassion for the physically horrible is more virtuous than the desire for the physically beautiful, therefore Ruskin would replace the one by the other; forgetting, even as the middle ages forgot, that the beautiful, the healthy, are the best and happiest for all of us ; that we are given sympathy with the physically evil only that we may endure its contact long enough to transform it into the physically good : that we compassionate disease only that we may cure it.

Thus this sophisticated sense of duty, which, applied

to artistic interests where it has no place, has merely
caused injustice of all sorts, and falsehood and unceasing
contradiction : which has condemned the artistically
pure for its juxta-position with the morally impure :
which has preferred the inferior in art because it
answered to the definition of the superior in morals :
which has placed Giotto above Michel Angelo because
the second could paint and the first only imagine : which
has condemned Greek art as long as it seemed beautiful
and acquitted it when it appeared ugly : which has
legitimated colour art with one verse of the bible and
anathematised linear art with another : which has so
often rejected the excellent in art because it wanted the
excellent in conduct : which has come to the point of
preferring that disease and putrefaction which, in the
physical world, are equivalent to sin and corruption in the
moral—this sophisticated sense of morality, originally
intended to sanction all that which in art is sanctioned
by its mere innocence and delightfulness, has at length
destroyed the very artistic system which it was to sustain.   For the divine elements of justice, and mercy, and
honour, cannot be wasted in this world ; entrapped and
imprisoned in order to consecrate by their presence the
already holy, rendered sterile and useless among those
artistic things with which they have no concern, they
have at last sought for their field of action, for their
legitimate objects, and have burst forth, shattering
the whole edifice of art philosophy in which they
were enclosed, mere useless talismans.   And it has
come home to Ruskin, once and again, that this virtue
thus expended upon cornices and lintels, upon lines
and colours, while evil raged outside, is no virtue : that

this sanctified art is not holy ; that, direct our intentions
as we may, think of God as much as we like, we cannot
make art one whit the less passive and egotistic ; it has
come home to him, and with the noble candour of doubt
which is his logical weakness and his moral strength, he
has confessed that he had never known one man really
and exclusively devoted to mere moral good, who cared
for art at all.   The elaborate system of ethical æsthetics,
the ingeniously far-fetched explanations of physical
beauty by moral excellence, the triumphant decision
that art is the kingdom of God, has, after all and at last,
failed to redeem the beautiful in the eyes of Ruskin.
He has seen a ragged creature die of starvation on a
dung heap ; and all the cathedrals of Christendom, all
the resplendent Turners and saintly Giottos in the world
have seemed to him black and hideous.   He has argued
and stormed, and patched up once more his tattered
theories, and talked more than ever of beauty being
virtue, and its appreciation religion, and God being in
all fair things ; but all this latter talk has been vain ;
into the midst of art discussions have for ever crept
doubts whether art should be at all.   The placid paradise of art, whose every flower and grass blade is a
generous thought, whose every fruit is a noble action,
where every bubbling of waters and every bird's song is
a hymn to the goodness of God, has become suspicious
to its own creator now that he realises by what it is surrounded ; to live in this sweet and noble impossible
paradise, where beauty is the mere visible expression of
virtue, while the foul world-swamp is stealthily being
eaten into, washed away, absorbed by the surrounding
flood of hell : is this not a sin, this quiet dwelling in

holiness, and a worse sin than any being committed in
the darkness and jostle below?

In this way has Ruskin, one of the greatest thinkers
on art and on ethics, made morality sterile and art base
in his desire to sanctify the one by the other.   Sterile
and base, indeed, only theoretically : for the instinct of
the artist and of the moralist has ever broken out in
noble self-contradiction, in beautiful irrelevancies ; in
those wonderful, almost prophetic passages which seem
to make our souls more keen towards beauty and more
hardy for good.   But all this is incidental, this which is
in reality Ruskin's great and useful work.   He has made
art more beautiful and men better without knowing it—
accidentally, without premeditation, in words which are
like the eternal truths, grand and exquisite, which lie
fragmentary and embedded in every system of theology ;
the complete and systematic is worthless and even dangerous, for it is false ; the irrelevant, the contradictory,
is precious, because it is true to our better part.   Ruskin
has loved art instinctively, fervently, for its own sake ; but
he has constantly feared lest this love should be sinful
or at least base.   Like Augustine, he dreads that the
Devil may be lurking in the beautiful sunshine; lest evil
be hidden in those beautiful shapes which distract his
thoughts from higher subjects of good and God ; he
trembles lest the beautiful should trouble his senses and
his fancy, and make him forget his promises to the Al-
mighty.   He perceives that pleasure in art is more or
less sensuous and selfish ; he is afraid lest some day he
be called upon to account for the moments he has not
given to others, and be chastised for having permitted
his mind to follow the guidance of his senses ; he trem-

P

bles and repeats the praise of God, the anathema of
pride, he mumbles confused words about "corrupt earth"
—and "sinful man,"—even while looking at his works of
art, as some anchorite of old may instinctively have
passed his fingers across his beads and stammered out
an *Ave* when some sight of beauty crossed his path and
made his heart leap with unwonted pleasure. Ruskin
must tranquillize his conscience about art; he must persuade himself that he is justified in employing his
thoughts about it; and lest it be a snare of the demon,
he must make it a service of God. He must persuade
himself that all the pleasure he derives from art is the
pleasure in obeying God, in perceiving his goodness: that
the pleasure he derives from a flower is pleasure not in
its curves and colours and scent, but in its adaptation to
its work, in its enjoyment of existence; that the enjoyment he derives from a grand view is enjoyment of the
kindness of God, and the enjoyment in the sight of a
noble face is enjoyment of the expression of harmony
with God's will; in short, all artistic pleasure must become an act of adoration, otherwise, a jealous God, or a
jealous conscience, will smite him for abandoning the
true altar for some golden calf fashioned by man and
inhabited by Satan. And to this constant moralising,
hallowing, nay, purifying of art, are due, as we have seen,
the greater number of Ruskin's errors; his system is false,
and only evil can spring from it; it is a pretence at a
perfection which does not exist, and which, like the pretence at the superhuman virtue of the anchorite and mystic, must end in lamentable folly: in making men lie to
their own heart because they have sought to clothe all
that is really pure in a false garb of sanctity and have

blushed at its naked reality; because it makes a return to nature a return to sin, since what is natural has
been forbidden and what is innocent has been crookedly
obtained; because it tries to make us think we are
nothing but soul, and therefore turns us to brutes when
we remember that we are also body, and devils when we
perceive that we are also reason.   Because, in short, it is
a lie, and only falsehood can be born of it.   For, in his
constant reference to a spiritual meaning, Ruskin has
not only wasted and sterilised our moral impulses, but
has reduced art to mere foulness; in his constant sanctifying of beauty he makes it appear impure.   Above all,
in his unceasing attempt to attach a moral meaning to
physical beauty, he has lost sight of, he has denied, the
great truth that all that which is innocent is moral; that
the morality of art is an independent quality equivalent
to, but separate from, the morality of action; that beauty
is the morality of the physical, as morality is the beauty
of the spiritual; that as the moral sense hallows the
otherwise egotistic relations of man to man, so also
the æsthetic sense hallows the otherwise brutish relations
of man to matter; that separately but in harmony,
equally but differently, these two faculties make our lives
pure and noble.   All this Ruskin has forgotten: he has
made the enjoyment of mere beauty a base pleasure, requiring a moral object to purify it, and in so doing
he has destroyed its own purifying power; he has
sanctified the already holy, and defiled with holy water,
which implies foulness, the dwelling of holiness.

    This is the lesson to be derived from the attempt at
noble self-delusion which Ruskin has practised upon
himself.   There is not in the world that harmony and

perfection, nay, that analogy of good to good and evil to
evil for which our higher nature seeks.   As we have
said, there is contradiction and anomaly : anomaly the
most horrible, since our logical sense must accept it, and
our moral sense cannot : anomaly of good springing
from evil, and evil from good, of pollution of the noble
and hallowing of the foul by the force of inevitable
sequence.   There is also isolation of one sort of good
from the other, and clashing of their interests.   All this
there is, and against it all our moral sense must for ever
protest, and against it, whether free in our endeavour or
merely pushed on by the universal necessity, we must
struggle.   We must seek for ever to resolve the discord
between good and good, to disentangle the meshes of
good and evil, to destroy the dreadful anomaly of things.
But we can do so, however partially, we can really
wish to do so, only if we have the courage to see that
the lamentable discord and the horrible tangle do exist :
only if we do not shrink from the battlefield of reality
into an enervating Capua of moral idealism.   And thus
we should admit that only morality is really moral, and
only virtue really virtuous ; that physical beauty intrinsically possesses but an æsthetic value quite separate
from all moral value ; that above it must always remain
a more generous world of feeling and endeavour.   If we
do not shrink from this painful truth we shall see that
physical beauty and its egotistic enjoyment have yet a
moral value of their own : the value of being, in the
lives of others, absolute pleasure, the giving of which is
positive good.   For in this world all is not completed
when we have destroyed evil ; it must be replaced by
good.   We must all of us work, but we must work in

different ways. One half of us are the destroyers of
evil, the wrestlers with all that is wrong in itself or be-
gets wrong, falsehood, injustice, disease, misery ; sent to
extirpate the bad, laboriously to weed it out blade by
blade, or boldly to plough and burn it up by the sheaf,
the field, the acre. But when this half of active mankind
has done its work, what would remain ? A mere joyless
desert of painless vacuity ; and the other half of the
workers must come and sow and plant absolute good,
positive joy in this redeemed life soil ; nay, even while
the work of destruction is far from completed, and most
of all, perhaps, then, do we require that in the very
shadow of the yet deep-rooted evil, the little tufts of
good should rise up, and console and strengthen us with
their sight and their scent. And of all these kinds of
egotistic good which we must needs sow while evil is
being cleared away, art is one of the noblest and most
necessary ; and woe betide those who, having the power
of creating beauty, would leave their allotted work and
join the destroyers of falsehood and of evil. The
amount of absolute good in the world is comparatively
small, and we must seek to increase it for ever ; but increased it cannot be except by the full employment of
our activities, and our activities can be fully employed
only in their own proper sphere. In every artist there
is a man, and the moral perfection of the man is more
important than the artistic perfection of the artist ; but,
in as far as the artist is an artist, he must be satisfied to
do well in his art. For, though art has no moral meaning, it has a moral value ; art is happiness, and to bestow
happiness is to create good.

A DIALOGUE ON POETIC MORALITY.

God sent a poet to reform His earth.—A. MARY F. ROBINSON.

"AND meanwhile, what have you written?" asked Baldwin, tickling the flies with his whip from off the horse's head, as they slowly ascended, in the autumn afternoon, the hill of Montetramito, which with its ilex and myrtle-grown black rocks, and its crumbling mounds, where the bright green spruce pine clings to the washed-away scarlet sand, separates the green and fertile plain of Lucca from the marshes of the Pisan sea-shore. The two friends had met only an hour or so before at the foot of the Apennine pass, and would part in not much more again. "And what have you written?" repeated Baldwin.

"Nothing," answered the younger man, drearily, leaning back languidly in the rickety little carriage. "Nothing, or rather too much; I don't know which. Is trash too much or too little? Anyhow, there's none of it remaining. I thrust all my manuscripts into my stove at Dresden, and the chimney took fire in consequence. That's the tragic history of all my poetical labours of the last two years." And Cyril, lying back in the carriage with his arms folded beneath his head, smiled half-sadly, half whimsically in the face of his friend.

But Baldwin did not laugh.

"Cyril," he answered, "do you remember on a birth-

day of yours—you were a tiny boy, brought up like a
girl, with curls and beautiful hands—one of your sisters
dared you to throw your presents into the garden well,
and you did it, before a number of admiring little girls:
you felt quite a hero or a little saint, didn't you?   And
then my little hero was suddenly collared by a big boy
fresh from school, who was his friend Baldwin, and who
pulled his ears soundly and told him to respect people's
presents a little more.   Do you remember that? Well;
I now see that, with all your growing up, and writing,
and philosophising, and talking about duty and self-
sacrifice, you are just the self-same womanish and uncontrolled *poseur*, the same romantic braggadoccio that
you were at seven.   I have no patience with you!"
And Baldwin whisked the whip angrily at the flies.

"Mere conceit: effeminate heroics again!" he went
on.   "Oh no, we must do the very best! Be Shakespeare at least! Anything short of that would be de-
rogatory to our kingly nature! no idea of selecting the
good (because in whatever you do there must be talent),
and trying to develop it; no idea of doing the best with
what gifts you have! For you are not going to tell me
that two years of your work was mere rubbish—contained nothing of value.   But, in point of fact, you don't
care sufficiently for your art to be satisfied to be the
most you can; 'tis mere vanity with you."

Cyril became very red, but did not interrupt.

"I am sorry you think so ill of me," he said sadly,
"and I dare say I have given you good cause.   I dare say
I am all the things you say—vain, and womanish, and
insolently dissatisfied with myself, and idiotically heroic.
But not in this case, I assure you.   I will explain why I

thought it right to do that. You see I know myself very well now. I know my dangers; I am not like you—I am easily swayed. Had those poems remained in existence, had I taken them to England, I am sure I should not have resisted the temptation of showing them to my old encouragers, of publishing them probably; and then, after the success of my other book, and all their grand prophecies, the critics would have had to praise up this one too; and I should have been drifted back again into being a poet. Now, as I wrote you several times—only, of course, you thought it all humbug and affectation—such a poet as I could be I am determined I will not be. It was an act of self-defence—defence of whatever of good there may be in me."

Baldwin groaned. "Defence of fiddlesticks! Defence of your vanity!"

"I don't think so," replied Cyril, "and I don't think you understand me at all in this instance. There was no vanity in this matter. You know that since some time I have been asking myself what moral right a man has to consume his life writing verses, when there is so much evil to remove, and every drop of thought or feeling we have is needed to make the great river which is to wash out this Augean stable of a world. I tried to put the doubt behind me, and to believe in Art for Art's own sake, and such bosh. But the doubt pricked me. And when suddenly my uncle left me all he had, I felt I must decide. As long as I was a mere penniless creature I might write poetry, because there seemed nothing else for me to do. But now it is different. This money and the power it gives are mine only as long as I live;

after my death they may go to some blackguard ; so, while I have them, I must give all my energies to doing with them all the good that I possibly can."

" In that case better give them over to people who know best what to do with them—societies or hospitals, or that sort of thing—and write your verses as before. For I don't think your thoughts will add much to the value of your money, Cyril. You've not a bit of practical head. Of course you may, if you choose, look on idly while other people are using your money. But I don't think it is specially worth doing."

Cyril sighed, hesitated, and then burst out rapidly—

"But it is the only thing I *can* do—do you understand? I can't write poetry any more. Perhaps that may be the only thing for which I was ever fit, but I am fit for it no longer. I cannot do what I have got to despise and detest. For I do despise and detest the sort of poetry which I should write—mere ornamental uselessness, so much tapestry work or inlaid upholstery. You believe in Art for Art's own sake—Goethianism—that sort of thing, I know. It is all very well for you, who have an active practical life with your Maremma drainings and mine diggings, a life in which art, beauty, so forth, have only their due share, as repose and refreshment. It was all very well in former days also, when the people for whom artists worked had a deal of struggle and misery, and required some pure pleasure to make life endurable ; but now-a-days, and with the people for whom I should write, things are different. What is wanted now-a-days is not art, but life. By whom do you think, would all the beautiful useful things I could write, all the fiddle-faddle about trees and streams and statues and love and aspiration (fine aspiration, which never takes a practical shape!) be read? ˙ By wretched overworked creatures, into whose life they might bring a moment of sweetness, like a spray of apple blossom or a bunch of sweet-peas into some black garret? Nothing of the kind. · They would be read by a lot of intellectual Sybarites, shutting themselves out, with their abominable artistic religion, from all crude real life; they would be merely so much more hothouse scents or exotic music (*con sordino*), to make them snooze their lives away. Of course it is something to be a poet like those of former days; something to be Tasso, and be read by that poor devil of a fever-stricken watchmaker whom we met down in the plain of Lucca; but to be a poet for the cultured world of to-day—oh, I would rather be a French cook, and invent indigestible dishes for epicures without any appetite remaining to them."

So saying, Cyril jumped out of the gig, and ran up the steep last ascent of the hill. He had persuaded himself of his moral rightness and felt quite happy.

Suddenly the road made a sharp bend between the overhanging rocks, grown in all their fissures with dark ilex tufts and yellow broom and pale pink cyclamen; it turned, and widened into a flat grass-grown place, surrounded by cypresses on the top and ridge of the hill. Cyril ran to the edge and gave a cry of pleasure. · Below was stretched a wide strip of Maremma swamp-land, mottled green and brown—green where the grass was under water, brown where it was burned into cinders by the sun; with here and there a patch of shining pond or canal; and at the extremity of this, distinguishable from the greyish amber sky only by its superior and intense luminousness, the sea—not blue nor green, but grey, silvery, steel-like, as a mirror in the full sunshine. Baldwin stopped the gig beneath the cypresses.

"Look there," he said, pointing with his whip to a dark greenish band, scarcely visible, which separated the land from the sea: "those are, the ·pine woods of Viareggio. It was into their sand and weeds that the sea washed Shelley's body. Do you think we should be any the better off if he had taken to practical work which he could not do, and declared that poetry was a sort of French cookery?"

Baldwin tied the reins to the stem of a cypress, and threw himself down on the warm sere grass on the brow of the hill, overlooking the tangle of olive and vine and fig-trees of the slopes below.

"In Shelley's time," answered Cyril, leaning his head and shoulders against one of the cypresses, and looking up into its dark branches, compact in the centre, but delicate like feather and sparkling like jet where their extremities stood out against the pale blue sky—"in Shelley's time, things were rather different from what they are now. There was a religion of progress to preach and be stoned for ; there was a cause of liberty to fight for—there were Bourbons and Lord Eldons, and there was Greece and Spain and Italy. There was Italy still when Mrs. Browning wrote : had she looked out of Casa Guidi windows now, on to the hum-drum, shoulder-shrugging, penny - haggling, professorial, municipal-councillorish Italy of to-day she could scarcely have felt in the vein. The heroic has been done—"

"There is Servia and Montenegro, and there are Nihilists and Democrats," answered Baldwin.

" I know—but we can't sing about barbarous ruffians,
nor about half-besotten, half-knavish regicides ; we can't
be Democrats now-a-days—at least I can't. Would you
have a man sing parliamentary debates, or High Church
squabbles, or Disestablishment, or Woman's rights, or
anti-communism? sing the superb conquests of man
over nature, &c., like your Italian friends, your steam-
engine and mammoth poet Zanella? The wonders of
science !—six or seven thousand dogs and cats being
flayed, roasted, baked, disembowelled, artificially ulcera-
ted, galvanized on ripped-up nerves, at Government
expense, in all the laboratories of Christendom, in order
to discover the soul-secreting apparatus, and how to cure
old maids of liver complaint ! Thank you. My muse
aspires not thereunto. What then? Progress? But it
is 'assured. Why, man, we can't even sing of despair,
like the good people of the year '20, since we all know
that (bating a few myriads of sufferers and a few centuries of agony) all is going to come quite right, to be
quite comfortable in this best of all possible worlds.
What then remains, again? Look around you. There
remains the poetry of beauty—oh yes, of pure beauty, to
match the newest artistic chintzes ; the poetry of artistic
nirvana, of the blissful sleep of all manliness and energy,
to the faint sound (heard through dreams) of paradisiac
mysticism sung to golden lutes, or of imaginary amorous
hysterics, or of symphonies in alliteration. And this
when there is so much error, so much doubt, so much
suffering, when all our forces are required to push away
a corner of the load of evil still weighing on the world :
this sort of thing I cannot take to." And Cyril fiercely
plucked out a tuft of lilac-flowered thyme, and threw it

into the precipice below, as if it had been the poetry of which he was speaking.

" Do you know, Baldwin," went on Cyril, "you have destroyed successively all my gods ; you have shown me that my Holy Grails, in whose service, one after another I felt happy and peaceful to live, like another Parzival, or Galahaso, are not the sacred life-giving cup brought down by angels, but mere ordinary vessels of brittle earth or stinking pewter, mere more or less useful, but by no means holy things ; ordinary pots and pans, barber's basins like Mambrino's helmet, or blue china teapots (worst degradation of all) like the Cimabue-Browns'. I believed in the religion of Nature, and you showed me that Nature was sometimes good and sometimes bad ; that she produced the very foulness, physical and moral, which she herself chastised men for ; you showed me whole races destined inevitably to moral perversion, and then punished for it. So I gave up Nature. Then I took up the fashionable religion of Science, and you showed me that it was the religion of a sort of Moloch, since it accustomed us to acquiesce in all the evil which is part and parcel of Nature, since it made us passive investigators into wrong when we ought to be judges. After the positive, I threw myself into the mystic—into the religion of all manner of mysterious connections and redemptions ; you showed me that the connections did not exist, and that all attempted sanctification of things through mysticism was an abomination, since it could not alter evil, and taught us to think it might be good. O my poor Holy Grails ! Then I took up the religion of love ; and you proceeded to expound to me that if love was restricted to a few worthy individuals, it meant neglect of the world at large; and that if it meant love of the world at large, it meant love of a great many utterly unworthy and beastly people. You deprived me of humanitarianism, of positivism, of mysticism; and then you did not even let me rest peaceably in pessimism, telling me that to say that all was for the worst was as unjust as to say that all was for the best. With a few of your curt sentences you showed me that all these religions of mine were mere idolatries, and that to rest in them for the sake of peace was to be utterly base. You left me nothing but a vague religion of duty, of good; but you gave me no means of seeing where my duty lay, of distinguishing good from evil. You are a very useful rooter up of error, Baldwin; but you leave one's soul as dry and barren and useless as sea shingle. You have taken away all the falsehoods from my life, but you have not replaced them by truths."

Baldwin listened quietly.

"Would you like to have the falsehoods back, Cyril?" he asked. "Would you now like to be the holy knight, adoring and defending the pewter basin or blue china teapot of humanitarianism, or positivism, or mysticism, or æstheticism? And what becomes of the only religion which I told you was the true one—the religion of good, of right? Do you think it worthless now?"

"I think it is the religion of the Unknown God. Where shall I find Him?"

"In yourself, if you will look, Cyril."

Cyril was silent for a moment. "What is right?" he said. "In the abstract—(oh, and it is so easy to find out in the abstract, compared to the concrete!)—in the abstract, right is to improve things in the world, to make it better for man and beast ; never to steal justice, and always to give mercy ; to do all we can which can increase happiness, and refrain from doing all which can diminish it. That is the only definition I can see. But how vague !—and who is to tell me what I am to do? And when I see a faint glimmer of certainty, when I perceive what seems to me the right which I must do, who again interferes ? My friend Baldwin, who, after preaching to me that the only true religion is the religion of diminishing evil and increasing good for the sake of so doing, coolly writes to me, in half-a-dozen letters, that the sole duty of the artist is to produce good art, and that good art is art which has no aim beyond its own perfection. Why, it is a return to my old æsthetic fetish worship, when I thought abstract ideas of beauty would set the world right, as Amphion's harp set the stones building themselves. . . . . Am I justified in saying that you merely upset my beliefs, without helping me to build up any ; yes, even when I am striving after that religion of right doing which you nominally call yours— ? "

"You always rush to extremes, Cyril. If you would listen to, or read, my words without letting your mind whirl off while so doing—"

"I listen to you far too much, Baldwin," interrupted Cyril, who would not break the thread of his own ideas ; "and first I want to read you a sonnet."

Baldwin burst out laughing. "A sonnet! one of those burnt at Dresden—or written in commemoration of your decision to write no more ? "

"It is not by me at all, so there's an end to your amusement. I want you to hear it because it embodies, and very nobly, what I have felt. I have never even

seen the author, and know nothing about her except that
she is a woman."

"A woman!" and Baldwin's tone was disagreeably
expressive.

"I know you don't believe in women poets or women
artists."

"Not much, so far, excepting Sappho and Mrs.
Browning, certainly, But, come, let's hear the sonnet.
I do abominate women's verses, I confess; but there are
such multitudes of poetesses that Nature may sometimes
blunder in their production, and make one of them of the
stuff intended for a poet."

"Well then, listen," and Cyril drew a notebook from
his pocket, and read as follows :—

> "God sent a poet to reform His earth
> But when he came and found it cold and poor
> Harsh and unlovely, where each prosperous boor
> Held poets light for all their heavenly birth,
> He thought—Myself can make one better worth
> The living in than this—full of old lore,
> Music and light and love, where saints adore
> And angels, all within mine own soul's girth.
> But when at last he came to die, his soul
> Saw Earth (flying past to Heaven) with new love,
> And all the unused passion in him cried :
> ' O God, your Heaven I know and weary of,
> Give me this world to work in and make whole.'
> God spoke : 'Therein, fool, thou hast lived and died.'"

Cyril paused for a moment. "Do you understand,
Baldwin, how that expresses my state of feeling?" he
then asked.

"I do," answered the other, "and I understand that
both you and the author of the sonnet seem not to have

understood in what manner God intended that poets
should improve the earth. And here I return to my
former remark, that when I said that the only true religion was the religion not of nature, nor of mankind,
nor of science, nor of art, but the religion of good, and
that the creation of perfect beauty is the highest aim of
the artist, I was not contradicting myself, but merely
stating two parts—a general and a particular—of the
same proposition. I don't know what your definition of
right living may be ; mine, the more I think over the
subject, has come to be this :—the destruction of the
greatest possible amount of evil and the creation of the
greatest possible amount of good in the world. And
this is possible only by the greatest amount of the best
and most complete activity, and the greatest amount of
the best activity is possible only when everything is seen
in its right light, in order that everything may be used in
its right place. I have always preached to you that life
must be activity ; but activity defeats itself if misap-
plied ; it becomes a mere Danaides' work of filling
bottomless casks—pour and pour and pour in as much
as you will, the cask will always be empty. Now, in
this world there are two things to be done, and two distinct sets of people to do them : the one work is the
destruction of evil, the other the creation of good. Mind,
I say the *creation* of good, for I consider that to do good
—that is to say, to act rightly—is not necessarily the
same as to *create* good. Every one who does his allotted
work is doing good ; but the man who tends the sick, or
defends the oppressed, or discovers new truths, is not
creating good, but destroying evil—destroying evil in
one of a hundred shapes, as sickness, or injustice, or

Q

falsehood. But he merely removes, he does not give; he leaves men as poor or as rich as they would have been, had not disease, or injustice, or error stolen away some of their life. The man who creates good is the one who not merely removes pain, but adds pleasure to our lives. Through him we are absolutely the richer. And this creator of good, as distinguished from destroyer of evil, is, above all other men, the artist. The scientific thinker may add pleasure to our lives, but in reality this truth of his is valuable, not for the pleasure it gives, but for the pain it removes. Science is warfare; we may consider it as a kind of sport, but in reality it is a hunting down of the most dangerous kind of wild animal—falsehood. A great many other things may give pleasure to our lives—all our healthy activities, upper or lower, must; but the lower ones are already fully exercised, and, if anything, require restraint; so that French cooks and erotic poets ought rather to be exterminated as productive of evil than encouraged as creative of good. And moral satisfaction and love give us the best pleasures of all; but these are pleasures which are not due to any special class created on purpose for their production. Oh, I don't say that any artist can give you the pleasure you have in knowing yourself to be acting rightly, or in sympathizing and receiving sympathy; but the artist is the instrument, the machine constructed to produce the only pleasures which can come near these. Every one of us can destroy evil and create pleasure, in a sort of incidental, amateurish way, within our own immediate circle; but as the men of thought and of action are the professional destroyers of evil, so the artists are the professional creators of good—they work not for those immediately around them, but for the world at large. So your artist is your typical professional creator of pleasure; he is fitted out, as other men are not, to do this work; he is made of infinitely finer stuff than other men, not as a whole man, but as an artist : he has much more delicate hearing, much keener sight, much defter fingers, much farther-reaching voice than other men; he is specially prepared to receive and transmit impressions which would be as wasted on other creatures, as the image in the camera on unprepared, ordinary paper. Now, what I maintain is simply this, that if, according to my definition, the object of destroying as much evil and creating as much good can be attained only by the greatest activity rightly applied, it is evident that a man endowed to be an artist—that is to say, a creator of good for the whole world—is simply failing in his duty by becoming a practical worker; that is to say, an amateur destroyer of evil. What shall we say of this artist? We shall say that, in order to indulge in the moral luxury, the moral amusement, of removing an imperceptible amount of pain, he has defrauded the world of the immense and long-lasting pleasure placed in his charge to give; we shall say that, in order to feel himself a little virtuous, this man has simply acted like a cheat and a thief."

Baldwin had spoken rapidly and earnestly, with a sort of uniform or only gradually rising warmth, very different from the hesitating, fluctuating sort of passion of his companion. There was a short silence; Cyril was still seated under the tall, straight cypress, whose fallen fruit, like carved balls of wood, strewed the sere grass, and whose compact hairy trunk gave out a resinous scent, more precious and strange than that of the fir : he felt that he was momentarily crushed, but had a vague sense that there lurked somewhere reasons, and very potent ones, which prevented his friend being completely victorious ; and Baldwin was patiently waiting for him to muster his ideas into order before continuing the discussion. A slight breeze from the over-clouded sea sent a shiver across the olives into the ravine below, turning their feathery tops into a silver ripple, as of a breaking wave ; the last belated cicalas, invisible in the thick plumy branches of the cypresses, sawed slowly and languidly in the languid late afternoon ; and from the farms hidden in the olive yards of the slope came faint sounds of calling voices and barking dogs—just sound enough to make the stillness more complete. " All that is very true," said Cyril at last, " and yet—I don't know how to express it—I feel that there is still remaining to me all my reason for doubt and dissatisfaction. You say that artistic work is morally justifiable to the artist, since he is giving pleasure to others. From this point of view you are perfectly right. But what I feel is, that the pleasure which the artist thus gives is not morally valuable to those who enjoy it. Do you follow? I mean that the artist may be nobly and generously employed, and yet, by some fatal contradiction, the men and women who receive his gifts are merely selfishly gratified. He might not, perhaps, be better employed than in giving pleasure, but they might surely be better employed than in merely receiving it; and thus the selfishness of the enjoyment of the gift seems to diminish the moral value of giving it. When an artist gives to other men an hour of mere enjoyment,

I don't know whether he ought to be quite proud or not."

Baldwin merely laughed. "It is droll to see what sort of hypermoral scruples some people indulge in now-a-days. So, your sense of the necessity of doing good is so keen that you actually feel wretched at the notion of your neighbours being simply happy, and no more, for an hour. You are not sure whether, by thus taking them away for a moment from the struggle with evil, letting them breathe and rest in the middle of the battle, you may not be making them sin and be sinning yourself! Why, my dear Cyril, if you condemn humanity to uninterrupted struggle with evil, you create evil instead of destroying it; if mankind could be persuaded to give up all of what you would call useless and selfish pleasure, it would very soon become so utterly worn out and disheartened as to be quite powerless to resist evil. If this is the system on which poets would reform the world, it is very fortunate that they don't think of it till they are flying to heaven."

"I can't make it out. You seem to be in the right, Baldwin, and yet I still seem to be justified in sticking to my ideas," said Cyril. "Do you see," he went on, "you have always preached to me that the highest aim of the artist is the perfection of his own work ; you have always told me that art cannot be as much as it should if any extra-artistic purpose be given to it. And while listening to you I have felt persuaded that all this was most perfectly true. But then, an hour later, I have met the same idea—the eternal phrase of art for art's own sake—in the mouths and the books of men I completely despised ; men who seemed to lose sight of all the earnestness and duty of life, who had even what seemed to me very base ideas about art itself, and at all events debased it by associating it with effeminate, selfish, sensual mysticism. So that the idea of art for art's own sake has come to have a disgusting meaning to me."

Baldwin had risen from the grass, and untied the horse from the trunk of the cypress.

"There is a storm gathering," he said, pointing to the grey masses of cloud, half-dissolved, which were gathering everywhere; "if we can get to one of the villages on the coast without being half-drowned while crossing the swamps, we shall be lucky. Get in, and we can discuss art for art's own sake, and anything else you please, on the way."

In a minute the gig was rattling down the hill, among the great blasted grey olives, and the vines with reddening foliage, and the farm-houses with their fig and orange trees, their great tawny pumpkins lying in heaps on the threshing-floor, and their autumn tapestry of strung-together maize hanging massy and golden from the eaves to the ground.

Baldwin resumed the subject where they had left it : "My own experience is, that the men who go in for art for art's own sake, do so mainly from a morbid shrinking from all the practical and moral objects which other folk are apt to set up as the aim of art; in reality, they do not want art, nor the legitimate pleasures of art : they want the sterile pleasure of perceiving mere ingenuity and dexterity of handling ; they hanker vaguely after imaginary sensuous stimulation, spiced with all manner of mystical rubbish, after some ineffable half-nauseous pleasure in strange mixtures of beauty and nastiness; they enjoy above all things dabbling and dipping alternately in virtue and vice, as in the steam and iced water of a Turkish bath. . . . In short, these creatures want art not for its own sake, but for the sake of excitement which the respectabilities of society do not permit their obtaining, except in imaginative form. As to art, real art, they treat it much worse than the most determined utilitarian : the utilitarians turn art into a drudge ; these æsthetic folk make her into a pander and a prostitute. My reason for restricting art to artistic aims is simply my principle that if things are to be fully useful they must be restricted to their real use, according to the idea of Goethe's Duke of Ferrara :—

> ' Nicht alles dienet uns auf gleicher Weise :
> Wer viel gebrauchen will, gebrauche jedes
> Nach seiner Art : so ist er wohl bedient.'

I want art in general not to meddle with the work of any of our other energies, for the same reason that I want each art in particular not to meddle with the work of any other art. Sculpture cannot do the same as painting, nor painting the same as music, nor music the same as poetry ; and by attempting anything beyond its legitimate sphere each sacrifices what it, and no other, can do. So, also, art in general has a definite function in our lives ; and if it attempts to perform the work of philosophy, or practical benevolence, or science, or moralizing, or anything not itself, it will merely fail in that, and neglect what it could do."

"Oh yes," continued Baldwin after a minute, as they passed into the twilight of a wood of old olives, grey, silvery, mysterious, rising tier above tier on either side

of the road, a faint flicker of yellow light between their
feathery branches. "Oh yes, I don't doubt that were I
a writer, and were I to expound my life-and-art philosophy to the world, the world would tax me with great
narrowness! Things are always too narrow for people
when they are kept in their place—kept within duty and
reason. Of course there is an infinite grandeur in chaos
—in a general wandering among the Unknown, in an
universal straining and hankering after the Impossible;
it is grand to see the arts writhing and shivering to
atoms, like caged vipers, in their impotence to do what
they cannot. Only it would be simpler to let those do it
who can; and my system is the only one which can work.
Despair is fine, and Nirvâna is fine; but successful and
useful activity is a good deal finer. Wherefore I shall
always say—'Each in his place and to his work;' and
you, therefore, my dear Cyril, to yours, which is poetry."

"I think your philosophy is quite right, Baldwin, only
—only, somehow, I can't get it to suit my moral condition," answered Cyril. "I do feel quite persuaded that
sculptors must not try to be painters, nor musicians try
to be poets, nor any of them try to be anything beyond
what they are. It is all quite rational, and right, and
moral, but still I am not satisfied about poetry. You
see a poet is not quite in the same case as any other
sort of artist. The musician, inasmuch as musician,
knows only notes, has power only over sounds; and the
painter similarly as to form and colours; if either be
something more, it is inasmuch as he is a mere man, not
an artist. But a poet, inasmuch as he is a poet, knows,
sees, feels a great many things which have a practical
and moral meaning: just because he is a poet, he knows

that there is something beyond poetry ; he knows that there are in the world such things as justice and injustice, good and evil, purity and foulness: he knows all this, which the mere musician, the mere painter, does not—and knowing it, perceiving, feeling, understanding it, with more intensity than other men, is he to sweep it all out of his sight ? is he to say to justice and injustice, good and evil, purity and foulness, ' I know you, but my work lies not with you ?' Is he to do this ? Oh, Baldwin, if he be a man and an honest one, he surely cannot : he cannot set aside these ideas and devote himself to his art for its own sake."

Baldwin listened attentively to the passionate words of his companion, and twitching at a sprig of olive as a branch swept across their heads in their rapid movement through the wood, he answered quietly :

" He will not set aside the ideas of justice and injustice, of good and evil, of purity and impurity, Cyril. He will make use of them even as the musician uses his sounds, or the painter uses his colours. Such ideas are at least one-half of the poet's material, of the stuff out of which he creates—the half which belongs exclusively to him, which he does not share with any other artist ; the half which gives poetry a character in many respects different from that of painting or music. I have always laughed at the Ruskinian idea of morality or immorality in architecture, or painting, or music, and said that their morality and immorality were beauty and ugliness. I have done so because moral ideas don't enter into the arts of line, or colour, or sound, but only into the subjects to which their visible and audible works are (usually arbitrarily) attached. But with poetry the case is different; and if the poet has got a keener perception (or ought to have) of right and wrong than other men, it is because a sense of moral right and wrong is required in his art, as a sense of colour is required in painting. I have said 'art for art's own sake,' but I should have been more precise in saying 'art for beauty's sake.' Now, in poetry, one half of beauty and ugliness is purely ethical, and if the poet who deals with this half, the half which comprises human emotion and action, has no sense of right and wrong, he will fail as signally as some very dexterous draughtsman, who should have no sense of physical beauty and ugliness, and spend his time making wonderful drawings of all manner of diseased growths. Of course, you may be a poet who does *not* deal with the human element, who writes only about trees and rivers, and in this case your notions of right and wrong are as unnecessary to you as an artist as they would be to a landscape painter. You use them in your life, but not in your art. But as soon as a poet deals with human beings, and their feelings and doings, he must have a correct sense of what, in such feelings and doings, is right and what is wrong. And if he have not this sense, he will not be in the same case as the painter or musician who is deficient in the sense of pictorial or musical right and wrong. The wise folk who have examined into our visual and acoustic nerves seem to think, what to me seems extremely probable, that the impression of æsthetic repulsion which we get from badly combined lines, or colours, or sounds, is a sort of admonition that such combinations are more or less destructive to our nerves of sight or of hearing; so, similarly, the quite abstract aversion which we feel to an immoral effect in literature,

seems to me to be the admonition (while we are still
Platonically viewing the matter, and have not yet come
personally into contact with it) that our moral sense—
what I may call our nerves of right and wrong—is being
disintegrated by this purely intellectual contact with
evil.   And, moreover, our nerves of right and wrong are,
somehow, much less well protected than our visual or
acoustic nerves : they seem to be more on the surface of
our nature, and they are much more easily injured : it
takes a good deal of bad painting and bad music to de-
prave a man's eye or ear, and more than we can well
conceive to make him blind or deaf; but it takes less
than we think of base literature to injure a man's moral
perception, to make him see and hear moral things completely wrong.   You see the good, simple, physical
senses look after themselves—are in a way isolated ; but
the moral sense is a very complex matter, and interfered
with in every possible manner by the reason, the imagination, the bodily senses—so that injuring it through
any of these is extremely easy.   And the people whom
bad painting or bad music had made half-blind or half-
deaf would be less dangerous to themselves and to others
than those who had been made half-immoral by poetry."

"But at that rate," said Cyril, "we should never be
permitted to write except about moral action ; if the
morally right is the same for the poet as the pictorially
right for the painter.   Baldwin, I think, I fear, that all
these are mere extemporized arguments for the purpose
of making me satisfied with poetry, which I never shall
be again, I feel persuaded."

"Not at all," answered Baldwin.   "I mean that the
moral right or wrong of poetry is not exactly what you

mean. If we were bound never to write except about good people, there would be an end to half the literature of the world."

"That is exactly what I saw, and what showed me the hollowness of your theory, Baldwin."

"Because you mistook my theory. There could be no human action or interest if literature were to avoid all representation of evil : no more tragedy, at any rate, and no more novels. But you must remember that the impression given by a play or a poem is not the same as that given by a picture or statue. The picture or statue is all we see ; if it be ugly, the impression is ugly. But in a work of literature we see not only the actors and their actions, but the manner in which they are regarded by the author ; and in this manner of regarding them lies the morality or immorality. You may have as many villains as you please, and the impression may still be moral ; and you may have as many saints as you please, and the impression may still be immoral."

The road had suddenly emerged out of the olive woods covering the lowest hill ranges, and in a few minutes they were driving through a perfect desert. The road, a narrow white ribbon, stretched across a great flat tract of country : field after field of Indian corn, stripped of its leaves and looking like regiments of spindles, and of yellowish green grass, half under water ; on either side a ditch full of water-lilies, widening into sedge-fringed canals, in which the hay of coarse long grass was stacked in boats for sheer want of dry soil, or expanding into shallow patches of water scarcely covering the grass, and reflecting, against the green of the meadow below, the boldly peaked marble mountains of Carrara, bare, intensely ribbed, veined, and the blue sky and rainy black clouds. Green brown fields, tufts of reed, hill and sky reflected in the inundated grass—nothing more, not a house, or shed, or tree for miles around—in front only the stormy horizon where it touched the sea.

"This is beautiful," cried Cyril. "I should like to come and live here. It is much lovelier and more peaceful than all the woods and valleys in creation."

Baldwin laughed. "It might be a good beginning for final Nirvâna," he said. "These are the sea-swamps, the *padule*, where the serene Republic of Lucca sent its political offenders. You were locked up in a tower, the door bricked up, with food enough to last till your keeper came back once a fortnight; the malaria did the rest."

"It is like some of our modern literature," answered Cyril, with a shudder; "Maremma poetry—we have that sort of thing, too."

"By the way," went on Baldwin; "I don't think we quite came to the end of our discussion about what a poet ought to do with his moral instincts, if he has any."

"I know," answered Cyril, "and I have meanwhile returned to my previous conclusion that, now that all great singable strifes are at an end, poetry cannot satisfy the moral cravings of a man."

"You think so?" asked Baldwin, looking rather contemptuously at his companion. "You think so? Well, therein lies your mistake. I think, on the contrary, that poetry requires more moral sense and energy than most men can or will give to it. Do you know what a poet has to deal with, at least a poet who does not confine himself to mere description of inanimate things? He has to deal with the passions and actions of mankind—

that is to say, with a hundred problems of right and
wrong. Of course, men who have deliberately made up
their mind on any question of right and wrong, are not
shaken by anything in a book; nay, they probably
scarcely remark it. But if you remember that in the
inner life of every man there must be moments of doubt
and hesitation, there must be problems vaguely knocking
about, you will understand that for every man there is
the danger that in such a moment of doubt his eyes may
fall upon a sentence in a book—a sentence to other men
trivial—which will settle that doubt for ever, rightly or
wrongly.   There are few of us so strong that the
moment does not come when we would ask, as a good
Catholic does of a confessor, what is right and what
is wrong, and take the answer which is one of the
two that have been struggling within himself, as
definite ; and to us, who do not go to confession, a
book, any book casually taken up, may be this terribly
powerful spiritual director. People used to exaggerate
the influence of books, because they imagined that they
could alter already settled opinions; now-a-days I deliberately think that they underrate this influence, because
they forget how it may settle fluctuating opinion.   The
power of literature is in this way very great."

  "It has been formerly—yes, I grant it," answered
Cyril; "but it is no longer what it was ; in our cut-and-
dry days it is necessarily smaller."

  "On the contrary, much greater now than perhaps
almost at any other time.   These are not cut-and-dry
days, Cyril, but the very reverse ; you must not let
yourself be deceived by a certain superficial regularity,
by railway journeys and newspapers, and a general

civilization of hand-books and classes.   In reality there
is more room for indirect moral perversion or enerva-
tion in our days than there has been for a good while;
for the upsetting of ideas, the infiltration of effete or
foreign modes of thought and feeling, is much greater in
this quiet nineteenth century than it was, for instance, in
the Renaissance or the eighteenth century.   With all
their scepticism, the people of those days had a great
fund of tradition about everything; they were floating
about a good deal, I admit, but they were fully persuaded
of the existence of certain very solid moral rocks, to which
they might always tie their boat when it grew over-
rough; rocks of religion or deistic mysticism, or of
social *convenances*, which we have now discovered to be
by no means granite, but some sort of sea deposit, of
hardened sand, whose formation we understand and no
longer rely upon.   The most arrant sceptics of the past
had always one great safety, that they were in a groove;
they saw, understood, sympathized with only their own
civilization.   What they thought right they had never
seen questioned—they never imagined any one could
regard as wrong; hence the most liberal thinkers of
former days always strike us, with their blindness to all
but their own civilization, as such Philistines.   Things
have changed since then; they began to change already,
as soon as men began to look at other civilizations; and
the suggestive first-fruit of this early ethnographic
eclecticism may be seen in Diderot's very beastly books:
he found that the South Sea Islanders had not, on the
subject of incest, the same views as Christian folk;
whereupon it struck him that those views might be due
to prejudice.   It was not the development of the natural

sciences, but rather of the historic and ethnographic, which upset people's ideas; it was the discovery of how our institutions, moral and social (hitherto regarded as come straight from heaven), had formed themselves, and how they were subject to variation. Speaking of poets, look at a pure man, I believe a very pure man, Shelley, if you want to understand the necessity of poets having a greater solidity of moral judgment than the mere Jones and Browns who stick to their shop, and are not troubled with theories. Add to the influence of scientific doubt, of the doubt created by books on the origin of ideas and institutions (showing of what moonshine they are often made), the utterly confusing effect of our modern literary eclecticism, our comprehension and sympathy with so many and hostile states of civilization, our jumbling together of antique and mediæval, of barbarous and over-ripe and effete civilizations, our intellectual and moral absorption of incompatible past stages of thought and feeling, with the follies and vices inherent in each;—sum up all this, and you will see that, with our science and our culture, our self-swamping with other folk's ideas, we are infinitely less morally steady than the good sceptics of the days of Voltaire, who always believed in the supremacy of their own century, their own country, their own institutions, their own conventionalities; who were in danger only from their own follies and uncertainties, while we are in danger from the follies and uncertainties of every past century from which we have inherited. And you will see, if you look, that that sceptical eighteenth century, which was very much more credulous and conservative than ours, was very little divided and upset in its ideas; certain things were universally admitted, and certain other things universally rejected ; in that day there was always the master of the ceremonies—Propriety. He knew exactly what could be permitted : in the dining-room, drunkards yelling filthy jests ; in the drawing-room, polite gentlemen stalking or tripping through their minuets. It is different now-a-days."

Cyril nodded. " I understand what you mean," he said ; " but I don't see the application yet."

" Well," answered Baldwin, " I will show you one instance of the application. Have you ever thought over the question of—how shall I call it ?—the ethics of the indecent ?"

Cyril stared. " No, it never struck me that there were any. I don't write indecent things, it doesn't amuse me. I feel not the smallest desire to do so ; if anything, I feel rather sick at such things ; that is all."

" That is all for you, but not all for other people. You don't feel attracted to write on some subjects ; well, other people not only feel attracted, but imagine that it is their duty even if they are not."

" They are swine ; I have nothing to do with them." And Cyril looked as if he had settled the matter.

" But they are not swine ; at least, not all of them ; or they are not entirely swine, by any means," insisted Baldwin. " You are not going to tell me that a man like Walt Whitman is a mere pig. Still there are things of his which to you are simply piggish. Either Whitman is a beast or you are a prude."

" That depends upon difference of nature," said Cyril quickly, vaguely desirous of putting an end to a discussion which brought forward an anomaly.

R

"That is merely repeating what I said," replied Baldwin. "But in reality I think it is *not* a difference of
nature. I think it depends on a difference of reasoned
opinion; in short, upon a sophistication of ideas on the
part of Whitman. I think it depends in him and the
really pure men who uphold his abominations upon a
simple logical misconception; a confusion of the fact
that certain phenomena have been inevitable, with the
supposition that those same certain phenomena are
therefore desirable—a confusion between what has been,
and could not help being, and what may be and ought
to be. It is the attempt to solve a moral problem by an
historical test."

"I don't understand in the least, Baldwin."

"Why, thus: our modern familiarity with the intellectual work of all times and races has made people
perceive that in past days indecency was always part
and parcel of literature, and that to try to weed it out
is to completely alter the character of at least a good
half of the literature of the past. Hence, some of us
moderns, shaken as we are in all our conventional ideas,
have argued that this so-called indecency is a legitimate
portion of all literature, and that the sooner it is re-in-
troduced into that of the present the better, if our literature is to be really vital and honest. Now, these people
do not perceive that the literature of the past contained
indecencies, merely because, being infinitely less self-
conscious, less responsible than now, the literature of those
days contained fragments of every portion of the civilization which produced it. For besides what I might call
absolute indecency, in the sense of pruriency, the literature of the past is full of filth pure and simple, like some

Eastern town ; a sure proof this, that if certain subjects
which we taboo were not tabooed then, it was not from
any conscious notion of their legitimacy, but from a
general habit of making literature, like the street of
some Oriental or mediæval town, the scene of every sort
of human action, important or trifling, noble or vile ;
regarding it as the place for which the finest works were
painted or carved, and into which all the slops were
emptied.   Hence, in our wanderings through the literature of the past, our feet are for ever stumbling into
pools of filth, while our eyes are seeking for the splendid
traceries, the gorgeous colours above ; our stomachs are
turned by stenches even while we are peeping in at some
wonderful rose garden or fruit orchard.   I think you
might almost count on your fingers the books up to the
year 1650, in which you are sure of encountering no
beastliness—choice gardens or bowers of the soul, or
sacred   chapels   kept   carefully   tidy   and   pure—viz.,
Milton, Spenser, the *Vita Nuova*, Petrarch, Tasso—
things, you see, mainly sacred or spiritualistic—sort of
churches where only devotion of some sort goes on ; but
if we go out to where there is real life, life complete and
thoughtless — Shakspeare, Rabelais, Molière, Ariosto,
Cervantes, Aristophanes, Horace—the evil odours meet
us again at every step.   Well, now-a-days this has all
been misunderstood.   People have imagined that an inevitable nuisance of the past ought also to be a deliberately chosen nuisance of the present : a line of
argument which appears to me to be similar to that of a
man, who, because the people of Lisbon used, in the
days of my grandfather, to practise a very primitive
system of sewerage, should recommend that the in-

habitants of modern London should habitually empty
their slops on to the heads of passers-by.   I am crude?
Well, it is by calling nasty things by beautiful names
that we are able to endure their existence.   I think that
people who should attempt such literary revivals ought
to be fined, as the more practical revivers of old traditions certainly would be."

Cyril paused a moment.   "I think that these sort of
offenders, like Whitman, are not evil-doers, but merely
snobs: they offend not good morals, but good taste."

"That's just such an artistic and well-bred distinction
as I should expect from you," answered Baldwin, rather
contemptuously.   "I wonder what that word 'good taste'
signifies to your mind?   Everything and nothing.   They
are offenders against good taste, you say.   Well, let us
see how.   If I hang a bright green curtain close to a
bright blue wall-paper, you will say it is bad taste; if I
set Gray's 'Elegy' to one of Strauss's waltzes, that is
bad taste also; and if I display all my grand furniture
and plate (supposing I had it) to my poor neighbour,
whose chintz chair is all torn, and who breakfasts out of
a cup without a handle, that also is bad taste.   Each for
a good reason, and a different one; in each case I am
inflicting an injury, too slight and inadvertent to be sin,
against something: the green curtain and blue paper
combination pains your eye; the Gray's 'Elegy' and
Strauss's waltz combination annoys your common sense;
the contrast between my riches and your poverty inflicts
a wound on your feelings; you see that all sins against
taste are merely a hurting of something in somebody.
So that, if writing indecent poems is an offence against
good taste, it means that it also inflicts some such in-

jury. That injury is simply, as the world has vaguely felt all along, an injury to your neighbour's morals."

" But," put in Cyril, "such a man as Whitman has no immoral intention, nor is he immoral in the sense that Ariosto and Byron are sometimes immoral. The man is not a libertine, but a realist. He wishes people to live clean lives ; all he says is, that everything which is legitimate, innocent, necessary in life, is also legitimate and innocent in literature. And although I should rather select other subjects to write about, and would rather he did so likewise, I cannot deny that there is logic in saying that there can be no harm in speaking of that which there is no harm in doing."

" Yes," said Baldwin, "that is just the argument of such men. And the answer is simply that there are things which are intended to be done and *not* to be spoken about. What you call logic is no logic at all, but a mere appeal to ignorance. It so happens that the case is exactly reversed—that there are a great many things which there is not the smallest immorality in speaking about, and which it would be the most glaring immorality to do. No one shrinks from talking about murder or treachery ; nay, even in the very domain of sexual relations there need not be the smallest immorality, nothing at all perverting, in a play which, like the whole Orestes trilogy, or *Othello*, or *Faust*, turns upon adultery or seduction ; no one also has the slightest instinct of immorality in talking about the most fearful wholesale massacres. Yet the world at large, ever since it has had any ideas of good and evil, has had an instinct of immorality in talking of that without which not one of us would exist, that which society sanctions and the

church blesses. And this exactly because it is as
natural as murder—of which we speak freely—is the
contrary. For, exactly because certain instincts are so
essential and indispensable, Nature has made them so
powerful and excitable ; . there is no fear of their being
too dormant, but there is fear of their being too active,
and the consequences of their excess are so hideously
dangerous to Nature itself, so destructive of all the
higher powers, of all the institutions of humanity ; the
over-activity of the impulses to which we owe our birth
is so ruinous of all that for which we are born, social,
domestic, and intellectual good, nay, to physical existence itself, that Nature even has found it necessary to
restrain them by a counter-instinct—purity, chastity—
such as has not been given us to counteract the other
physical instincts, as that of eating, which can at most
injure an individual glutton, but not affect the general
social order. Hence, the slightest artificial stimulus is a
danger to mankind, and the giving thereof a crime ; for
the experience of all times tells us what modern psychology is beginning to explain—viz., the strange connection
between the imagination and the senses, the hitherto
mysterious power of awakening physical desires, of almost reproducing sensation, possessed by the mind, even
as the mention of dainty food is said to make the mouth
water, and the description of a surgical operation to
make the nerves wince. So that the old intuition, now
called conventionalism, which connects indecency with
immorality, is entirely justified. Crime may be spoken
of just because it is crime, and our nature recoils therefrom ; indeed, I think that now-a-days, when our destructive instinct (except in small boys and professors of

physiology) is becoming effete, there has ceased to be any very demoralizing influence in talking even of horrors. But the immorality of indecency is quite unlike the immorality of—how shall I distinguish?—of ordinary immorality. In the case of the latter the mischief lies in the sophistication of the reason or the perversion of the sympathies ; as, for instance, in Machiavel's 'Prince,' or any of a hundred French novels. In the former case, that of indecency, the immorality lies in the risk of inducing a mood which may lead to excess—that is, to evil. And, as a rule, I think this inducing of a mood is the commonest source of moral danger, whether the mood be a sensual or a destructive one."

" I don't see how you make that out ; although I now understand what at first seemed to me mere inexplicable instincts—founded on nothing."

"Some things are inexplicable, perhaps, but be sure instincts are not founded on nothing. Misconceptions are mere false conceptions ; but a good half of what people call social convention is based upon a perfectly correct conception, only mankind has forgotten what that conception was. Well, I should place the various sorts of demoralization of which literature is capable in this order : No. 1, and least dangerous, sophistication of judgment ; No. 2, and more dangerous, perversion of sympathy ; No. 3, and most dangerous, inducement of questionable frame of mind. And I place them thus because it seems to me that this is the order of facility, and, consequently, universality ; I mean that fewest people can be found who depend sufficiently on their deliberate ideas, and most effort is required to sophisti-

cate them ; whereas, least effort is required, and most
effect produced, in the matter of inducing a mood ; the
perversion of sympathy is half-way. Of course, if we
could imagine (as once or twice has actually been the
case) that the moral ideas of a whole people were
sophisticated, that would be the worst, because the least
remediable ; but, in the first place, people act but little
from ideas, or few persons do, and it is difficult to alter
people's ideas ; and, in the second place, the sophistication of conscience of single individuals is kept in check
by the steadfastness of the mass of mankind, and, consequently, as in such men as Diderot, reduced to mere
talk, without corresponding action. But a mood is easily
induced without the reason even perceiving it, and the
more necessary the mood is to nature, the more easily it
will be aroused—the more unnatural an evil, the less
danger of it ; the more an evil is the mere excess of the
necessary, the more danger there is of it."

"It is curious how you marshal ideas into their right
places," said Cyril. "There remains one thing to be
said about the ethics of impropriety. The people who
go in for writing upon subjects which thirty years ago
would have distinctly been forbidden, do not all of them
write as Whitman does : they are not all what I should
call openly beastly. They do their best, on the contrary, to spiritualize the merely animal."

"That is just the most mischievous thing they could
possibly do," interrupted Baldwin. "I know the sort of
poets you mean. They are the folk who say that things
are pure or impure, holy or foul, according as we view
them. They are not the brutal, straightforward, naturalistic school ; they are the mystico-sensual. Of the

two, they are infinitely the worse. For the straightforward naturalistic hogs generally turn your stomach
before they have had a chance of doing you any harm ;
but these persuade themselves and you that, while you
are just gloating over sensual images, you are improving
your soul. They call brute desire passion, and love lust,
and prostitution marriage, and the body the soul. Oh!
I know them ; they are the worst pests we have in
literature."

"But I don't think they are intentionally immoral,
Baldwin."

"Do you think any writer ever was intentionally immoral, Cyril ?"

"Well, I mean that these men really intend doing
good. They think that if only some subjects be treated
seriously, without any sniggering or grimacing, there
ceases to be any harm in them. They say that they
wish to rescue from out of the mire where prudery has
thrown it, that which is clean in itself; they wish to
show that the whole of Nature is holy; they wish to
purify by sanctifying."

Baldwin listened with a smile of contempt. "Of
course such words seem very fine," he said ; "but a
thing is either holy or is not holy : all the incense of
poetry and all the hocus-pocus words of mysticism cannot alter its nature by a title. And woe betide us if we
once think that any such ceremony of sanctification can
take place; woe betide us if we disguise the foul as the
innocent, or the merely indifferent as the holy ! There
is in Nature a great deal which is foul : in that which
men are pleased to call unnatural, because Nature herself
chastises it after having produced it : there is in Nature

an infinite amount of abominable necessity and abominable possibility, which we have reason and conscience to
separate from that which within Nature itself is innocent
or holy. Mind, I say innocent *or* holy ; for innocence
and holiness are very different things. All our appetites,
within due limits, are innocent, but they are not therefore holy ; and that is just what mystico-sensual poetry
fails to perceive, and in giving innocence the rank of
holiness it makes it sinful. Do you know what is the
really holy ? It is that of which the world possesses too
little, and can never possess too much : it is justice,
charity, heroism, self-command, truthfulness, lovingness,
beauty, genius—these things are holy. Place them, if
you will, on a poetic altar, that all men may see them,
and know them, and love them, and seek after them life-
long without ever wearying. But do not enshrine in
poetic splendours the merely innocent ; that which
bestows no merit on its possessor, that which we share
with every scoundrel and every animal, that which is so
universal that it must for ever be kept in check, and
which, unless thus checked by that in ourselves which is
truly holy, will degrade us lower than beasts. For in so
doing—in thus attempting to glorify that in which there
is nothing glorious—you make men think that self-indulgence is sanctity, you let them consume their lives in
mere acquiescence with their lusts and laziness, while all
around is raging the great battle between good and evil.
Worst of all, in giving them this worship of a mystic
Ashtaroth or Belial, you hide from them the knowledge
of the true God, of the really and exclusively holy, of
good, truth, beauty, to know and receive which into our
soul we must struggle lifelong with the world and with

ourselves ; yes, struggle for the sake of the really holy
with that mere innocence which is for ever threatening
to become guilt."

Baldwin paused ; then resumed after a moment: "I
believe that mankind as it exists, with whatever noble
qualities it possesses, has been gradually evolved out of
a very inferior sort of mankind or brutekind, and will, I
hope, be evolved into a very superior sort of mankind.
And I believe, as science teaches us, that this has been
so far effected, and will be further effected henceforward,
by an increased activity of those nobler portions of us
which have been developed as it were by their own
activity ; I believe, in short, that we can improve only
by becoming more and more different from the original
brutes that we were.   I have said this to explain to you
my feelings towards a young poet of my acquaintance,
who is very sincerely smitten with the desire to improve
mankind ; and has deliberately determined to devote a
very fine talent to the glorification of what he calls pure
passion, pure in the sense that it can be studied in its
greatest purity from the cats on the house tops."

Cyril made a grimace of disgust.

"No, indeed," continued Baldwin, "that poet is not
one of the æsthetic-sensual lot you seem to think.   He
is pure, conscientious, philanthropic ; but he is eminently
unreasoning.   He is painfully impressed by the want of
seriousness and holiness with which mankind regards
marriage, and his ambition is to set mankind right on
this subject, even as another young poet-philanthropist
tried to improve family relations in his 'Laon and
Cythna.'   Now, if you were required to use your poetical
talents in order to raise the general view of marriage, in

order to show the sanctity of the love of a man and a woman, how would you proceed ? "

"I have often thought about that," answered Cyril ; " but it has been done over and over again, and I think with most deliberate solemnity and beauty by Schiller and Goethe in the 'Song of the Bell' and in 'Hermann and Dorothea.' Well, I think that poetry can do good work in this line only if the poet see where the real holiness of such love lies ; in the love not of the male and the female, but of the man and the woman. For there is nowhere, I think, greater room for moral beauty and dignity than in the choosing by a man of the one creature from whom only death can separate him ; of the one friend, not of a phase of his life, but of his whole life ; of the one soul which will grow and mature always by the side of his, and having blossomed and borne fruit of good, will gently fade and droop together with his. But this is not the most holy part of the choice, for he is choosing also the mother of his children, the woman who is to give half their nature, half their training, to what children must mean to every honest man : the one chance he possesses of living as he would have wished to have lived, of being what he should wish to have been, his one chance of redeeming his errors, of fulfilling his hopes, of realizing in a measure his own ideals. And to me such a choice, and love in the sense of such a choice, become not merely coldly deliberate, but passionately instinctive, are holy with the holiness that, as you say, is the only real one ; holy in all it implies of recognized beauty and goodness, of trust and hope, of all the excellence of which it is at least the supposed forerunner ; and its holiness is that upon which all other holiness, all the truthfulness and justice and beauty and goodness of mankind, depends.   This is how I view the sanctity of the love between man and woman ; how all the greatest poets, from Homer to Schiller, and from Schiller to Mrs. Browning, have viewed it ; and it is the only possible view that I can conceive."

Baldwin nodded.   " This is how I also see the question.   But my young poet is not satisfied with this : he wishes to make men believe in the holiness of that which is no more holy, and far oftener tends to be unholy, than eating or drinking ; and in order to make mankind adore, he lavishes all his artistic powers on the construction of an æsthetical temple wherein to enshrine, on the preparation of poetic incense with which to surround, this species of holiness, carefully separated from any extraneous holiness, such as family affection, intellectual appreciation, moral sympathy ; left in its complete unmixed simplicity of brute appetite and physical longing and physical rapture ; and the temple which he constructs out of all that is beautiful in the world is a harlot's chamber ; and the incense which he cunningly distils out of all the sights and sounds of Nature are filthy narcotics, which leave the moral eyes dim, and the moral nerves tremulous, and the moral muscle unstrung. In his desire to moralize he demoralizes ; in his desire to sanctify one item of life, he casts aside, he overlooks, forgets, all that which in life is already possessed of holiness.   Thus my young poet, in wishing to improve mankind, to raise it, undoes for the time being that weary work of the hundreds of centuries which have slowly changed lust into love, the male and female into a man and a woman, the life of the body into the life of the soul ; poetry, one of the highest human products, has, as it were, undone the work of evolution ; poetry, which is essentially a thing of the self-conscient intellect, has taken us back to the time when creatures with two legs and no tail could not speak, but only whine and yell and sob—a mode of converse, by the way, more than sufficient for the intercourse of what he is pleased to call the typical Bride and Bridegroom."

They had got out of the strange expanse of brown and green swamp, and after traversing a strip of meagre re-deemed land, with stunted trees and yellowish vines, had reached the long narrow line of pine woods which met the beach. They passed slowly through the midst of the woods, brushing the rain-drops off the short, bright, green pines, their wheels creaking over the slippery fallen needles embedded in the sand ; while the setting sun fell in hazy yellow beams through the brushwood, making the crisp tree-tufts sparkle like green spun-glass, and their scaly trunks flush rosy ; and the stormy sea roared on the sands close by.

" I think your young poet ought to be birched," re-marked Cyril ; and if anything could add to my aversion, not for poetry, but for the poetic profession, this would which you have just told me. You see how right I was in saying that I would have more moral satisfaction in being a French cook than in being a poet."

" By no means," answered Baldwin. " In the first place, my young poet ought not to be birched ; he ought to be made to reflect, to ask himself seriously and simply, in plain prose, what ideal of life he has been setting be-fore his readers. He ought to be shown that a poet, inasmuch as he is the artist whose material is human

feeling and action, is not as free an artist as the mere
painter, or sculptor, or composer; he ought to be made
to understand that now-a-days, when the old rules of conduct, religious and social, are for ever being questioned,
every man who writes of human conduct is required, is
bound, to have sound ideas on the subject: that, because
now-a-days, for better or for worse, poetry is no longer
the irresponsible, uncontrolled, helter-skelter performance of former times, but a very self-conscious, wide-
awake, deliberate matter, it can do both much more
harm and much more good than it could do before."

They were slowly driving along the beach, among the
stunted pine shoots and the rough grass and the yellow
bindweed half buried in the sand, and the heaps of sea-
blackened branches, and bits of wood and uncouth floating rubbish which the waves had deposited, with a sort
of ironical regularity, in a neat band upon the shore;
down-here on .the coast the storm had already broken,
and the last thin rain was still falling, dimpling the grey
sand. The sun was just going to emerge from amidst
the thick blue-black storm-clouds and descend into a clear
space, like molten amber, above the black, white-crested,
roaring sea; it descended slowly, an immense pale luminous globe, gilding the borders of the piled-up clouds
above it, gilding the sheen of the waves and the wet sand
of the shore; and as it descended, the clouds gathered
above it into a vast canopy, a tawny orange diadem or
reef of peaked vapours encircling the liquid topaz in
which the sun moved; tawnier became this garland,
larger the free sky, redder the black storm masses above;
till at last the reddening rays of the sun enlarged and
divided into immense beams of rosy light, cutting away

the dark and leaving uncovered a rent of purest blue.
At last the yellow globe touched the black line of the
horizon, gilding the waters ; then sank behind it and
disappeared. The wreath of vapours glowed golden, the
pall of heaped-up storm-clouds flushed purple, and bright
yellow veinings, like filaments of gold, streaked the pale
amber where the sun had disappeared. The amber grew
orange, the tawny purple, the purple a lurid red, as of
masses of flame-lit smoke; all around, the sky blackened,
until at last there remained only one pile of livid purple
clouds hanging over a streak of yellow sky, and gradually
dying away into black, with but here and there a death-
like rosy patch, mirrored deadlier red in the wet sand of
the beach. The two friends remained silent, like men
listening to the last bars, rolling out in broad succession
of massy, gradually resolving chords, of some great
requiem mass—silent even for a while after all was over.
Then Cyril asked, pointing to a row of houses glimmering white along the dark lines of coast, below the great
marble crags of Carrara, rising dim in the twilight—

"Is that the place where my friends will pick me up?"

"Yes," answered Baldwin, "that's the place. You will
be picked up there if you choose."

"I must, you know." And Cyril looked astonished, as
if for the first time it struck him that there might be no
must in the matter. "I must—at least, I suppose I ought
to—go back to England with them."

"You know that best," replied Baldwin, shortly. "But
before we get there I want to finish what we were saying
about the moral value of poetry, if you don't mind. I
gave you the instance of Whitman and the mystico-
sensual school merely because it is one of the most

evident; but it is only one of many I could give you of
the truth of what I said, that if a poet, inasmuch as he is
a poet, has—what the painter, or sculptor, or musician,
inasmuch as they are such, have not—a keener sense of
moral right and wrong than other men, it is because his
art requires it.　Consider what it is deliberately to treat
of human character and emotion and action; consider
what a strange chaos, an often inextricable confusion of
clean and foul, of healthy and pestilent, you get among, in
penetrating into the life of the human soul; consider that
the poet must pick his way through all this, amidst very
loathsome dangers which he often cannot foresee; and not
alone, but carrying in his moral arms the soul of his reader
—of each of his thousands of readers—a soul which, if he
see not clearly his way, if he miss his footing, or tread in
the soft, sinking soil (soft with filthy bogs), may be be-
spattered and soiled, perhaps for ever—may be sucked
into the swamp pool or poisoned by the swamp air; and
that he must thus carry, not one soul, but thousands of
souls, unknown to him—souls in many cases weak, sometimes already predisposed to some loathsome moral
malady, and which, by a certain amount of contact with
what to the poet himself might be innocuous, may be
condemned to life-long disease.　I do not think that the
poet's object is to moralize mankind; but I think that
the materials with which he must work are such that,
while practising his art, he may unconsciously do more
mischief than all the professed moralists in Christendom
can consciously do good.　The poet is the artist, remember, who deliberately chooses as material for his art the
feelings and actions of man; he is the artist who plays
his melodies, not on catgut strings or metal stops, but

S

upon human passions; and whose playing touches not a mere mechanism of fibres and membranes like the ear, but the human soul, which in its turn feels and acts; he is the artist who, if he blunders, does not merely fatigue a nerve, or paralyze for a moment a physical sense, but injures the whole texture of our sympathies and deafens our conscience. And I ask you, does such an artist, playing on such an instrument, not require moral feeling far stronger and keener than that of any other man, who, if he mistake evil for good, injures only himself and the few around him? You have been doubting, Cyril, whether poetry is sufficient work for a man who feels the difference between good and evil; you might more worthily doubt whether any man knows good from evil with instinct sure enough to suffice him as a poet. You thought poetry morally below you : are you certain that you are morally up to its level?"

Cyril looked vaguely about him : at the black sea breaking on the twilight sands, at the dark outline of pine-wood against the pale sky, at the distant village lights—vaguely, and as if he saw nothing of it all. The damp sea breeze blew in their faces, the waves moaned sullenly, the pines creaked in the wind; the moon, hidden behind clouds, slowly silvered into light their looser, outer folds, then emerged, spreading a broad white sheen on the sands and the water.

"Are you still too good for poetry?" asked Baldwin; "or—has poetry become too good for you?"

"I don't know," answered Cyril, in the tone of a man before whose mental eyes things are taking a new shape. "I don't know—perhaps."

POSTSCRIPT OR APOLOGY.

I HAVE had the sense that now, before these foregoing pages be definitely printed—before what have been living thoughts and feelings be irrevocably composed and stiffened, embalmed, distinctly and unmistakably prepared to last, as things are permitted to last, only in death—I have had the sense that while yet I can, I must say one or two more things. But now, I can scarcely tell why, it seems to me as if there could by no means be anything to say. It is a mood, due to the moment and place. All about me there is broad, scarce-flickering shadow on the grass, and stirring of sunlit tree-tops and vague buzzing of bees in the limes; and across the low ivied wall comes from the black, crumbly-stoned chapel faint music of organ and white-sounding voices, which swells and pierces through the silence (as a green reed bud swells and pierces its soft scaly core) and dies away, making you suddenly very conscious of twitter of sparrows and chucking of jackdaws; bringing suddenly close home to you, with the silence, a sense of solid reality. So, instead of saying what I wished, it seems to me most evident that there is nothing to say, that there scarcely could have been anything worth saying. It is enervate, I suppose; but so it is. I wonder how any one can ever have felt inclined to write about art—how art can ever have been worth writing about. Every-

thing around seems so incomparably more interesting
does it not, than art; so entirely beyond the power of
writing to convey or imitate.   Above, high up, there are
two great branches of lime, apparently printed distinctly
on to the pale blue sky, black wood dividing and sub-
dividing and projecting, green leaves and light yellow
blossom, the sun shining straight through; it seems so
simple.   But try and paint it: those two branches, which
seem at first so well-defined, so close together, so closely
clapped against the sky, do you now see how far apart
they really are, how separated by a gulf of luminous air,
how freely suspended, poised, at infinite distance, in the
far receding pale blue; those green leaves and yellow
blossoms, which are not green nor yellow, but something
shadowy and at the same time luminous, are clearly defined and yet undefinable; the sunshine which we
thought at first one plain beam of light is now a white,
vague sheen, a shimmer; now one light spark, one
tremulous star between the leaves, or a waving network
of rays, long, then short, white, coloured, iridescent,
shaking, shifting, dancing.   Paint it, describe it if you
have a mind to, my friend the poet, my friend the
painter; I have not.

   This is one of those moments when reality, and the enjoyment thereof, fill one with a sense, self-contemptuous,
sceptical, almost cynical, and yet pleasureable and
stoically self-flattering in the recognition of our own importance, a pervading illogical sense of the futility, the
unreality, the museum-glass-case uselessness of art.   It
seems as if art were enjoyed because it has been produced, not produced because it is to be enjoyed; as if
mankind had acquired an elaborate pleasure in its own

works because they are its own works; as if all of us, instead of passively receiving the impression of beauty in the same way that we passively perceive the rustle of the branches, the twitter of the birds, the light upon the grass, our soul staying quietly, as it were, at home, and receiving these things as visits from nature; went forth, when art appeals to us, on a sort of journey or grand tour, well provided with guide-book knowledge, schooled beforehand which road to take, what turnings of feeling to expect, what baggage of poetic and historic association to lug with us, what little mole-hill eminences of thought and feeling to stand upon, morally on tiptoe, looking down upon an artistic scene upon which we have never before set eyes, and which is yet as wellknown, as drearily familiar to us as is the inside of our pocket.

Such is my present mood; fickle, contradictory, unworthy, slightly apostatising and blasphemous to my own deeper convictions, to my own written ideas, you say; you, my friend, the poet, who insist upon people being steadfast, unchangeable in all their feelings, because you poets keep your own moods quite steady, as photographers keep their victims, until you have taken the concentrated likeness, and can shift your souls into another equally steadfast, unchangeable pose. Such is my present mood, and you may call me what names you please for having it. All that concerns me is that most certainly this present mood of mine happens to be the one, of all others, in which I am least likely to be able to muster up those two or three remarks upon art with which I ought to conclude, and finally despatch into the limbo of things printed this collection of studies. The things must be said. If I carry my papers home, sit down at my table, fix my eyes upon the patterned wall-paper, I shall, in all probability, get back within five minutes all that the usual ideas, the usual feelings about art, in the contemplation of that patterned blankness ; all that phantasmagoria of art appreciation for which we carry all the necessary mechanism, self-manufac-tured (yet very neat) out of fragments of culture and philosophy, in a sort of little travelling case appended to our soul. A fact this, which is suggestive ; for does not our modern, imaginative appreciation of art, do not all those wondrous beautiful and horrible dreams and night-mares, suggested to us by a quite plain and unsuggestive picture, statue, or piece of music, depend a little upon our contemplation of the methodical, zig-zag and twirli-gig patterned vacuity of modern life ? For I suspect that, in former days (I confess I do not know exactly when), art may have been perceived pretty much in the same manner in which we perceive nature : that the en-joyed perception of a beautiful statue, of a picture, of a grand song, may have come interrupting, with pleasant interludes of quiet self-unconscious pleasure, the matter-of-fact, but not monotonous business of life ; even as my work now, my conscientious, deliberate, attempted work, is for ever being interrupted by the flicker of the lime-leaf shadows, light and clear, on my paper, by the breeze which sweeps the branches and carries away the drying manuscript on the grass.

Now it seems to me quite evident that art cannot be any such thing, as long as its enjoyment or supposed enjoyment is a sort of deliberate mental gymnastics, which our desire for well-balanced activity, or our wish

to display a certain unnecessary gracefulness of intellectual motions, impose upon us ; setting aside a certain
portion of our time for counteracting, in the artistic
gymnasiums (rows of soaped poles, and hurdles, and
ladders, and expanses of padded floor, quite as unlike as
may be from the climbable trees and jumpable brooks
which we ought to meet in our walks), called galleries,
concerts, etc., the direful slackening of our muscles and
stiffening of our joints, almost inevitable in our cramped
intellectual shop life of to-day. We writhe, clinging
with arms and legs, up the soaped poles of æsthetic feeling, slipping and rising again, straining and twisting, to
plop down at last on to the padding and the sawdust ;
we dangle, with constrained grace, high in æsthetic contemplation, flying, with a clutching swing, from idea to
idea : distant, oscillating in mid air, like so many
trapeze acrobats ; and then we think that an hour or so,
every now and then, of such exercise is all (except brutal
slumber) that can be required as repose in our intellectual life. For we are all of us getting more and more
into the habit of enjoying, not so much art, as the feelings and thoughts, the theories and passions, for which
we make it the excuse. "Nay," you will say "you yourself have written, are printing, correcting, and publishing
a whole volume of whims and ideas about art, you yourself are for ever theorising and becoming angry on the
subject—what right have you to object thereto in others?"

None, perhaps ; I have never pretended that I am
not as bad as my neighbours ; but the whole gist of
these my theorisings is that people should try and take
art more simply than they do ; that, if not called upon
to try and persuade others to simpler courses, they

should not theorise themselves. By theorising, I mean,
incorrectly perhaps, all manner of irrelevant fantasticating, whether it take the shape of seeking in art for hidden
psychological meanings or moral values, or of using art
merely as a suggestion of images and emotions, the perception of which infallibly interferes with, and sometimes
entirely replaces, the perception of the art itself. To
you, I know, all that I have written seems extremely
narrow, seems to limit excessively the powers of art, the
enjoyments we can derive therefrom. But I think otherwise ; I understand fully that, in the first place, there is
included, under the general name of art, the result of
ever so many intellectual activities : activities of mere
psychological perception, of mere mechanical imitation
and handling, which, though belonging quite equally to
other concerns, such as science or handicraft, are yet
pleasurable both to him who exerts and to him who perceives them ; I understand that there are so many different sorts of pictures, statues, and poems, and so many
different kinds of minds to see and read them ; I see
that so many questions of mental and physical why and
how are connected with every sort of visible or audible
thing, that there is nothing, however utterly bad and
idiotic and abortive, among the productions of mankind (and, consequently, among the things called works
of art), out of which some sort of intellect may not derive
very keen enjoyment. The enjoyment, however, may
be merely similar to that with which a physiologist
studies a disease, or a psychologist a form of vice ; and,
to my mind, this sort of enjoyment, which does not depend upon any perception of beauty, is no more artistic
than would be that of such men of science. And my

wish is merely that such pleasure be not substituted where there is an object to afford, or a mind to receive, the mere simple, honest pleasure in beauty. Moreover, with regard to your imputation of narrowness, I think, on the contrary, that, could we break ourselves of our habit of replacing or alloying real artistic interests with irrelevant matters, we should (and this is to my mind a great reason for so doing) be ridding ourselves of a great number of imaginary restrictions to our enjoyment. For in many, nay, most artistic things there is, in greater or less degree, beauty and enjoyableness; nor should we always despise the less, since we cannot always obtain the greater. I do not mean that all art is equally valuable; such intellectual democracy, Walt. Whitman-ish assertion of the equality of body and soul, good and evil, high and low, being just the most brutal rob-Peter-to-pay-Paul dishonesty that I know; but I think that in most art there is something valuable, and that we ought to make the most of it, and doubtless should, did not our eternal theorising interfere, with its arbitrary standard and requirements. Were we guided solely by our feelings, we should not be ashamed of taking a certain pleasure in the half-dapper, half-grotesque stone nymphs and tritons, with golden-lichened tresses and beards of green pond ooze, who smirk among the ill-clipped hedges, and puff at their horns among the flags and lilies of every abandoned Prince-Bishop or Margrave's garden, where the apricots ripen against the palace wall, and the old portraits fade behind the blistered palace shutters; we should not be ashamed of being just a little the better pleased for some common dance tune, heard vaguely, and between our work, from the neighbouring

houses ; we should not be ashamed of liking our village
church all the more for the atrocious stained glass which
we have decried as vandalism, when the sunlight falls
rosy, and golden, and green, through its monstrosities on |
to the extremely chaste, but excessively dreary, grey
arches and pillars.   We should not be so hypocritical to
ourselves, so exclusive in our adoration of only the best
pictures, and statues, and music, to appreciate rightly
whose great merit we ought (but do not), to appreciate
also the small, more appreciable merit of the less perfect
things of art.   When, instead of enjoying, we fantasticate
in theory, we not only remove a proportion of our attention from the work in hand, but also exclude ourselves
from getting the good we might from other things ; one
man will positively whip his soul out of enjoying the
sweet solemnity of Claude's sea sunsets, the tragedy pomp
of Poussin's black rustling ilex-groves, and ominous
green evening skies, because he seeks in painting a moral
sincerity which is incompatible with a false shadow or a
lumpishly rendered cloud.   Another man thinks music
ought to be the expression of dramatic passion, and
closes his ears to the splendours of poor Rossini's vocal
arabesques, theory-blinded to the sense that the powers
of creating beauty of the composer of *Tristram*, is after
all akin to the beauty making genius of the composer
of *Semiramis*.   Meanwhile, he who merely enjoys is
able to enjoy; is able (oh wonder of wonders) to be
what the man of theories never can be : just, because he
can be grateful for every amount of bestowed good.

There is another objection which you may make,
which (though perhaps unformulated) you certainly will
feel, against me and my book. You have an uncom-

fortable sense that in some way, although our artistic
life may gain, a certain amount of life which goes on in
or about art—we do not clearly know which—is being
cramped : a life of the fancy and feelings, which weave
between ourselves and the things which surround us and
the things which are absent, between the present
moment and the long-gone past, strange crossed and
recrossed threads, webs of association, infinitely fine,
iridescently connected by almost invisible filaments,
floating and oscillating in the vacuum of our lives, for
ever changing, breaking, reknotting their sensitive filaments. For in most of the things which we see and
hear with free, unpractical mind in the moments when
we belong to ourselves and to the present, there exists a
capacity for importance, nay for fascination, quite independent of beauty and of the pleasures which beauty
can give. There is in such things more than what they
can give alike to every one ; there is also what they can
give to each separate ; they have, besides the clear
language of form, which is equally intelligible to all men,
a half articulate language for every individual man, a
language of associations, vague, poor, if you will, broken
by something which might be a laugh or a sob ; an imperfect irrational language, which is yet, even when
spoken by some trifling thing, by a bar or two of trivial
melody, by a door such as we have many times passed
through, or a chair such as we have looked at when not,
as now, empty ; by a mere scent or touch ; is yet, this
mumble-jumble language, more dear to us than all the
eloquence and poetry which our soul hears from a great
work of art. I grant you all this. But I do not think
that such things need be interfered with by looking at

art simply and with straightforwardness; interfered with
they cannot be.   Nor could I wish it to be otherwise.
For in some ways I do think that almost better than
the mere perception of the work of another, than the
mere perception of statue or picture or poem, is this
evolving from out of ourselves of vague beauty and
goodness : our fancy and our feelings do not create anything enduring, but they are active, they create.   You
artists, you poets must be broad awake, for you can and
are bound to give to us the sober realities of beauty;
but we who cannot, we can yet sometimes dream, if but
for a moment, of an intangible, vague fairyland ; and of
this we must not be cheated.   Out of the broken, fragmentary realities of life there must arise, ever and again
for all of us, strange involuntary visions, which have
greater power over us, more charm for us, than all the
art in the world.   And of such things art has no right
to be jealous ; they are beyond it.   And thus, I will confess to you, as I fasten together these last pages of my
book, and rise from the grass, sere in the sunshine, and
sprinkled with daisies in the shadow of each tree, I will
confess to you that more nearly appealing to me, dearer
also, than antique bas-relief or song of Mozart, has been
the vague remembrance, evoked by trivial word or sight,
of that early winter afternoon on the ilex girded battlements of Belcaro, looking down upon the sere oak-
woods, flushed by the low sun, upon the hazy olive
slopes and walls and towers of Siena.   And, moreover, I
will even confess (as severest self-chastisement to a writer
on art, as complete expiation of æsthetic dogmatism and
fantastications), while we walk across the warm grass and
out through the low archway of black and flakewise

crumbling stone, that I foresee that many a time in the future there will arise between me and the fresco or picture at which I am looking, a vision of this old world garden, of the ivied chapel buttress, the flowering lime, the daisied grass, the copper beech leaves, ruddy and diaphanous, against the pale, moist English sky; that, sometimes, there will come into my head something— something ill-defined, pleasurable, painful—which will make me read only with my eyes; which will make me (worst humiliation) lose the thread of my theories, of my thoughts, of my sentence. And, after this confession, I think I can say no more.

OXFORD, *July* 21, 1881.

S. Cowan and Co., Strathmore Press, Perth.